14 May '5

PANORAMA OF AUSTRIA

With Glimpses of Bavaria and Switzerland

By JAMES REYNOLDS

An experienced traveler with an eye for the unusual, the colorful, and the significant, in his new book Mr. Reynolds wanders agreeably through one of Europe's most fabled regions. After visiting the picturesque villages of Upper Bavaria and the magnificent if synthetic castles of Ludwig II, he turns to the Salzkammergut with all its rich baroque lore, architectural, historical, and musical. The old cities along the Danube, the rich lands of Styria and Carinthia, Vienna, sacred to Maria Theresia and the family Strauss—all of these storied sites are fitting subjects for Mr. Reynolds' pen and brush in this beautiful book.

There are also excursions to the Tyrol, including imperial Innsbruck, and finally to Switzerland, mecca for the Anglo-Saxon tourist and lover of splendid scenery

(Continued on back flap)

(Continued from front flap)

since the eighteenth century. The wealth of material here, natural and man-created, is incredible, but the selectivity and finesse of the author keep this voyage in the best of company from becoming too cloying or hectic.

This is a personal guidebook to a peculiarly varied and interesting region, to lands many Americans are now thinking of for sport and diversion. The occupation of Austria is a thing of the past, the life of Vienna, still a world capital, is at its best. Who could ask for a happier combination of subject and enthusiastic author than in this case? Austria and the two surrounding regions covered in this book could hardly be more sympathetically and attractively presented.

THE AUTHOR

James Reynolds has won a reputation as painter, writer of ghost stories, and costume designer. His travel series now includes books on Spain, Italy, and England, to which *Panorama of Austria* is a splendid addition.

GÖTTWEIG MONASTERY
VIEW FROM STEIN·ON·THE·DANUBE.

James Reynolds

PANORAMA OF AUSTRIA

IN WHICH I RELATE ALSO SOME PLEASURES
TO BE EXPERIENCED WHILE TRAVELING IN
BAVARIA AND SWITZERLAND

G. P. Putnam's Sons   New York

MANUFACTURED IN THE UNITED STATES OF AMERICA

VAN REES PRESS • NEW YORK

SEXTON

Farm

Notable Horsewoman

Reynolds, James, 1891–
 Panorama of Austria, in which I relate also some pleasures to be experienced while traveling in Bavaria and Switzer-land. New York, Putnam [1956]
 350 p. illus. 25 cm.

51956

1. Austria—Descr. & trav.   I. Title.

G& 9My57

DB26.R48   914.36   56–10242 ‡

Library of Congress   [15]

Contents

9

CONTENTS

Introduction

No MATTER how frequently I travel in the various countries of the world I never lose a sense of excitement, an expectancy, a latent eagerness for new experiences to be encountered on crossing a frontier. This guardian line that divides one race of mankind and its individual way of life from another can, with magical suddenness, change the entire picture within one's focus. A frontier line of demarcation varies greatly in form. It may be invisible to one's eyes, perhaps just a frill of grass lazily bending to the breeze on some upland ridge. Or it may startle the eye with the grandeur of nature, like the Alpine spur called Haute Savoie, a rocky bastion eternally tipped with ice and snow dividing France from Italy.

Recently I crossed the frontier from Germany into Austria by a bridge over the storied Rhine. A hot sun shone on the terraced vineyards. I left the heady fragrance of grape blossoms starring the vines in Germany, to taste upon my tongue the cool freshness of pine and spruce and larch drifting down from the shadowy heights of forest-clad Austrian mountains.

Austria is an inveterate and masterly showman, presenting as a background the rich, vital colors of various traditional costumes and the sparkle of its architecture, a great deal of which, sharply silhouetted against the mountain forests, appears to hang suspended between heaven and earth. I believe the feeling I have always entertained for Austria and the Austrians is aptly borne out by a remark made by the late General Patton. It was just after the ceremony on May 7, 1945, when General Patton placed the Spanish Riding School of Vienna under the special protection of the American Army. An elderly gentleman in the crowd of onlookers approached the General, who was himself a notable horseman, and with genuine emotion thanked him for making this great gesture to Austria. The General replied, "My deep interest in horses aside, what less could I do for the warm and friendly Austrians who so staunchly uphold their glorious traditions?"

The terrain of Austria is unique in formation. Seen from the air it presents a picture of towering mountains either dark with trees that are evergreen or gray with serried rock crags cradling deep, wide valleys that sparkle with the sharp greens and gold of fertility. These are laced with swiftly flowing rivers and splashed by exquisitely slender waterfalls. As one drives along the roads it is these immensely spacious valleys with their scattered ancient villages that fill the eye. To my mind it is the valleys that take over in Austria; in some way more compelling than its renowned mountains. Save for the Province of Burgenland, that region of marshy pastures and reedy lakes lying next to the windy prairies of Hungary, the entire face of Austria is crosshatched by these mountain-walled valleys: Vorarlberg—Arlberg —Pinzgau—Tyrol (or Tirol)—Zillertal—and the far-reaching Salzkammergut, a lake-strewn valley flanked by Salzburg at one end and Almtal in Upper Austria at the other. If for no other reason—and there are scores—Salzgammergut is uncommonly distinguished by the Dachstein Glacier which can be seen flashing imperially above Alt Aussee. The shimmering effects of changing colors on this gleaming marvel of nature, over which thunder rolls mysteriously no matter how bright the day, must be seen; no words can describe it, just as no artist dares attempt to paint its color variations.

While the extraordinary force of its natural beauty claims first attention, I feel that the quite personal architecture of the Austrian countryside not only complements nature but, to a singularly impressive degree, becomes one with its richly green panoramas. The number and diversity of castles and fortified manor houses, dominating the landscape in every province in the land, loom large in Austrian history. They are rooted deeper in the soil than the sacred buildings, the great abbeys and monastic retreats with which Austria is so richly endowed. The church lands seek to retire, the *schlösser* (castles) to dominate and defend. Usually the site is a lofty elevation, like Schloss Rabenstein thrusting upon a crag above the River Mur in Styria, though another famous masterpiece of Austrian Baroque architecture, Schloss Eggenburg, containing the only hunting museum in the country, occupies a grassy plain surrounded by vast hunting preserves.

In the Provinces of Carinthia, Styria, Arlberg, the Burgenland and Tyrol the *schlösser* are predominately Medieval in design of 11th, 12th and 13th century construction. A keep tower rises arrogantly into the sky attracting all eyes in the valley to this warning finger of power. In the age of chivalry, it was the powerful prince who was pre-eminent in the land. The castle he built was purely to defend. The name of the reigning prince's castle was applied to the whole countryside. "He who cannot protect himself needs a protector." So ran the legend that to every countryman in the valleys was a shield and buckler of safety.

Descending centuries wrought great changes in the mode of life of prince or peasant. Now it is the historic and artistic blending that have preserved these castles not only as works of art in themselves but as repositories of art and historical curiosities. Schloss Ambras near Innsbruck, an 11th-century fortress, is a notable example of this schloss museum. Rebuilt by Archduke Ferdinand II into a magnificent Renaissance château, the Archduke traded its warlike eminence for a more elegant aspect but retained one of the great galleries of the world, the painted "Spanish Hall" and the original 11th-century armory presently visited by tens of thousands of tourists a year.

From earliest times Austria has been one of the richest sources of Catholic culture. During the ages of the great migrations, Christian monks converted the barbarian leaders whose descendants created the great feudal houses which ruled Europe through many centuries. In the golden age of Irish faith and learning, monks from the monasteries of the Western Isles traveled into Austria and along the Danube to Switzerland and Bavaria, bringing the light of Faith with them. All over Austria, in remote mountain villages or the busy market towns of the valleys, this is apparent. In the hundreds of great abbeys in every province that stand sentinel to a devout people, in place names, in legend and memory, the work of these Irish monks survives. Actually they were called "Scots," the Ireland of that age having been known as "Scotia Minor."

Traversing the valley roads in Austria one is often treated to fascinating glimpses of tiny graystone Medieval hermit chapels which perch perilously on wooded hillsides. Many of these were originally pilgrimage shrines erected by early Irish monks. So steep are these miniature mountains, with no path visible among the rough grasses, it would seem that only an experienced Alpinist could ever reach the aerial altars. But the Austrian is a deeply devout soul.

For another instance in the territory covered by this book, one of the most splendidly appointed cathedrals in Switzerland is to be found at St. Gallen, a spacious town set on a plateau not far from Lake Constance amid the undulating fruit orchards of Switzerland. It was founded in 612 by St. Gallus, a monk from Ireland who originally fashioned a hermitage out of a rude stone lair from which he had driven wild beasts. Today St. Gall vies in religious stature and architectural splendor with the basilica-monastery, the Pilgrimage of Einsiedeln near Lucerne.

While in some of the more ancient towns in Austria, Bavaria and Switzerland one still finds Romanesque, or Early and Late Medieval churches, it is the lustily ornate Baroque order in religious architecture that prevails. In Austria, the great scale of its vigorous scrolls and counterfoils, its wide bolection-molding cornices and architraves in the form of floriations surrounding doors and windows is completely individual. Swiss Baroque presents a stern face, the flow of line is disciplined, the scale of proportion less grand. Certain medium-size town houses in the Canton Vaud, or more particularly in the city of Neuchâtel, combine aristocratic elegance with livableness to achieve some of the finest examples of Baroque and Rococo style in existence.

Bavarian Baroque is exuberant, florid. Bavaria's princely hunting lodges were built by lavish-handed Electors and Hereditary Grand Dukes, each edifice large and spectacular enough to be called a palace. Many are semi-ruinous now, others still somewhat sketchily lived in, all are on show. The Rococo and *chinoiserie* apartments and alcoves in the Amalienburg Pavilion in the gardens of Nymphenburg Palace, the work of the great French designer François de Cuvilliés, are considered the finest in this style to be seen today.

And so the roster streams out, Austria, Bavaria and Switzerland, each neighbor creating its own individuality in all things—art, architecture, music. A love of music prevails in all three countries. There are music festivals in Salzburg, Bregenz, Lucerne, Geneva; in Munich and Bayreuth. Each is noted for its love of sports, to be enjoyed summer and winter in the lovely reaches of an agreeable countryside. Imaginatively contrived Winter Sports Carnivals are to be found at Garmisch-Partenkirchen, Zermatt, St. Moritz, Gstaad, Mürren. St. Anton in the Arlberg Valley, renowned as a ski capital of the world, vies with adjacent Vorarlberg and Tyrol resorts to give winter sports enthusiasts the best entertainment on the slopes by day, with traditional music and dancing in the inns and *bierstubes* at night. Semmering, near Vienna, is proud of its staunch habitués. It proclaims "a century of winter sports and the oldest mountain railway in Europe." Its big luxury hotels are world-famous for superlative cuisine in the great Viennese tradition, its *gasthäuser* and numerous pensions excellent.

I have always contended that a summer spent in Austria, with side trips into Bavaria and Switzerland providing contrast in food and exploration, can be the ideal holiday. Even the many beautifully situated spas devoted to curing a sufferer of whatever ails him are never lugubrious. There is ample provision for pleasure.

And finally in addition to this landscape so prodigal with mountains, lakes, valleys and rivers, one has for balance three of the most agreeable cities in the world to visit—Vienna, Munich and Geneva.

JAMES REYNOLDS

Schloss Rabenstein
Frohnleiten
Styria

PANORAMA OF AUSTRIA

Chapter 1

THE VORARLBERG, VALLEY OF AUSTRIAN LEGENDS

WHEN visiting Austria for the first time, I suggest that if it can be managed the traveler should enter through the frontier portal of Bavarian Lindau. Leaving the mainland the railway trains and motorcars still cross one of the longest stone and timber bridges in Europe. For this frontier depot, guarding the Austro-Bavarian marches, is an island. The quiet, romantic old Roman port, walled and battlemented, towered and turreted, is prideful of its antiquity. Originally this island was a mighty fortress. Today one sees a Gothic town of high, gabled houses leaning conversationally across narrow, twisting cobbled streets as if mumbling old scandals and memories of past wars. The Diebsturm, the high German-Gothic watchtower sprouting four balconied turrets, overlooks a wide, stone-paved marketplace surrounded by the fine Baroque houses of rich burghers.

The Altes Rathaus, its magnificent step-gables reminiscent of Dutch-Renaissance grand scale, is an architectural curiosity. On Wednesdays and Saturdays the Stift Platz is raucous and vividly alive with shouts of market-stall vendors crying fish, vegetables, fruits and cheeses. Great baskets of flowers crowd up the steps of the imposing Renaissance church. Groups of nuns always moving two-by-two, wearing the Madonna-blue habits with fly-a-way white linen coifs of the Bavarian sisterhoods, weave among the market stalls. A most striking lion in sculptured granite sits atop an armorial throne—the Lion of Lindau, arrogantly surveying all ships that enter the lighthouse-sentineled port.

On my most recent visit to Austria, in 1955, I had arrived from Paris via the Orient Express. After a necessary change of trains in the forenoon at Ulm in Germany, it is only a short journey to Lindau. The countryside is like nothing so much as an illuminated page from a book of old tales of chivalry, the castles still rearing machicolated towers on the surrounding mountain crags. This air of knightly days sets the mood for fully savoring Bregenz, the first city on Austrian soil, gateway to the inviting province of Vorarlberg—"Before Arlberg"—lying between Lake Constance (known in German as the Bodensee) and the edge of the Alps.

From Lindau to Schloss Hofen at Lochau-bei-Bregenz is a short drive. Once I left the lake road I saw Schloss Hofen embraced in pine trees, high on a green knoll sparkling in the midday sun as if it were a painting on glass. The long line of its pink-washed stucco walls follows the subtle curve of a Saracen scimitar. Under an archway letting into the stables, which act as a gate lodge, we swung into a long driveway up the hill terminating in a paved courtyard. Masses of claret-red peonies and bushes of greenish-white snowballs surrounded the court.

Quite apart from its advantageous position commanding a tremendous view of lake and surrounding mountains, Schloss Hofen has a distinguished history, one of importance and interest to all students of the Baroque period, its modes, manners, and particularly its architecture. The Renaissance castle Burg Hofen was built in 1586 by the family von Raitenau, whose most celebrated member was Wolf Dietrich, a Medici through the male line. He was first created cardinal at the age of twenty-eight, and later rose in eminence as Lord Archbishop of Salzburg. This enthusiastic promoter of the Austrian-Baroque motif in architectural art, which was to emblazon his name as a personal device for posterity, passed his boyhood in Burg Hofen, although he was born at Alt Hofen, the early fortress of the lords of Raitenau.

A short walk up a mountain path behind the Schloss leads through fern brakes to a larch-encircled mound thrusting out into space like the prow of an ancient barge. Rising from dense undergrowth the vine-latticed ruins of the old castle reveal a dilapidated *enceinte* wall and a crumbling keep tower.

In the Vorarlberg Museum in Bregenz I found a number of illuminating prints and old paintings which considerably clarified the Wolf Dietrich von Raitenau story. When only a youth he designed and consecrated the chapel at the end of the west wing of the existing Schloss. This is reached by an outside staircase leading to a gallery supported by Gothic arches, an architectural feature typical of the older Austrian *schlösser*. Wolf Dietrich was a remarkable man in his age. From his various exploits, I believe he would have been judged extraordinary even in this age. Once he became cardinal, his life was one long blast of sound and fury caused by envious prelates. He did not attempt to allay calumny but simply disregarded it, although he was accused by the pope of "paganism" because he indulged his love of giving great banquets with highly provocative entertainments.

I suggest that anyone traveling in the vicinity of Bregenz will be rewarded by paying a visit to Schloss Hofen even if it is only for a look around or possibly for a meal. I recommend the food as extremely good. In the large dining room hangs a stunning collection of Dürer and Holbein prints which reflect the early period of the castle's history. Of exceptional interest among the Dürer prints is a long panel in sepia ink depicting the marriage procession of Maximilian I, "The Great" (beloved by his Tyrolean subjects as "Kaiser Max") and Maria of Burgundy. The procession of floats wound five miles long. Such fantastic splendor had never been seen at any European court. Certainly it was the most romantic wedding and richest entourage ever recorded. Maria was of tall and stately build; her brilliant golden hair, parted in the middle, hung to the ground in thick tresses. It is said that when Maximilian, who was at heart as much a poet as he was the intrepid "Great Huntsman," first saw his bride standing in a window embrasure in full sunlight, he exclaimed, "I will ride in sheathed silver mail to reflect the beauty of my Golden Bride." And so he did, clad from crown to mailed shoe in burnished silver mail.

At Schloss Hofen the ceilings in all the reception apartments and what was once the state bedrooms are richly coffered and painted. The ceiling in the dining room where the Dürer prints embellish the pale gray walls is particularly noteworthy. The deeply recessed coffering forms intersecting triangles and octagonal lozenges laid off in honeycomb design. All this is painted in three shades of rusty-pink, gray and violet.

Bregenz-am-Bodensee (Lake Constance) is the principal town of Vorarlberg where in reality "the mountains and the waters meet." Both the lake and the Rhine River water its mountain-slope meadows cradling the farms that lie on three sides of the town. The soaring pines, so straight, so resilient and tough in fiber, which have for centuries been used for the masts of ships sailing the Seven Seas, march in great battalions up the flanks of the Pfänder. In a matter of minutes the summit of this peak (3,491 feet) can be reached by suspension railway from the town. The Roman governors who lived in sybaritic luxury in log villas sumptuously carved and painted in garish colors on the lower slopes of the Pfänder, when Bregenz was the Brigantium of the Romans, were only reproducing in more sumptuous style the dwellings of barbarian chieftains that ringed a fortress stockade town of Celtic origin centuries older than Brigantium. There are traces of a Celtic fortress rent from the stone of Gebhard Peak, and archaeologists have found axheads and other battle gear in Pfänder and Gebhardsberg caves that baffle antiquarians, since these implements appear to antedate the early Celts.

Bregenz is of ancient lineage. Long embattled, too, situated as it is at an angle of the Swiss and German frontiers. The Oberstadt, the old walled quarter, a quadrangle of vine-hung houses halfway up the hill, raises a massive tower called Martinsturm. At least, that is the official name. But the day that I wandered around the narrow cobbled streets of the Oberstadt I started to mount the covered wooden stairs winding upward on the outside of the deeply gouged stone walls. A small boy, armed with a self-made catapult fashioned in the form of a Medieval crossbow, asked if he might conduct me to the top of the tower. He proved a garrulous, inventive and informative guide. The first thing he showed me were some stone door lintels deeply incised in all the flourish of old German script. *The Tower of Warning,* read one. The other, *Tower of the Bloody Steps.*

The broad Rathausstrasse terminates in a narrow roadway that climbs between high lichen-gilded walls to the castle gateway Martinsthor. This portcullis barbican is a small museum in itself. Windows facing a *platz* inside the walls are screened in beautifully preserved examples of the Medieval scrolled ironwork for which Bregenz is famed. Traces of color and gilt can still be seen. The skull of a stag, sprouting a formidable set of antlers and bearing a crucifix crossed with St. Martin's staff between the antler points, strikes a dramatic note above the Roman arch. Various stone images, warriors in armor, saints, and a pair of horrendously grimacing mountain trolls are placed at various levels half-embedded among the heavily foliaged ivy.

To me the most interesting object displayed has an appealing history. The Mermaid of Bodensee, dry as parchment and doubled up in a contortionist attitude, swings by a chain in the arch. It is said that in the 13th century Bregenz suffered a series of disasters in recurrent sieges by German warrior barons and decimating plagues. One night a fisherman in the Bodensee drew in his net to find a writhing creature with the head and torso of a maiden. In place of legs slapped a scaly tail and ribby fins. Horrified that this was devils' work, the fisherman was about to toss the creature back into the lake when a voice from out the dark waters cried: "Take my daughter and hang her in the arch of Martinstor. She is begat of a land woman and is of no use here." Fearing the evil consequences if he disobeyed the Spirit of the Waters, the man did as he was commanded. Early next morning a man-at-arms found the slimy creature dead, writhed into the queerly distorted shape we see hanging in the portal today. And in the old chronicles of Bodensee the story solemnly declared that "from that day out Bregenz enjoyed a century free from siege, famine and plague."

In the *platz* facing Martinstor stands an attractive inn, Gasthaus Storchen, displaying one of those handsome signs of wrought and gilded iron seen all over Austria. In this case it takes the form of delicate scrolls supporting a white stork in full flight.

The Vorarlberg Landesmuseum in Rathausstrasse harbors Roman and Medieval armor, Gothic altars, and animals carved from olive wood. Some of them, the size of life, I found oddly naïve in execution, with the haunting charm of primitive art. A wonderfully well-chosen collection of textiles and handicrafts of this region I admire for the floss-silk embroidery in scenes of farming and the chase. Skirts, aprons, bodices, waistcoats and jackets shimmer with every imaginable hue that silk can be dyed, all this pinked out with metal threads. The ceremonial headdresses, fit for a pagan goddess on her votive feast day, are alone worth a visit.

The Bregenz Music Festival is held in August on a semicircular stage built over the lake, fronting the Seestrasse. Such operas as *Tales of Hoffman* and Johann Strauss's *Thousand and One Nights* are presented with great effect, particular attention being paid to settings and costumes that light up well when seen from a distance. In this presentation of open-air opera, reflections of light and color in rippling water heighten the scene immeasurably.

Kornmarkt, a wide paved space ablaze with heterogeneous wares, displays under brilliantly striped awnings a kind of racial "Ballet of Abundance." On Saturdays the mountain folk appear in full costume, the women from Dornbirn in halo headdresses decked with bows of embroidered ribbons, dark velvet bodices aswing with gold and silver heirloom chains. The men sport skirted coats with silver buttons, high choker collars, and bell-crowned top hats worthy of a Regency dandy.

Hotels in Bregenz offer wide variety. I prefer the Weisses Kreuz, its gray and white Baroque façade adrip with hanging baskets of bleeding hearts and petunias. The Fohrenburg has an enviable reputation for big comfortable rooms, and its restaurant is famous for roast game from the adjacent mountain forests, served with great flourish by "foresters" in costumes of green piped in red. The lime-green painted Krone Hotel, its doorway surmounted by a huge gold ducal crown, is also highly regarded by travelers.

Gasthäuser and cafés abound. Café Löffler, in the picturesque Römerstrasse, offers entertainment by dancers from the Bregenzerwald. Dressed in beguiling costumes, they play the old "mountain music" on trumpets and accordions. This music denotes a special language used in Bregenzerwald, Arlberg and Tyrol to convey messages across the valleys. A forester in an isolated mountain hut, eager for news of a "neighbor" residing miles across the valley, can carry on a conversation by trumpet notes without moving a foot.

Although Dornbirn is advertised as "an Industrial Center with 17,000 happy workers engaged in the manufacture of textiles, embroideries, silk fringes and skiing outfits," there is no smoke. "White coal" (electricity) never pollutes the crystal mountain air. The "Garden City," as the townsmen proudly call Dornbirn, is girdled round with a green kirtle of pine forests. Above these rise the everlasting snow crowns of the Churfirsten, Appenzell, and the ice-tipped peaks of Sentis. Every house, no matter its size or condition of occupant, whether in the heart of Dornbirn or mounting the slopes to Bödele, is set in a considerable garden, usually divided between vegetables and flowers. For magnificent panoramas, go up to Bödele—its Alpine Lodge is a famous haunt of top-flight Alpinists and skiers.

I set out for Bludenz on a morning when all the "old mountain gods" one hears so much about in these parts were hurling thunderbolts, jagged spears of lightning and cyclopean buckets of water at each other. Mountain peaks would suddenly appear purple-black on one side, livid, lightning-yellow and green on the other, to ride high above the drifts of heavy silver mist shrouding the valley. Suddenly the sun would shine through a deluge of rain, turning half the valley to molten gold, the other half to streaming silver. Then lightning would take over, painting the whole picture a green of such brilliance that when the flashes subsided the Stygian blackness, mantling the mountains for a space of minutes, would slowly turn the deep, clear, celestial blue of lapis-lazuli. In its palest shade this is the blue of a clear sky over Alpine peaks.

Recognizing a famous landmark—the long, covered bridge built of interlaced bronze-brown timbers across the Rhine—I entered the now sun-latticed streets of Lustenau to the sound of band music, the players grandly decked out for festival, playing full force at ten o'clock in the morning. In this ancient town shadowy streets, narrow as alleys, wind under the deep-eaved houses to debouch into encroaching fruit orchards.

It is an oft repeated tale in the Vorarlberg that following in the train of the first Roman Legions to settle Bregenz (Brigantium) and along the Rhine Valley there came a tribe of gypsy horse traders, numbering thousands, from the wild Carpathian Mountains. These gypsies remained after the Romans withdrew, and settled in a "city of tents" where now stands Lustenau. The townspeople are today re-marked for blue-black hair, tall and lean build, their black eyes set aslant above high, Slavic cheekbones. Secondly, they are famous for their musicianship. Every man is a composer and his music has a strong Eastern flavor. Young boys are taught early in life to play the Magyar zither with abandon, until the strings literally leap with the vitality of the swift gypsy music.

The road winds like a switchback through flowery countryside. Fruit orchards crowd right up to the villages, almost obscuring from view the clusters of houses known as dorfs, usually centered by the inevitable pink, ivory-yellow or sky-blue church frescoed with out-size figures of saints. These chapels seem about to keel over, top-heavy from the disproportionately long, needle-point spire invariably tipped by the disheveled nest of twigs and grasses scrabbled together by the fierce Alpine hawk, reprobate of the air, who cannily builds his nest within swooping distance of the farmyard chicken run.

My road now ran along the Ill River, bordered on both sides by battalions of deep pink and white marshmallow and the spikes of dark-brown cattails, austere as ramrod-straight governesses disapproving of the flightiness of their charges. The ballet-skirted, flirtatious mallows, most feminine of flowers, fluttered in the breeze.

Still following the Ill, I came into Bludenz to be greeted, as in Lustenau, by a blaring brass band. It was St. Angelica's day, and banners and pennants, some painted with her image, fluttered from windows of houses above arcaded streets. The Medieval air is strong here. The Unicorn of the Forest, legendary equine, is emblazoned on the arms of Bludenz. A unicorn appears in some form—stone, carved wood or painted fresco—on every hand. But in this much decorated town the chief fresco is an ancient one, as fresh today as it must have been when first painted, depicting the story of Frederick of the Empty Pockets. A kind of Lord Bountiful of the countryside, a good Samaritan of eaglelike profile and heroic physique, Frederick stalked the roads and mountain passes in all weather giving succor in guidance, money and food to the needy.

The marketplace of Bludenz is certainly "overlooked" by mountains. Rising from the Ill marshes, the two highest peaks in the Rhätikon Alps—Panuelerhornspitz (9,482 ft.) and Scesaplana (9,734 ft.)—dominate the scene at this point. From the Altturm in Bludenz or, an even grander sight, from the battlements of Schloss Gaienhofen, riding the ridge of a hill close to the town, is the view of lonely and serene Brand, shining like a silver galleon in the sky. Brand is a far-famed winter resort. The ski slopes hereabouts are definitely not for the timid, nor the unsure. In the vast maw of a fireplace at Alpine Hütte-Brand, a whole deer can be roasted while a strong red Vöslau wine is poured over the sizzling haunches. Roast haunch of deer served with brandied currant conserve—a Bludenz specialty—red cabbage kraut, and all the Vöslau you can hold make a memorable meal when eaten before the fire after a day's skiing, or on the wide balcony overlooking a world of radiant mountains on a soft October night, with memories of a great day of shooting to spangle the conversation.

It was dark when I arrived in the walled town of Feldkirch. Later I went to the wine cellar of Schloss Schattenburg. Against the walls of this long, vaulted cellar are arranged carved oak benches and trestle tables so blackened by centuries of candle smoke that the original grain is burnished with a patina like black bronze. The room is dominated by a remarkable forest-green and white tiled stove hugely scaled to complement the raking proportions of the stone chamber.

When they pour the wine—the red Vorarlberg, the fragrant white native Tyrolean wines, or the supreme Prälaten so rare to come by—the waiters enact a little ceremony. Each fellow turns his round embroidered cap back to front for good luck with his left hand. Then with his right hand he lifts the bottle at arm's length and without spattering a drop, pours into the glass a stream of wine so thin as to be nearly invisible.

It was in this very wine cellar above the ancient crypt that the Swedes who sacked and looted Feldkirch in 1647 held Count Rudolf Habsburg prisoner, with a sword point at his throat, until he agreed to pay an exorbitant indemnity to the Swedish captain for sparing the castle. It is told that to meet this demand it took every treasure the count possessed. Altar vessels from the chapel, his wife's jewelry, even gold buttons from the gowns of the ladies of his household, were heaped on the floor as tribute. But Schattenburg was saved.

Although Feldkirch on the Ill is no longer dominated by the Habsburg dynasty who held it as part of their vast territories for hundreds of years, it was Habsburgs who built the lordly houses that surround the tree-shaded squares. The great wall for defense, now a rampart of vines showering red, yellow and orange nasturtiums, was enlarged by them and kept in defensive condition long after this feudal precaution was necessary. The Churer Tor, a massive barbican gateway, and the Katzensturm (tower) were part of the original wall. One of the most important institutions of learning in Austria is the beautifully mellow Jesuit college, Stella Matutina, once called by Napoleon "a nursery for Imperial diplomats" and noted for the singular open-mindedness of its teachers regarding world affairs.

Many fine inns line the massively cobbled streets. In the 14th century a Habsburg tyrant, one Otto the Bold, taking a leisurely stroll in the town, was run down by a swiftly galloping horseman. He forthwith commanded all streets of Feldkirch to be repaved in such a way that no horseman could ever again go dashing hell-for-leather through the town without breaking his neck. Each cobble laid down was the size of a goodly cannon ball. (Some of the side streets retain these ankle bruisers to this day.) Furthermore, each stone was marked with an intertwined O. von H. deeply incised.

I was now set for a feast of high altitude scenery, heartened by the good surface of the Bodensee—Arlberg Road. This connects the regions of Lake Constance, the Rhine Valley, Walgau, Klostertal, the Arlberg and Bregenzerwald. The round trip can be started and finished at Bregenz or by branching off at Schröcken, taking the newly completed Hochtannberg Road to Lech, a silent town where time seems to have hibernated in some cave and all the ancient Vorarlberg customs in the roster are in daily use.

TWO VIRGINS OF SCHRUNS TRADITIONAL CROWNS

Now the road climbs ever higher, often through drifting clouds of mist, until it reaches an improbably high Alpine altitude at the heart of Bregenzerwald. A refreshing world of clouds and mountain peaks spreads before me. Far off lie Silvretta and Vermunt reservoirs glittering in sunlight. The Silvretta high Alpine pass reaches its highest point at the Bielerhöhe. This skyland is famous ski terrain all the way to Montafon. Here at the Winter King Christmas Carnival the costumes worn by the women are sumptuous—black satin, heavy gold galloon and crimson embroidered aprons and bodices crowned by a kind of archbishop miter headdress in gold filigree, sewn with garnets.

The feminine element of Montafon regard Sunday as peculiarly their own. For meals cold food, prepared on Saturday, is in order. Sunday is a day for church and relaxation, which means gossip. It is a day for show of heirloom finery. I watched a long line of women, walking in couples, mounting the steep path to the church. Their garments, so costly at the start, so treasured through the years, never alter in design from one generation to another.

The interiors of their Baroque churches are resplendent with much gold, painted frescoes, and bejeweled figures of the Madonna, her attendant angels and a galaxy of saints. Against the burnished gold carving and white plaster foliations of the nave in the church at Schruns in Montafon the women appear unconsciously regal in their beautifully imagined and painstakingly wrought traditional costumes; I watched these mitered figures standing stiffly in rows singing or kneeling to pray. The susurrus of silk, black, plum-purple, deep garnet-red, encrusted with bands of gold galloon, whispered richly as the wearers genuflected. In striking contrast to this sumptuousness were the placid faces, calm eyes gazing upon the altar crucifix. Clear, untroubled eyes of workers in the houseplace and in the fields. I found this an awesome sight, this scene of simple devotion, the mood immeasurably heightened by the worshipers clothed in all the magnificence of a Byzantine enamel altarpiece.

Chapter 2

THE HAUNTED BREGENZERWALD, ARLBERG MUSIC OF THE SHEPHERD AND THE HUNTER

O N A morning early, with a determined sun struggling to assert its brilliance through veils of mist, I came out of a rocky defile to see lying before me the immensely ancient town of Hohenems. In the watery light, which was neither quite sunshine nor all-enveloping mist, the houses of patrician families surrounding the Marien Kirche thrust their peaked roofs palely above the remnants of the Medieval wall. The roofs are as steep-pitched as a ski run, the dormer windows set in prim rows, one tier above another—so indicative of the urban architecture of this region. The plaster walls are tinted pale gray, deep rose and pink.

The antiquity of Hohenems is so apparent, so forceful, it looms like a presence, a mysterious knight, armored cap-a-pie, visor lowered. A huge bracken-covered mound with craggy stonework still visible is said to be a Celtic fort. Later the area surrounded by the Medieval wall was a Roman cavalry depot. In Medieval times a ring of small castles perched on the curiously formed buttresses of serried rock abutting on the road over which I had just come. I learned that these were built to guard the approach to Schloss Alt Ems, riding high on a wooded knoll, its age indeterminate, its compelling, monolithic style of architecture unique in all Austria. These guardian castles are ruined now. From flame-riven keep towers, empty windows gape toward Hohenems or the scarlet and gold carpets of poppy-strewn wheat fields that lie all about Götzis crouching in the valley floor, its houses wide and low, the brown roofs sprouting wind-blown grasses that shelter family and livestock in perfect harmony.

Empress Elizabeth of Austria used often to stay in the linden-tree-shaded Schloss Hohenems. It is said that when she first came to stay here for summer holidays she was gay and beautiful. Then—she did not come again for many years. Unheralded, in mourning, she came again, after the suicide by drowning of her beloved companion-cousin, Ludwig of Bavaria. Still supremely beautiful if wan with grieving, she was no longer gay. In the last restless years of Elizabeth's life when she traveled almost constantly, incognito, she took, for "my shadow self" as she wrote to Richard Wagner, the feudal title Countess Hohenems. There is an entertaining story concerning this incognito of the Empress when she used to visit Ireland. Three years in succession she leased Lord Longford's house Summerhill for the fox-hunting season. A fearless woman to hounds, the Empress, posing as Countess Hohenems, by her beauty and her charm won the admiration and the hearts of the Irish. The country people knew that out in the great world this lady was of first importance, but were not quite sure just *who* she might be. So they settled the question typically by a play on her incognito and her title, referring to her as Countess Who?

I wandered about Hohenems at midday. At the foot of the hill leading up to Schloss Glöpper I arranged my sketching paraphernalia. In 1363 the House of Habsburg acquired a small estate at Götzis "for raising of wheat and other viands," a chronicle reads, the first toe-hold in what later became vast holdings in fertile Vorarlberg. At that time the hilltop castle, its builder or its origin unknown, frowned down on the new landlords. Today it still frowns from habit. History of the castle has been varied, from a stronghold for defense to centuries of peaceful agricultural pursuits in its encircling meadows. As I started to sketch I thought of the curiously shaped fungi I have sometimes come upon walking in a primeval forest. Invariably these wonders of forest flora grow into tall, conical shapes, gnawed by wood creatures or pecked by birds into vague semblance of castles. Here before me in giant-size, hoary with age and battling man and the elements,

Glöpper resembles a weirdly colored fungus with its tall, rake-wall towers and ragged roof line. The castle is lived in, the main portal still swings on huge wrought-iron hinges, and there is a notable example of a Medieval covered outside stairway set on rough-hewn stone buttresses. The timbers sturdily cling to the wall facing the valley. Half smothered in rusty ivy and trumpet vines, the foundations of the

castle are obscured, so that the mottled, yellowish-white walls rise from rank vegetation. From the valley road the effect is that of a scaly old monster from out the age of pre-history, attempting to escape to the mountaintops yet clawed back by gnarled vines to the earth it has so long inhabited. I believe, as I sketch its massy contours, that it will stand among its rapacious vines, breasting the centuries as long as the companion mountains salute its towers at night and morning.

Last rays of saffron-red sunset kindled a mighty blaze of light on the church spires and casement windows in the clustered houses of sky-borne Tschagguns in Montafon. This faraway village was once a famous pilgrimage to the Shrine of the Miraculous Image of Mater Dolorosa, but today the villagers seem more concerned with further-ing its enviable reputation as a winter sports resort. Completely snow-bound days are frequent here, so it is a satisfaction to find the inns—Sporthotel Adler, Gastof Sonne, to name only two of the numerous inns and pensions—all comfortable, with well-stocked larders ready for a long siege of *totentäge*, the dead-days of inactivity, the bane of ski enthusiasts.

It is a proud boast in Tschagguns that in one night it is not unusual for seventy inches of snow to fall softly. At dawn each roof is mantled deep in spotless ermine. Then, they say, the village resembles the Capital of the Snow Queen, whose annual coronation at New Year's festivities attracts guests from all over the world. Always a girl of flaxen beauty is chosen for the Snow Queen.

A rival resort is Grabs, situated 4,800 feet above sea level. There is an old tale that a white Montafon eagle, "an immortal bird," nested for centuries on a crag above Grabs. A kind of ghost eagle seen only in winter, he defied capture. Frequently a dove snatched from one of the valley farms would be found on the snow of Grabs, bleeding from talon marks, but oddly these doves never died. It became the custom for a male of Grabs—all ardent hunters dedicated to bringing down the "phantom" eagle—to wear embroidered on his jacket a *weisse adler* and just so a woman embroidered on her bodice a *weisse taube*. White eagle and white dove of the snows.

In a district known as the Vorarlberg Garden, gateway to the Bregenzerwald, the town of Rankweil wears its judicial mantle from the Early Middle Ages with dignity. This storybook town cherishes its distinction of having played an unusual role in the history of the province from 1200 into modern times. The entire population acting as a tribunal, the jury arranged in tiers of bleachers, sat garbed in the awful solemnity of black robes. Since the 15th century the Pilgrimage

34

Church of the Visitation has been one of the great pilgrimage centers of this Catholic province.

The setting of Liebfrauenkirche has an uncommonly fanciful aspect. Rising in slender elegance, lifting double towers to heaven, the Gothic edifice lies protected within the walled precincts of Felsenwarte, an Early Medieval citadel topping the fern-grown crag of rock that rises unexpectedly from gardens and fruit orchards of Rankweil.

I first saw Rankweil on a day of Pilgrimage. As I approached, the Medieval mood was present in the air of pageantry. A forest of tall "pinions" or pennant poles supported long, pointed banners of wide vermilion and white stripes, the ancient banner of Vorarlberg streaming on the breeze. Although the Liebfrauenkirche is of Gothic style built in 1657-82 (as were most of the town houses and those of the prosperous farmers in this region during the great architectural revival of 1620-1700), nave, alcove-chapels and the altar are richly Rococo, employing superb color in painted lunettes, the whole enriched with gold leaf. The shrine ensconcing the miraculous figure of the crowned Virgin standing with the Child in her arms is a wood carving of the 15th century, silvery olive in tone.

The houses of Rankweil, loosely grouped, form a sort of *cordon d'honneur* at the foot of the mount. Red, brown and gold lichened roofs slant away from the lively colored plaster walls, drenched with berry bushes trained on trellises and espaliered fruit trees, a noticeable feature in the Vorarlberg Garden.

When I wander along the roads and hill paths of the valley, I am constantly being entertained by some inadvertent incident which greatly enlivens the scene. A case in point is this. At mid-morning I had topped a rise near Bezau. As I walked farther up the mountain path, the slopes shortened. A wide belt of pines grew so thickly that I could scarcely press on between the scaly trunks. Suddenly the dense stand of pines ended and I came out into a magic acre—an upland farm entirely screened from the valley below. An emerald-green and golden place, worlds away in time. On a ridge was perched a wide-eaved house, softly colored in all shades of brown from seal to the sepia of the siding boards, to rose-brown and the pale, rain-washed gold of the solid shutters roughly cut out by jig saw in flights of birds. In the mountain meadows, pitched to my mind at an impossible angle for harvesting, worked an entire family with the greatest of ease. A large family of sturdily handsome sun-bleached blond fairness. Each one smiled widely, calling out to me *"Grüss Gott,"* the usual greeting of good nature. Here, I thought, is perfect pastoral beauty, if ever I saw it. A kind of ballet of the gleaners.

I walked on ever upward past long festoons of fragrant, newly scythed hay hung on wooden palings shaped like the Cross—hay so thickly sown with red clover that the air was redolent with the illusive sweetness of field grasses and the headier tang of pine needles. And here, high above Schröcken, so whitely gleaming, set like a village of alabaster beside the Köbersee, which reflected the dark forest and the ravines of Braunarlspitze in bottomless depths, I came suddenly upon a *marterl* of exceptional beauty. I have before now, particularly in the Salzkammergut, seen remote *marterl* crudely made, usually neglected and wind battered. But here in this mountain fastness the richness of the crucifix was startling. The Cross was at least fifteen feet high. The sensitively carved Christ, the features depicting sorrow beyond bearing, was the size of life, the flesh delicately painted in sallow tones. The peaked hood that sheltered the head, crowned in a wreath of iron thorns, was painted in scrolls of red, green and blue. But what filled me with wonder was the carefully tended, lonely garden. Who was it that came to this remote place to tend the garden, to plant, to weed and to change the flowers in the jars? The plot was protected by upright boards of pine to enclose a variety of Alpine flowers, fresh as if just picked, that were arranged in half a dozen glass jars. I was just about to turn away when I caught sight of printing on a card slipped down behind one of the glass jars. I stooped to read.

HERE ON THE BRAUNARLSPITZ LIES KURT RAINER,
1888-1913, AGED 25 YEARS.
*He was hurled to his death by the horns of
a wounded chamois.*

I shall always wonder who tends this boxed garden under the patient Saviour. Too, I can see in my mind's eye a young hunter out shooting on the ridge, perhaps bending over a chamois which he thought he had shot quite dead. Perhaps there was a struggle for footing on this precarious ledge, the sudden fury of the wounded animal rising and butting the too eager young hunter into eternity with his curved horns.

In the church at Schwarzenberg in Bregenzerwald I saw the frescoes painted by Angelica Kauffmann when she was eight years old. Her sense of color and her draftsmanship even at that age were admirable. She was completely self-taught. She became a famous decorator of ceilings and wall panels for such noted architects as Robert Adam at Osterly Park in England. In her native land her subjects, taken from the classic myths and Shakespeare's plays or Austrian history, are widely known.

And now a subtle stir was apparent in the air of the Bregenzerwald. I sensed the hurry and excitement of preparation, for tomorrow would be June 9th, with Fronleichnam (Corpus Christi) processions forming in every village to wend their way up and down the mountain roads all day long, in some localities far into the night.

I arrived in the Kirchplatz at Alberschwende in time to witness the stirring military ceremony which annually precedes the religious one. Alberschwende is rife with historical associations instinct with all the glamour and excitement of having once been a hunting preserve of the counts of Montfort, later Hohenems and Habsburg. Under an oak tree of tremendous girth and reach of branches, its heavy foliage the nesting place for myriad cuckoos, the emblematic bird of Bregenzer-wald, a brace of brass cannon is placed. To punctuate the ceremonies, salutes are fired which reverberate among the rocky ravines and peaks like Olympian thunder.

Young men of the Bregenzerwald and Montafon district have for centuries been known for their conspicuous height, strength and stamina, the typical mountaineer physique. But of this region entire it has always been the strapping sons of Alberschwende (indicated on an early 19th-century map as "Crossroads of the Hunters") that topped the list for inches. Prince Eugen of Savoy, High Commander of the Imperial Armies during the reign of Empress Maria Theresia, witnessed a review of recruits at Bezau. He was so impressed by the strapping contingent from Alberschwende that he forthwith created a special regiment to act as Imperial Household Guards at the imperial palace, the Hofburg. The uniform designed, during the reign of Emperor Franz Josef, for a regiment of foot from the same village is the one presently worn on parade for ceremonies such as Fronleichnam.

Although of correct military pattern, the sense of freedom peculiar to the mountaineer and intrepid hunter is stressed in the colors employed. Rich bronze of pine needles that carpet the wooded aisles; gray of the pine and spruce tree bark. Tunics, the dark burning green of firs, never changing under shadow or under the sun, show a crimson piping at the seams. A narrow brim curls slightly at the sides of high crowned hats of black felt. A dashing plume of cock feathers is posed at the left side, the iridescent fronds sweeping the shoulder.

I had taken a place in the shade cast by the great oak tree and was sketching this nostalgic scene. Six stalwarts marched into the square. A lot of ground was covered by each man's stride, his high black field boots striking sparks of blue fire from the cobblestones. Six muskets were raised and aimed at a point in the sky above the topmost branch of the oak tree. A sharp order, "Fire," and the earth rocked as if convulsed by a minor earthquake. The kick of these weapons, which are said to cause terrific havoc in battle, lethal as that of a small cannon, seemed not in the least to faze these giants in aprons of white butcher's linen. Three volleys they fired in honor of three famous battles in which their regiment had covered itself with glory.

Each village in Bregenzerwald has a personal distinction in dress. In Bezau the married women wear long, skirted gowns of black knife-pleated linen treated with a "secret" process—"dipped in a sort of lacquer" was all I could find out on inquiry—lending the material a high polish like patent leather. Short bolero jackets, their tight finger-tip sleeves piped and embroidered in scrolls or flower designs of royal blue, identify women of this village. Here, too, the black felt hat shaped like a large inverted funnel is worn low and straight across the brow. For unmarried women the five-inch crown is of gold lace, embroidered in gold sequins and arranged slightly tipped forward over the eyebrows.

WOMEN OF BEZAU
BREGENZERWALD.
CORPUS CHRISTI PROCESSION

Of the many variations that I have seen, I have sketched for this book the costume I most favor for its sheer dramatic impact. It is worn by women when attending a funeral for an adult. A cortege of ten women was chosen to wear it in the procession because of the significance of the Corpus Christi ritual. The particular woman I sketched I shall never forget. The geniality of her broad countenance was etched by understanding, humor and patience. Note the Medieval white wimple and the long, pleated tabard of dull black wool resembling a slashed cape that reaches to the knees. Behind this woman walked a young girl who wore an elaborately folded linen headcloth in Medieval mood. Unmarried women, however, do not wear the sweeping cape over the usual shiny black linen dress. It is these differentiations, each detail having a meaning that stems from ancient usages hidden from the uninitiated, that to me makes the study of traditional costumes the world over so intensely interesting. Throughout Austria these costumes are still worn in the daily round.

Shortly after leaving Bezau, I met a brass band. The men wore dark-green knee breeches, heavy white wool stockings, and black silver-buckled shoes. The jackets were varied in hue—plum, gray, brown or black heavily braided in self color. Instead of the bell-crowned top hat, today it was broad-brimmed cavalier hats with low round crowns that completed the men's costumes of the Bregenzerwald, worn with the assurance that this style of dress becomes them.

In the windows of village houses in Alberschwende and all over the mountains the lights from candles shone like stars fallen among the dark pines. In every house a window is opened. In this is set an altar with either a crucifix or a statue of the Virgin surrounded by wreaths and garlands of flowers. When tall candles are lighted at either side, it is as lovely a sight as one will ever see. Extending across the second floor of Gasthaus Taube, there is a *jagdzimmer* or hunt room. The walls are sheathed in pine planks carved in motifs of the chase. A frieze depicting historic hunts that have taken place in the mountains round about is painted on canvas with proper attention paid by the artist to presenting his narrative with characteristic vitality and drama. One hundred and fifty persons have been banqueted in this room after a hunt.

Monumental amounts of wine have been drunk to accompany roast game prepared in the vast kitchen, itself a museum piece. I ordered a game ragout served with fried noodles and braised celery root, the wine a light Vorarlberg.

I left Bregenzerwald by way of a mountain-locked village. Gargellen of the Silences, it is called. Such immensities of fir-clad mountains rise, and dark ravines plunge, threaded with hundreds of exquisite waterfalls. Always the silence. It seems articulate. A voice telling me that this is the way the world looked the day after Creation. Inhaling the cool, crystal air, my eyes searching the dark emerald forests and the cerulean arc of the empyrean, I know that the elements rule here. So, I believe what the silence tells me—this "thunderous tongue of silence," as dying Tamerlane cried out in the night watches. To me there is no greater ecstasy or no greater loneliness than contemplating the timeless mountains.

From Gargellen, Alpinists start to climb the Rötbühlspitz (9,346 ft.), or the notoriously difficult walls of Valzifenzgrat (8,036 ft.). If ascent of these granite giants does not interest you, there are still the pleasures of the Madrisa, a famous inn noted as the purest example of carved and painted peasant-style interiors in this region, renowned, too, for its food.

To every skier the name Arlberg is magic—white magic. The name derives from a connecting link between Tyrol and Vorarlberg, as well-known in Medieval times as it is today. The approach to the "Temple of the White Art," as skiing is called with reverence hereabouts, is through narrow passes glinting with black and white marbled bark of silver birches. Anyone who has spent a fortnight at St. Anton, Lech, or Zürs, all admired winter sports resorts, will agree that it is a never-to-be-forgotten experience. The winding pass of Klostertal is a tortuous way, a maze of viaducts, tunnels and breath-taking curves, but if the trip can be managed the scenic splendor, winter or summer, is too exciting to be foregone.

Langen-on-the-Arlberg is the axis for any number of rewarding excursions into the land of sky and mountains. One particular favorite of mine is the great Walser Valley, the villages of crosshatched larch-wood houses hardly distinguishable from the sun-scorched grasses and amber moss sheathing the rocks. Here is the land of the avalanches, a spectacular winter force in the Arlberg. Late spring is their crashing time when snow, which sometimes does not entirely disappear during the summer, is carved into improbable shapes by the moving sabers of ice. One's imagination takes wings as the eye traces palaces and pavilions, snow galleons sailing rippled seas and whole cavalcades of gigantic knights in armor, thrashed up against the blue sky, only, perhaps, to be assailed by another avalanche and tossed crashing into deep ravines, the black rocks glistening with ice spray. Long after an avalanche has subsided, buried somewhere from sight in the deep crevasses, the thunderous roar continues. I have often found some safe vantage point to watch the whole day through. I once counted nine avalanches in one day; six I saw and three were invisible but I could hear them distinctly, roaring on the other side of the mountains.

Above Hirschegg and Riezlern the green slopes of pastures seem to climb into the clouds. It is here that a race of nomad shepherds live lonely lives tending their flocks and herds, always on the move, grazing the upland pastures far above what is loosely termed "the comforts of civilization." In winter the shepherds hibernate in the valley at the foot of the mountain, housed under the same roof with their flocks. Come "true spring," or "violet time," as it is extolled in their songs, when the snow melts to disclose swathes of deep purple violets sweeping the slopes, they leave the valley for their *maisäss* or "May residences" for perhaps two months until the elements relent and send the long sunny days of "true summer" when the meadow roses blow. I spent a few days in a *maisäss*, a farm owned by Wolf Wildgan. The panorama viewed from my box-bed, built into an angle in the wall of my chamber under the eaves, was a miracle of nature. At sunrise, at sunset, and by the light of a late rising Alpine moon.

On a balcony I ate curds and whey from a wooden bowl, using a mammoth wooden spoon nearly as big as the bowl. I was given a cheese as round as a bushel basket, all to myself. My personal cheese, the rind stenciled with my name in indigo dye, it was intended to last me for the length of my stay. Had I stayed the whole summer I could not have eaten half of it. One night, with a full hunter's moon painting the mountains and valley a rich red-gold, we roasted a roebuck whole over a bed of charcoal out under the stars. Frau Wildgan broached a sealed jar of apple and apricot conserve, a delicacy for which she was famous, to serve with the roast game. We drank no wine with this repast, but ice-cold spring water. All I had to do was walk a few steps from the table and fill a pottery mug from a spring formed by a waterfall tumbling down the mountainside.

For over half a century St. Anton-am-Arlberg, situated in a wide bowl of pasture lands between the mountains called High Arlberg, has been world famous for summer and winter pleasures. The wild glacial waters form whirlpools from which by a phenomenon of nature they divide, forming thousands of rivulets to leap the crags and to form rivers, some of which bear storied names—the Inn, the Danube, and the Rhine. The people of St. Anton will often say, "We are famous for three things: Hannes Schneider and his Arlberg technique of skiing downhill—making us the ski capital of the world; our Hotel Post, as famous to travelers as the Paris Ritz; and the pretty houses built on the meadow slopes by foreign ladies who bring a new husband here each year."

The walks around St. Anton lead through groves of pine, larch and mountain ash beside rushing streams. Up one climbs at an angle not too steep for enjoyment. Tea and cakes are served at *hütten* scattered along the ascent. Here is a walker's paradise. The beautiful Fervalltal walk up the larch-fringed paths is rewarded for being an unusually stiff pull by the large *hütte* Constanza which welcomes you to its broad terraces for coffee and fabulous pastries. Sit long over whatever it is you order and watch the sun set and, if you are lucky, the moon rise over the silently slipping Rosanna. A glacial river, it winds serpentine around St. Anton toward the hospice of St. Christophe and the magnificent wildness of the gorge where with sound and fury it unites with the Trisanna to flow in unexpected harmony to join the Inn. There are hotels in plenty to suit every taste—Hotel Valluga, Hotel Schwarzer Adler. The spacious Alpenrose seems always in festive

43

WINTER ERMINE
ST. ANTON·AM·ARlberg

mood, painted roses sprawling over its eaves and balconies, and fat bolsters and coverlets, puffed on the windowsills to air, as gay as a field of poppies.

Whenever I enter the Arlberg over the passes of Flexen-Fern, Hochalpenstrasse, Silvretta, or the dramatic wildness of the Arlberg–Orient route, I am elated by the sight of rivers at full flow foaming in torrents, or running deep and swift through fern-grown gorges, the icy waters dark as obsidian from reflecting the ever-present stands of larch and pine. Above these waters the stag ruts, the red deer leaps, the wily capercailzie struts, and the blackcock dances his comic wooing waltz. I have an old fondness for rivers. I like rivers to be well watered no matter whether the river is great or small, a creek or brook runneling grasses. In Austria, because of frequent rainfall and the source of so many streams, a sky-borne watershed, the rivers are invariably in full spate.

Standing on a ridge above Prutz in the Oberinntal, it seemed that I stood alone in time, possessor of the world. Spreading away from me were rivers in silver-channeled ravines by the score. I gazed across deep watered valleys. Pine clad and snow crested, the mountains seemed to stretch away to misty horizons. I stood knee-deep in gentians. From the long, dagger-shaped leaves the mountaineers brew a potent, aromatic liqueur. As if a vast Persian floral carpet had been tossed over the ridge of rock, every Alpine flower in the roster appeared to flower in multitude. I picked a few blossoms so that I might later learn their names. The blushing Alpenrose (*Rhododendron Ferrugineum*). The turquoise and violet frilly Flockenblume (*Centaurea Montana*). Loveliest of all I think is the varicolored Leinkraut (*Linaria Alpine*) resembling the garden columbine, its violet, blue, pale gold and pink petals aquiver as if dancing in the breeze. I painted the dark wine-purple Frühlingsenzian (*Gentian Verna*) for the vigorous double-star formation of its petals. I noticed that the flower predominant in the Arlberg floral galaxy is the exquisitely fragile, heliotrope-pink Zyklamen (*Cyclamen Europaeum*). Great bunches of this flower are gathered before dawn, the dew still sparkling, by young men who have been chosen to join a wedding party. They toss these

45

flowers over the head of the bride to insure the lasting freshness of her complexion.

The next morning, bound for Tyrol, I visited Tösens, a brown and white village perched on its emerald-green, grassy knoll, seeming as contented as a broody hen warming her set of eggs. Then on to Pfunds sunk in solitude, hardly a soul abroad, where the high-fronted pink and green plaster houses are frescoed with ribbons and scrolls perpetuating in boldly painted script verses from the poems of Pfunds' most celebrated son, the Arlberg poet Senn. I went on through leafy lanes, finally reaching Oetz.

The highlight of this large town is Gasthof Stern, an inn dating from Gothic times, one of the chief existing treasures of Arlberg Medieval architecture. A large oriole window surrounded by a frame of iron-work enriches the façade. The exquisite delicacy of design convinced me that it is from the hands of those Medieval craftsmen who so greatly embellished Innsbruck and Salzburg with balconies and hanging signs of ornamental ironwork. The entire front of the inn is frescoed in a manner extraordinarily sumptuous. Surprisingly fresh in color, too, the painted procession winds upward between the tiers of windows. The scene depicts noble lords and ladies in grand array preceded by pages bearing heraldically emblazoned shields and banners proclaiming their style and title. Groups of portly burgesses in dark robes, furred wealthily, crowd huntsmen laden with spoils of the chase, who in turn are jostled by arrogant prelates in bejeweled gold miters. One bishop seems to be deviously whispering—possibly a plea for advancement—into the ear of a hovering archangel. Above this window the star performer in the painted pageantry looms large— St. Christopher, carrying on his heavily muscled shoulders a delicate pink and white Christ Child eating an apple.

In the raftered and frescoed *speishalle*, or main dining room, I ate *huhne im nudl-suppe*, a sort of chicken fricassee in broth garnished with herb- and onion-flavored dumplings.

My last view of the majestic peaks of the Kaunsertal-in-Arlberg, illumined rose-gray and silvery gold in long rays from the setting sun, included at closer range a living picture that is the subject of many a frescoed inn front hereabouts. A hunting party of ten or a dozen men were returning leisurely from a day's shooting, wearing the traditional forest-green and gray jackets and the black or green Tyrolean hats rakishly bedecked with silver badges, brush, and cluster of oak leaves denoting that the wearer had brought down whatever quarry. Behind this shooting party came a group of young boys carrying on pine-branch litters the spoils of a good day's sport. Suddenly the forest aisles echoed to the winding of a horn. A long, lovely whirl of notes strangely like wind among the pines soared to a crescendo; then to the gentle cadence of falling water. "Arlberg Music," the call familiar to every forest hunter, a signal—"come you all together"—to gather at a previously arranged meeting place.

I went away down the path, listening. I could still hear far off in the fastness the answering sound of a hunting horn, wound by some belated hunters, to say, "We come, await us, we come." And then, mingling with this music, I heard a more distant call, the rippling notes of a shepherd's pipes summoning his herd together. All about me the air was musical. Thus I departed from the High Arlberg to the sound of its traditional music.

HATS
WORN IN
TYROL

Chapter 3

SPARKLING TYROL, SUN
ON A HUNDRED ALPINE PEAKS,
GILDED ROOFS AGAINST
A SAPPHIRE SKY

IN THE Tyrol, how brightly everything gleams in the sunlight. Palest pink and lavender mountain chalets accented by vivid red geraniums and purple *veilchen*, or Alpine violet. The metallic white of shimmering, distant peaks that never lose their mask of ice or snow. The deep green, the silvered blues of pine, spruce, cedar and larch, cobwebbed with crystal in the dawn mist. Shiny red faces of the Tyrolese, glistening with health and glowing from brisk scrubbing with cold spring water. Land of Tyrol, the villagers say, is divided into as many localities as Switzerland is into cantons, but many of the boundaries exist only in the minds of the inhabitants. In Obergurgl on the Italian frontier, where black and golden eagles eternally battle to the death in the gentian-blue skies, fighting in a shower of tattered plumage for supremacy of the crags, the curious dialect of the chamois hunters—for this is pre-eminently chamois country—is a tantalizing blend of Hoch Mitteldeutsch (correct Middle Ages German), northern Italian and "Deep Green" Tyrolese. The tall, robust inhabitants of what they call the Deep Green Tyrol, an area bounded by St. Anton, Imst, Nauders and Reutte, are so energetic that a grizzled old hunter will tell you with a glint of humor in his narrow, upslanted, icy blue eyes, "We are always too busy working for our old age to give time to sleep." He will tell you that since ancient days, when this was a country of the earliest known mountain passes, when Celtic and later Roman pack mules laboriously climbed the Alpine tracks, his people of the Deep Green Tyrol have been the blood stream of the race. A pulsing, richly red blood stream to strengthen an inherently virile race.

The wanderer in Tyrol, and wandering at will is the reason for coming to this province, comes upon sudden changes of mood in the people and in the extraordinary variety of traditional costumes, in many localities worn even in the daily round. Perhaps most noticeable of all are the superstitions, a legacy from pagan worship. I find this mood more prevalent in Tyrol than in any other Austrian province save Carinthia. Old ones in the mountains will nod in their chimney corners and say, "It is all because of the mad Föhn"—that south wind so unpredictable, so variable, that every illness, sudden death, misfortune of any kind, is blamed on the Föhn. The Föhn may cause the temperature to rise to 80 degrees Fahrenheit in January, turning icicles into the "ice rain" which bodes no good. Often in August when all is serene, the cows contentedly grazing in Alpine meadows, the women "cruddling" cream for their bland yellow cheeses, hundreds of which will be stored away until Christmas, the Föhn will meet his rival north wind. The Föhn invariably wins, but during the struggle the "gasps" of the north wind will drive the temperature down close to zero.

I drove from Stanz to Landeck deeper into what a large sign rearing next to a roadside shrine informed me was THE HOLY PROVINCE OF TYROL. The device was painted with a score of heraldic quarterings, surrounding the Red Eagle of Tyrol. I climbed by a series of serpentine rises to view one of the most exciting panoramas the Tyrol has to offer. The Gründe of Mayrhofen splits into valleys, like the spread fingers of a hand, to reveal sweeping vistas of deciduous trees, all the blues and greens in the spectrum, and the glitter of snow and ice rising above the timber line. There is drama here, a great stage setting for the whimsical pleasures or catastrophes of the Old Gods of the Mountains, represented in Tyrolese legend as North, South, East and West Winds. Black-cloud ramparts piled over Zwieselstein. This is a small secretive village of frescoed houses drowsing under a hunting castle once a favorite residence of Maximilian I, familiarly known as "Hunter Max." But more vividly is this place remembered for its connection with the wife of Archduke Ferdinand of Tyrol, the beautiful Philippine Welser. Around her memory shine more legends, each one contradicting the other, than there are moon rays in the diadem of the Madonna of Ambras in Schloss Ambras chapel, a statue for which the lovely, incredibly fragile Philippine is said to have posed. A persistent legend has it that soon after the statue was finished, the lady died of poison administered in a cup of wine by a spurned suitor.

The slopes of the Ötz rise in steps which give the effect of cyclopean hanging gardens. Sölden, Unhausen, Langenfeld and Ötz. My road wove upward through stands of larch, the needles of the fernlike branches quivering in the Föhn wind and catching the last rays of livid, before-the-storm sunshine, to flame in every shade of green from pale chartreuse to vivid emerald. At Vent I sought shelter from the deluge in a farmhouse crouched on a high, grassy escarpment, hanging out over a torrent-riven gorge at what, I thought, even in ordinary weather would seem a perilous angle. It was an old house, "carved, waxed and painted" in curious symbols. The roof was shingled in great slabs of pine bark so encrusted with a rich crop of gold lichen that it obscured the good-sized boulders arranged in checkerboard pattern to weight the roof. Now, with tempest winds lashing the crag, I looked at the date 1645 carved over the entrance door and wondered how this mountain retreat had endured through three centuries. But I was assured all would be well. This was "just that Föhn." The man told me his daughter lived in a house two hundred years older than this one "up the mountain"—he pointed into the rain—at an altitude of 6,000 feet. I had heard of these cloud-borne Ötz farms where the mountaineer farmers do not come down into a valley village but twice a year, in the spring and in the autumn.

I came into Schwaz at late sunset hour, as all the church bells were ringing. It was a sunset of russet gold that evening. I thought how appropriate that I should behold the ancient town thus. For it was on the silver and copper mines of Schwaz, "The City of the Mint," that one of the greatest banking fortunes the world has ever known was founded. The five Fugger brothers, among their other achievements, founded the courier system, as such, and amazingly efficient it was, with deputies in every town of any size in any land where trading or "the business of making money" could be carried on. Peace correspondents. War correspondents. The House of Fugger working later from Augsburg in Germany kept files which reveal that in 1650 they had 15,000 men in their employ "at a wage." The original five brothers were known by a kind of title, Die Münzreiche—"The Rich in Coin."

In one of the cobbled streets of Schwaz stands an old corner house, actually a tower. A niche is cut out of one angle to recess a statue of striking curiosity. A figure roughly hewn in stone portraying Georg von Freundsberg, called variously "The Ferocious" or, because of his rutting habits with women, "The Uncouth." He is, nevertheless, a local hero, the famous mercenary soldier leader of the Peasant Revolt. (The Castle of Freundsberg, ancient "lair" of his family, imperially powerful in this region, sits impregnable, high above the town on a thrusting spur of rock reached by the hardy climber via a tortuous path.) The warrior appears to have been in stature a squat creature, as massive-shouldered as a gorilla. His statue shows him clothed entirely in plate armor save for a helm, which it is said he spurned to wear, even in battle.

The impressive yet curiously dark and forbidding Gothic Schloss Siegmundslust near Schwaz was built by Duke Siegmund in 1440 when he was renowned throughout Europe as the richest prince of his day. In the great beamed halls of the castle there are traces of the former extravagance in decoration. Frescoes, carving and gilding, all paid for by riches from the mines of Schwaz.

Hall-im-Tyrol, or Solbad Hall-on-the-Inn, is another town of proud ancestry. In the Middle Ages, wealth from salt mines raised it to such eminence that it was called "Hall, the envy of princes." This was one of Duke Siegmund's favorite possessions. He built the old Münzerturm (Mint Tower). The high, round belfry with its overhanging Nuremburg Gothic-style "penthouse," vast pointed dormer windows and encircling galleries, is in itself a veritable village on high. The tower is said to have been used as a model by Albrecht Dürer as the central motif in many of his paintings. The original fortifications were built by the Romans, who also erected a Temple to Poseidon and established the most "fashionable" baths of the time.

The approach to Innsbruck, the road wending along the richly green valley of the Inn, is as inviting, as felicitous, as any approach to a storied city I have ever entered. Acting as a benediction to the Glory of God and one's pleasant sojourn in Innsbruck, the Abbey of Stams reposes amid a grove of chestnut trees. Stams is not in the ordinary way open to the public. The abbot, living in seclusion, most graciously grants an invitation to a small party. Stams is now a cloistered retreat for men who wish to retire from the world, to live out in abiding quiet whatever span of years is left to them.

Granted that the Abbey has been altered to suit various personal tastes and to conform with architectural styles of the times since its founding six hundred years ago, it now presents a Baroque face of unrivaled beauty. The frescoes, in deep smoldering color, featuring all reds, purples and the green of mountain pools, depict the Tree of Life, a phantasmagoria of movement framed in Baroque carving by Franz Krichmayer, the Giant of Tratzberg. He used to delight in cutting a notch on a doorpost to show his height as eight feet. On his deathbed he "confessed" to his townspeople that gossip had been right. As a youth he had "sold his soul to the Devil." Why? "Why, always to have enough money to buy tools and wood to carve."

I entered Innsbruck by the Maria Theresienstrasse under the Triumphal Arch. In the center of the street rises the lovely shaft of nearly translucent rose-pink marble, the Annasäule. The column is dedicated to St. Anne; the figure on top is St. Mary. In a relaxed attitude St. Mary stands viewing the city, her cloak trails gracefully down, the hem entangled in a naturalistic way among the rich floriations of acanthus leaves forming the Corinthian capitals. Along this romantic street, lights were coming on. The ornate façade of the Thurn and Taxis Palace was ablaze, setting agleam the coronal of stars forming a nimbus around the saint's head.

Late twilight was upon me when I arrived at Hotel Maria-Theresia in the Altstadt (Old Town) to change before an engagement for dinner at the Stiftskeller, where one dines either out under the trees or inside a richly gold and mahogany dining salon, actually three big rooms. In 1600, mahogany destined for paneling and floors in the palace of an Austrian sugar nabob was sent from Santo Domingo to Innsbruck. The palace was never built and the mahogany planking reverted to the Court and Franciscan Church, of which this restaurant is an adjunct.

I found food at the Stiftskeller excellent, as I have so often done in the past. The night was starry-eyed but sharp, with an Alpine snow-chill in the air—mid-July no matter—so I ordered my Schnitzle Maria-Theresia served in one of the dining rooms. This dish is a veal steak sautéed in butter. Tomatoes, cauliflower cut into "nosegays," and onions are grilled under the flame and dusted lightly with paprika. If you take heed you will see that this dish reveals the Austrian national colors, red and white with the addition of the Imperial gold. (Sautéed to the proper turn, the veal steak appears golden.) Gold was the Empress' favorite color for her wardrobe.

In a corridor joining two of the dining rooms one wall is covered from baseboard to cornice by a "blazoning" in carved wood, stunning for sheer bravado in heraldic ornament, of the Imperial arms of Austria, quartering Lorraine. This device, carved openwork in three-quarter-round, is covered in burnished gold leaf. When the Empress Maria Theresia came to the Hofburg to celebrate the marriage of her son, she presented to the City of Innsbruck a gigantic barrel equal to four "tuns" of the best Gumpoldskirchner. This armorial plaque in massive, now hanging on the wall of Stiftskeller, was fixed to one end of the barrel. An extraordinarily decorative ornament of imperial aggrandizement, it is perfectly lighted for close inspection. Some idea may be gained of the immensity of the barrel, as well as the extrava-gance in which the habitually closefisted Empress indulged herself as a sort of glorification of her adored son Leopold. The barrel was hauled on a gun carriage through the streets. Dancing, carnival and "weintrinken" knew no restraint. Within a few weeks, while the wed-ding festivities were just on the wane, Emperor Francis I died suddenly at Hofburg "from a chill," or so the Court Calendar advised the populace. The Empress had come so joyously to Innsbruck, always a favorite city, whence she had once written to her daughter Marie Antoinette in Versailles, "I come to Hofburg set in the cup of Alpine mountains to refresh my eyes on the snows of Heaven." She stayed to attend her husband's funeral.

It is extensively documented in word and picture that this ceremony was a show of imperial pomp and circumstance, every bit as splendid as the wedding celebrations had been, albeit draped in gloom. Immediately after the funeral Maria Theresia caused the Triumphal Arch to present two vastly different faces. On the side where the bridal pair had entered the city are the original scenes of joy and life, carved in marble plaques. On the side that faces the St. Anne shaft, looking down the length of Maria Theresienstrasse, are depicted dreary scenes of mourning. An Arch of Triumph.... triumph over Life and over Death.

At Hofburg, I find that visitors to Innsbruck are awestruck by the immense sweep, lovely fresh color, the splendor of painted rooms, wealth of spirited portraits, and the fanciful tile stoves so indicative of the Tyrolean scene. The Giant's Hall, a vast but skillfully proportioned apartment, was considered, at the time of the famous wedding ceremony for Leopold, a marvel of the age. Couriers were sent from half the courts of Europe, with instructions to look, listen, and if allowed, copy down details.

The ceiling paintings by Franz Anton Maulpertsch, done in 1775, are unique in art, combining architecture in false prospective or Italian chiaroscuro rising in tiers of colonnades with figures in diminuendo. In the pale distance Olympian deities, flouting every law of gravitation, congregate on templed clouds. The effect is of unlimitable space and luminous clarity. As a foil to these limpid pinks, violets, primrose yellows and cerulean blues, and every value of white, a parade of heroes famed in Tyrolean history, banners streaming upon the breeze, armor flashing, destriers rearing on strong muscled hocks—a lusty crew painted in rich dark colors—stresses, as I have never seen before, the unassailable distance between the immortal godhead of legend and flesh-and-blood characters of documented history.

The life-size portraits of the Imperial children, painted separately in full *grande toilette*, are revealing as to character as well as being brilliant documents of the fashions and foibles of the period. "Primal" (primrose), childhood name for Marie-Antoinette, is exquisite in wide panniers of heliotrope and apple green traced with silver lace. But in all the castle collection, it is the full-length portrait by Winterhalter of Empress Elizabeth of Austria, in a star-sprinkled gown, a net of stars loosely confining her night-dark hair, that evokes most nostalgia for a ravishing beauty that is no more.

Besides providing a sumptuous residence for sovereignty, the Hofburg has the air of a small village nearly self-contained: the Stiftskeller (church restaurant), shops showing diverse wares in the arcaded street lining the Hofgarten courtyard, the castle apartments of state, and the intimate living quarters which rest directly in the arms of the church. The Court Church of Innsbruck, impressive in magnitude and its aura of ancient history, is a part of a "household," a rarity in religious houses. Acting as an anteroom to the church proper is the Silver Chapel, subtly fragrant with the odor of fresh flowers on the altar and scarcely more than the remembrance of azure smoke from centuries of incense wreathing from the silver censers that are arranged in ordered rows around the walls, partially accounting for the name of this sanctuary. In the Silver Chapel it is the "reborn" antiquity that adorns this radiant repository of Ferdinand, the great Renaissance prince, and his wife, the patrician beauty Philippine Welser.

It was Alexandre Colin, the leading sculptor of his time in Austria, who executed these recumbent effigies in silver, and black marble. The precious Silver Lattice altar, uncommonly compelling, is wrought in the most delicate hand-tooled silver, and strikes me as a kind of personal diary showing signs of the Zodiac and replicas of various residences, their fountains and gardens, beloved by Ferdinand and his wife. The small cedar-wood organ presented to Ferdinand by the pope is one of the rarest curiosities of the musical world. An Italian instrument of the 16th century, an organ of "great tone," it can be carried on horseback.

The nave and side ambulatories of Court Church seen from the

Silver Chapel gallery, embracing a score of alcove chapels, arrest the eye in a breath-catching parade of past history in bronze portraiture of twenty-eight personages frozen into immovability, only momentarily it would seem, so that the visitor may fittingly behold in detail the armor and jeweled damasks in which during life they confronted the world. Locally called "the black men," the bronze having aged to a smoky patina resembling obsidian, they form a grave crew of watchers. With hooded, narrowed or bulging eyes, they gaze across the empty red marble sarcophagus where Emperor Maximilian I had planned, with the greatest care, for this magnificent retinue to watch over him in perpetuity. But this did not come to pass. The bronze figures were not finished until almost a century had elapsed. By that time the mortal remains of Maximilian had been interred in a simple church in his native town of Wiener Neustadt.

On the imposing red marble sarcophagus is the kneeling figure of Emperor Maximilian, resplendent in coronation robes, wearing the heavily jeweled Imperial crown and Mantle of St. Stephen, his hands folded in prayer. He is guarded by four angels bearing articles particular to the performance of Holy Communion. All this is protected by a forest of bronze gilt Madonna lilies. As I stood gazing down at the empty sarcophagus, I thought how Maximilian had endeared himself to his people of Tyrol. It is not as the last of the *chevalier sans peur sans reproche* of Europe that he will be remembered by future generations of Tyrolese, but as one of themselves. A handsome fair-haired giant. A bold hunter and mountaineer who had laughed with their ancestors, had drunk their wine and passionately loved their beautiful daughters. Perhaps most of all he will be remembered for his gallantry. A woman from whom I bought postcard views of a hunting lodge (now a semiruined tower near Schloss Ambras), built by "Hunter Max" because he had been saved by divine intercession from an avalanche on that spot, said to me, "He was a noble and courteous gentleman."

It is impossible to give in detail more than a resumé of the splendor and ingenuity of detail in the technical realization of this bronze assemblage of long-dead emperors, kings, queens and prelates. Mary of Burgundy, first wife of Maximilian, wears her wedding dress and the tall *hennin* (steeple) headdress of Burgundian origin. Her face is full-fleshed, the features set in proud stern lines for one not eighteen years old at her marriage. But "my golden lily," as infatuated Maximilian ordered embroidered in cabochon topaz on the canopy borne over Mary in their bridal procession, was overproud of purse and lineage.

Various artists of note designed these statues. The one-legged "Drunkard of Munich," Gilg Sesselschreiber, was brought in a litter from Munich to do some of the work. He was superseded by Peter Vischer. Albrecht Dürer himself executed the statue "idyllic of legendary chivalry" presenting King Arthur of England, superbly proud of stance. As a case in point, the jeweled gorget ending in a collar displaying the pendant dragon of St. George, the sheep, representative of the Order of the Golden Fleece, and the epaulets of winged dragons about to take flight are considered in the first rank of important German Renaissance craftsmanship.

Theodoric, King of the Goths, is again by Dürer. The raised visor of his helm casts a deep shadow, out of which gaze the mournful eyes of the "dreamer of great dreams." Graf Albrecht of Habsburg appears rather the court jester in a Medieval masque than an anointed knight and fearless warrior, as history judges him to be. He is all flounces and jigged-jaggedry in knee garters, flowing sleeves, a corseted waistline and a luxurious walrus mustache.

Philip the Good has tremendous presence. His face is thoughtful and more than a little lined with weariness. Inordinately pious, fanatical to the point of spending the last years of his life as an anchorite on his knees in prayer. Godefroy of Bouillon, King of Jerusalem, leader of the First Crusade, has a rock-hewn face heavily bearded. The Cross of Malta in *profondo*-carved jewels covers his broad chest. He carries his head proudly, a wickedly sharp Crown of Thorns encircling his brow. Ferdinand the Catholic, his armor emblazoned with the Lion of Castile and the "Twain Castles" thereof, turns away his face, lined with pain from his suppurating wounds which never healed, from Joanna the Mad, so heavily bedecked with jewels of shells, starfish and creatures of the sea that her shoulders bow under the weight. Her mouth seems simpering, her eyes peer unfocused in a vacant stare. Maria Bianca Sforza of Milan, second wife of Maximilian, is a buxom woman, woefully plain of visage. Her attire however is sumptuous. The deeply incised design of pomegranate fruit, and acanthus leaves simulating cut-Genoese velvet, the texture softly burnished, the folds darkly rich, is a *tour de force* in skillful modeling. But it is the modeling of her slender hands, the fingers held as if she were describing the length of a meter of silk, that call for applause. The face of Rudolf of Habsburg, founder of the dynasty, is that of an aristocratic rodent. Crafty, petulant, purposely cruel. On his egg-shape skull, with meager locks plastered down into a pageboy bob, a fanciful crown, high as a dunce cap, sits precariously.

For sheer drama, a battering ram for impact on the imagination, give me Ferdinand of Portugal. His "pig-snout" helm is topped by a refulgent royal crown, actually a second casque, from which springs a rampant panache of "Turkish" plumes of the ostrich, straight not curled. It is the surprise of boldly carved infant satyrs astride flame-snorting dragons which form Ferdinand's plastron collar and *enplaque-ture* on his corselet that fills the eye. Going out into the sunlight of Medieval streets does not destroy the mood of these personages who lived "when panoply was real."

In the Old Town—Herzog Friedrich Strasse—the street is flanked for three quarters of a mile by *lauben* (vaulted arches), The Stadtturm (Town Tower), the house called Goldener Dachl (Golden Roof) and the house at Number 35 Blutbannadler (Blood Ban Eagle) featuring on its blood-red walls an Imperial Eagle on whose feathers the coats-of-arms of the various Estates are arranged in groups of four. The eagle holds in its talons two judges' swords. The owner of this house, built in 1485, was granted by the Emperor the right to pass the death sentence at will without right of trial, correcting a ruffian in the street by truncating him if he so wished. It is the only visible display of the "Blood Eagle" still existent in Austria, or in any German-speaking country. Dungeons were kept full of miscreants under this house. Today the place is said to be haunted to the last corbel by shrieks, groans, the sound of whiplash on naked flesh.

In Innsbruck, every time I ask the history of this house, or that castle, legends stream. The house called Golden Dachl wears an aura of legend second only to that forming a glittering diadem around the memory of Philippine Welser. One legend says that Duke Frederic— who owes his nickname of "the Empty Purse" to the fact that he had been outlawed, a fugitive in distress—had previously built the house, and that he added the balcony with golden metal shingles to prove his purse had been "mysteriously refilled." I believe the truth lies in the fact that the house appears in the chronicles of the town as having been built in 1500 by Emperor Maximilian in perpetual commemoration of his wedding with Maria Bianca Sforza, but also as a "box" for the onlookers at the shows of mountebanks, gypsies from Hungary, "circuses out of Italy" and tourney held in the town square. The canopy or roof of gold-leaf metal tiles laid in overlapping scales, like those of Minerva's Aegis of Wisdom, were intended solely to draw the attention of foreign visitors to the splendor of Maximilian's Court.

The Giant's House in Hofgasse (Court Street) was given to Nikolaus Haidl, the court giant. An old sandstone statue of this "lovable and merry" giant, towering nearly ten feet, stands on a parapet. Close by is the Rennweg, to my mind easily the most beautiful old square in the town. The ancient houses are stately, proud, and frescoed and carved with imagery.

Innsbruck is particularly happy in hotels and restaurants, cafés and *weinstuben,* to entertain her guests in the best Tyrolean style. Goldener Adler (Golden Eagle) in Herzog Friedrich Strasse is anciently famed for its fine cuisine. Its guest book, in which I was asked to make a sketch of an eagle (instead of my usual horse), is only one of sixty volumes accumulated since long before Maria Theresia "took a portion of wine" there during the famous wedding celebrations for Leopold. Near St. Anne's column is an ancient house, Alt Innsbruck, an inn with a great bay window decorated with two bronze replicas of the statues by Dürer and Vischer in the Hofkirche. The food here is in the best Tyrol tradition. But I prefer to stop at the old Hotel Maria

Theresia, though the Europa is excellent too. The new hotels, like Hotel Tyrol, which is practically in the railway station, are too noisy and always overcrowded. Perhaps the most memorable food to be had in Innsbruck is at Grauer Bär, a little way out of town but easy of access. I highly recommend the food and the view.

On my way out to Schloss Ambras I stopped at Wilten Abbey. A superb gesture in volatile Baroque enrichment, it has a proud Roman past. There have been buildings of religious nature standing here for nine hundred years. And before that a "retreat" for Roman patricians is mentioned in Roman scrolls. Tiberius called it Veldidena. In the museum are Roman relics in bronze.

The Madonna, called "Our Lady Among The Four Pillars, Sancta Mater," above the High Altar, my favorite Mary in Austria, sits within the crescent of a silver new moon. The Christ Child stands balanced a trifle uncertainly on one knee. Mary Mother seems more like a big sister told to sit still and mind her baby brother, than a mother of a child. Her heavy jeweled diadem is almost a papal miter, surrounded by a nimbus halo of silver stars. Her mantle is silver, lined with sapphire blue. To me she resembles a woodland nymph, a faun, or the King of Elfland's daughter. Her faint smile is the quizzical one of an old soul. What gives to Madonna and Child the illusion that they are floating in celestial spheres is the tremendous sunburst of silver-gilt rays, in number to defy counting, that forms a frame for the figures, the radius at least twenty feet high and over half as wide. Light from the afternoon sun streamed in through an ogival window. In its rays, trillions of golden moats flitted like scattered sequins in front of the Madonna, enthroned by the rays of her own private sun. Here to me was pure beauty, lift of the spirit in sanctity.

If anyone holds the opinion that Nature ever takes a rest from creating diversions bordering on the fabulous, or that her imagination ever falters and grows stale, he has only to pay a visit to the ice caves of Gletscherhöhle near the Berlinerhütte at Ginzling in the Zillertal, 6,732 feet above Innsbruck. One enters the pillared colonnades of this Palace of Perpetual Winter through a Gothic portal of ice, to walk for many furlongs through a shimmering, pale-green and silver world of vaulted naves and long winding ambulatories, the roof supported by twisted or fluted columns of pure ice, luminous as if lighted from within. There are benches of ice to sit on; tables hewn from ice on which to spread a picnic lunch if one is so inclined. Each morning, children come down from the heights to present to the custodian of the caves bouquets of Alpine flowers. These are thrust into apertures cut into the pillars and the walls. The huge bunches of flowers—Alpine roses, mountain gentian and the fragile pink and yellow Alpine orchid—retain their pristine freshness in the caves for a fortnight. An ice palace of many marvels, possibly the greatest is the marvel of temperature. Take your lunch leisurely, in an atmosphere bracing but only mildly cool.

When the two hundred and eighty-five variously ancient castles of the Tyrol are being discussed, the Castle of Ambras is generally conceded the palm. Star of the Tyrol, because of the star formation of the great bastion of rock from which rise its walls, it rides high above the surrounding valley, at all times silhouetted against the sky, the lights from its towers at night seeming to form a part of the starry firmament. By day the majestic "presence" of Ambras dominates the Valley of the Inn for many leagues. Approaching Innsbruck from Brenner Pass, from Passo Giovo or valley highways, this gigantic thrust of pale yellow masonry fills the eye and holds one's attention. Each of the countless windows is hung with solid wooden shutters painted white, bearing as device the Crusader's Cross in brilliant vermilion. The roof levels form a veritable village in themselves, presenting a patchwork of tiles from palest pink to deep red and raisin-brown, rimed with lichen or frilled in acid-green moss. Some of the tiles date from the 11th century. The patching is still going on, for I noticed workmen hoisting to the roof rose-red tiles to add still a fresher shade of red to this mosaic of colored clay. Verily an aerial picture in Dürer's style set against the stark whiteness of a cloud-piled sky.

The Counts of Andrechs early in the 11th century founded the town of Innsbruck. First, two proud warrior brothers Andrechs erected a timber bridge across the Inn. Each intended to build himself the mightiest castle ever seen in these parts, but history clouds over

GUARDIAN OF
THE VINEYARDS.
BRENNER.

at this point, for there is no record of *two* castles Andrechs. Only the embattled history of Castle Ambras survives, originally a mighty fortress of rough dressed stone. (The gigantic purplish-brown stones one sees in the ancient Roman bridges and fortress-castles. Boulders in early days were hauled out from the rocky debris of landslides to build "impregnably.") In 1515 Archduke Ferdinand II caused the castle to be entirely rebuilt into the Renaissance château one sees today. A *lustschloss* for merrymaking, or "pleasure palace," what the Plantaganet builders in Early Medieval England called a "*faire plaisaunce*." This development of defense castle into richly appointed residence was, of course, "a subtlety of Ferdinand's" for the purpose of dazzling his bride, Philippine Welser of Augsburg, stupendous beauty of the age, with a palace more luxurious than any other hitherto conceived. That he momentously succeeded, historians down the ages have agreed.

The archduke laid the foundation for an extensive collection of art treasures and arms which attained to world-wide renown under the name "Ambraser Sammlung." There are paintings by Lucas Cranach, Jan Vredeman de Vries, and the remarkable "Gale at Sea," considered the masterpiece of Jan Brueghel the Elder. Sculpture is set in a gallery situated in the highest part of the castle. The greatest treasures here are a series of mythological figures in bronze by the vital Giovanni da Bologna.

To me the armory is the heartbeat of the castle. Here I find sound and fury and great design. Here is displayed one of the foremost existing collections of arms for man and horse presented in such a way that knighthood in all its exciting pageantry leaps instantly to life the moment the great steel shutters that cover the tall windows on both sides of the gallery are flung back. In two long, high, vaulted Gothic rooms the procedure of jousting, as practiced between 1460 and 1580, is exemplified in models the size of life. In one room the visitor witnesses the joust or tourney at full gallop, knights intent, lances lowered at the thrust, visors down, torso crouched at balance to receive the impact of the opponent's lance point. One horse is caparisoned in housings of white linen blazoned with blue eagles and wide blue chevron stripes. Blue and white heron plumes are wired to give the effect of streaming out upon a steady wind. The second challenger is Red and White. Housings are quilted silk crosshatched red "bracelets" upon a white ground. The crest upon the helm of this knight is a winged red dragon poised for lift, its forked tongue spitting streams of red-silk flame. The room fairly reverberates with the sense of speed. The great destriers, superbly modeled at full-out gallop, seem about to crash into one another. Here is an exciting, evocative picture arrested in motion to raise the hackles on one's neck.

In another room one can view the sumptuous armor of Archduke Ferdinand, wrought in 1582 in honor of his wedding, of gold, silver, copper and black steel by Jakob Topf of Innsbruck, "Armorer to Princes" (so the archduke styled the man in gratitude for such craftsmanship).

A most entertaining display are five figures of children, Austrian princes, ranging from four or five years to perhaps ten or twelve, in full armor, even to visors lowered and sword or lance in hand. These effigies are arranged in a circle around the figure of Harmon of Hall-im-Tirol, the famous "palace giant." A ludicrous picture indeed, for he towers more than nine feet above the five versions of Jack the Giant Killer princes. (His burial casket measured nine feet, ten inches.) It is recorded that when the armorer who fashioned "full body armor to sheath Harmon of Hall" had finished his mighty task, he sent in a bill equivalent to that for six suits of armor for the average-size man.

The great expanse of wall in the Spanischer Saal (Spanish Room) seems peopled with an eloquent assemblage of potentates from out some Eastern land. Twenty-six figures portraying kaisers of Austria, (always it has been emperor in Austria) and princely personages are painted in glowing colors. Some appear in what would seem to be fancy dress, but what is in reality the richest and most exotic imperial raiment that court tailors in whatever century could devise for the coronation of the Kaiser, so that he and his guests would outshine any previous king or emperor and entourage. I noted a red fox cape flung back to reveal the lining, an artfully patterned design formed from the breast plumage of kingfishers. A flaxen-haired kaiser wore as a draped mantle the skin of a Nubian lion, mane left intact, the eyes, claws and gorget collar set with pigeon-blood rubies, sapphires like stars, and cabochon-cut emeralds. An unidentified stripling prince wore a vast turban in the Turkish taste, so asprout with the feathers of every kind of parrot, lyre-bird and bird-of-paradise, red, orange, yellow, saffron-gold and pink of coral, that the sun setting behind the spires of Innsbruck, its last rays streaming into the room, seemed dull and lack-luster in comparison to the painted turban of Kaiser Max.

Spanischer Saal is said to be the earliest large hall to be built in the monumental Renaissance style in Central Europe. It was built in 1570 by Giovanni Lucchese. Seventy-five feet long and thirty-five feet broad, the magnificent intarsia work in varied marbles is the art of the famous cabinet-maker Conrad Gottlieb from Hall-im-Tyrol.

The apartments of Philippine Welser are much admired for the beauty of carved woods, walls of ebony inset with ivory and red cedar, the painted ceilings, and even a "cabinet" or boudoir with panels of coral branches and mother of pearl. Her bathroom excites great interest. In her day it was the first bath ever heard of in Tyrol since the days of the Roman Emperors, when Diocletian and Trajan had had sunken baths of marble. In effect, the bath of the Venus of Augsburg, as one ardent poet styled the lady in song, is of Roman design. A long, deep sunken pool is reached by a flight of carved wooden steps. The walls of the room are of linden wood intricately carved in birds and Alpine flowers. It is said that the shutters (no longer in place) were a lattice of mother-of-pearl. The Venetian glass panes could be changed at will from amber, to simulate sunlight on a dull day, to rose-red, to lend a flush of dawn-rise beauty to white flesh.

The park of Castle Ambras abounds in grottoes, secluded pavilions, fountains and aquatic flowers in pools. Philippine's favorite flowers were water lilies or lilies of any description. As this was a palace of her desire, her desires are still everywhere manifest.

Kitzbühel is one town in Tyrol that never has a quiet moment. In summer there is a "chalet colony" that may care little for winter sports. The Hahnenkamm ski lift rises to the famous Hahnenkamm ski run which one can also enjoy in summer for the magnificent views.

I spent a fortnight at Schloss Lebenberg, the hunting-lodge castle of Count Schlick, run with supreme ease and charm as a private hotel. Large, comfortable rooms, food served, if the weather is agreeable, in an open colonnade under ancient Gothic arches. The castle is built on a hillside, so within there are all sorts of interesting levels. If it is cold or rainy, meals are served in a dining room, the walls so covered by entertaining memorabilia of the chase and activities during the great days of the Empire at Hofburg in Vienna that it is difficult to keep one's mind on the food, excellent as it is.

The Grand Hotel is perhaps the best in town, but there are any number to choose from either in the town itself or set in gardens on the slopes. The peasant dress is distinctive. Festivals and ceremonials must be observed for every saint in the calendar, for, it would seem, they are forever being honored. I heartily advise a traveler in Austria to give a few days to Kitzbühel.

Kufstein is one of those villages one comes upon suddenly in Austria when a roadway debouches from long forest ways or curves to reveal what has been hidden from view behind a mountain. I like to stop and admire the picture for a while before entering the narrow streets under an archway or across a bridge. Kufstein is a Medieval town at its best, where the castle, dreaming on its eminence, nevertheless quietly dominates the town and the surrounding countryside. Here is the perfect Dürer "castled town, sustained by towers." The castle, known as Festung Geroldseck, embraces many features I have never seen before in castle construction. The immensity in girth of its central bastion tower I recall only having seen equaled in the great Conqueror's Tower at Windsor Castle in England, or the circular keep of Castle Bellver in Majorca.

Built in 1260, Geroldseck was originally called a "castle for contemplation," although it served equally as constant refuge from enemy attack. Owned by the purse-proud and notoriously devious Bishops of Regensburg, it was besieged and conquered by Maximilian I in 1504. The Emperor rebuilt the castle as a fortress, adding the mighty bastion. He also used it as a "banqueting house" and hunting lodge, which accounts for the richness and variety of the decorations in its great rooms. It was only abandoned as a garrisoned fortress in 1882. Today it is a national museum and among other notable treasures, besides its striking frescoes, contains the famed "Heroes' Organ." Not alone is this instrument famed as the world's largest organ; it is accredited with supernatural powers. With no human hand involved, it is said to burst into triumphal music, a kind of mysterious death march, at the precise moment a national hero dies. Geroldseck needs a day at least to see it properly. The elevated terrace gardens in themselves are like progressing through centuries of Austrian history.

In recent years when I have been in Innsbruck and wished to drive through the region of South Tyrol, then up and over the Passo Giovo to Merano or Bolzano in Val d'Adige, I have always been warned "Road under construction—no thoroughfare." Now all this is changed. A fairly wide, not too tortuously curved road is open, and a great experience in what might be called "mountaineering" by roadway awaits the traveler.

The spectacular elephant-hide, serrated peaks of the South Tyrol Alps change character to merge near Bolzano into the "quartz mountain" Dolomites. These storied peaks have always presented a nearly impassable barrier between South Tyrol and the Italian frontier. Passable, but extremely dangerous to negotiate except with the smallest of vehicles. Now I find Passo Giovo an exhilarating contrast to the flat valley road of Brenner Pass which has, since Roman sappers laid it out, been the accepted way to travel from South Tyrol into this part of Italy which was, until 1919, Austrian.

The villages in the South Tyrol valley appear to be farm-holds lying in fertile fields of grain and orchards of apple, pear and peach. The rapier-sharp spire of a white plaster church, its walls vividly frescoed in a striking Biblical episode, is the only landmark to distinguish these communities as a "dorf."

Early autumn, the salubrious season of harvest and vintage, overlays the land. I motored through South Tyrol to Vipetano and up, up—ever climbing—to the summit of Passo Giovo over two thousand meters; then down along wide sloping grades so that I could enjoy the panorama of Val d'Adige and, far away to the north, Val d'Aosta. The

YOUNG
BETHROTHED
SOUTH
TYROL

mountain villages clinging to the serried rock above the timber line, or those half-hidden away in forests primeval past which the road now winds, are a newly discovered wonder. I marveled at the massive Roman architecture. Stone buttresses, worthy of a fortress, added protection against chasm winds for the simplest houses. Roman bridges still in perfect repair arched across ravines and led off the roads to allow a waterfall to drop unimpeded from great heights to a lower level. Curiosity-ridden eagles wheeled to dart close to the car; then, satisfied that this object was not of their world, zoomed up and out of sight. Wild mountain goats mingled with the milch-nanny of the villages. Shepherds appeared to have risen straight out of the pages of Homer. One giant of a fellow was lazily combing a tangled chestnut-red beard with a crudely carved bone comb as big as a hack saw. The costumes of the women attracted me because they were far out of the ordinary. The long, elaborately embroidered lace mitts pure Directoire and the hats uncommonly wide of brim. Sometimes the brim was turned up on one side to be caught with a huge pin of wrought silver, the crown swathed in silver chains.

A great deal of heavy metal jewelry is worn in this section, suggestive of the hieratical "goddess women" of Salamanca in Spain. The young girls affect a heavily embossed silver girdle worn loosely about the hips, a sort of chastity belt, heirlooms stemming from Medieval times. I was told these suggestive girdles are worn as a "satire." When a girl becomes betrothed there is a public ceremony in which she makes a great show of presenting her future husband with a "key" made of twisted gold wire.

At the summit of Passo Giovo, still in Austria, I looked down into Italy. The valleys, the rivers, the vineyards, and across to the rose and violet Dolomites. The Italy of Merano, ringed by twenty-nine Tyrolean castles, is set among its thousands of acres of terraced vineyards—Merano that was once Meran in Austria, as Bolzano was Bozen, pride of the Southern Tyrol.

Chapter 4

SALT, HEART AND RICHES OF LAND
SALZBURG, AND THE ANCIENT
LAKE VILLAGES

IN OBERTRUM on the Mattsee, a tall white building standing out into
the lake on stiltlike pilings, its steep-pitch roof diapered with scores
of narrow dormer windows, bore a huge painted shield of the province:
the rampant black lion on a yellow ground supported by the wide
vermilion and white stripes of the Austrian national flag. Described
in large black letters on a red and white ground was a single word
SALZFABRIK (salt works). Instead of the usual whistle or siren, a large
copper bell is rung at seven o'clock in the morning to summon workers
to their places and again at five o'clock in the evening, a sort of "now
for beer drinking" invitation. The picturesque methods used to refine
the salt for table use are nearly as primitive as the discovery of the
salt caves themselves.

Later I stopped in the sunlit square of Hallein on the river Salzach
to sketch the gabled houses, the fronts crosshatched in a maze of black
timbering; houses that cling, as if for dear life, to the silvery, granite
mountain slopes. From Hallein the time-honored roads, blazed by
Roman generals and later widened by the soldiers of Charlemagne,
lead into neighboring Bavaria, to Berchtesgaden and the magical,
shadowed fastnesses of the Königsee. But the real fame of Hallein, so
favored by Charlemagne as a "resort to recuperate from the bandages
of war," results from its salt mines in the depths of Dürnberg, the
oldest mines in Central Europe.

As I walked through the streets of Hallein a flash of fire caught my attention. I traced its source to the window of a shop where the sun's rays were dancing among what at first I thought to be huge, uncut diamonds. Amazed at the size of these stones, I went into the shop. I picked from out the window a "square-cut" gem. It was *salt*, but of a clarity, a greenish-white brilliance that was startling. Salt gave the province, the town and the river their names. Celts mined salt three thousand years ago in these mines, as is attested by prehistoric finds— mining implements, weapons of defense and even copper Celtic jewelry, all to be seen in the underground musem. After the Celts, industrious denizens of the Middle Ages cut long arterial galleries which cover an immense area to encompass an underground lake. Thousands of clustered torch-lamps are bracketed in the gleaming salt walls, reflecting like myriad stars, recreating their own brilliance in the obsidian black waters. Crossing this mysterious underground lake in "stand-up" handrail barges is an unforgettable experience for every visitor to the salt mines.

Usually on Saturday afternoon during the spring and summer season the salt miners perform their celebrated Hallein Sword Dance, by torchlight. Dressed coolly in white duck shirts and breeches, red sleeveless jackets, black caps and wielding long wooden swords of "two handed" Medieval design, the agile dancers leap, parry, thrust, whirl and thrust again, their shadows hugely writhing on the walls.

He who craves something different in Land Salzburg, who seeks a landscape and sport of Dolomite character, will be agreeably surprised if he goes from Bischofshofen via Mühlbach to the Arthurhaus, a comfortable, charmingly appointed hotel at the Mitterberg. A famous ski-jump world champion, Bradl, trains the younger generation of keen hero-worshipers to "jump the sky" in his own incomparable way.

Saalbach is an emphatically sports-minded village, "all the world away" in its quietness. A pleasing paradox, remote, proudly unsophisticated, yet easy to reach. Catering to hunters, fishermen and die-hard mountaineers, it attracts a mixed bag of enthusiasts as fellow visitors. Even those who wish to scale the mountain heights, but cannot do so under their own power, may enjoy the seemingly unattainable with ease, for the chair-lift runs daily all through the summer season.

The local brass band, recruited from tall, serious-faced young mountaineers, fishermen and game hunters—many of the latter are expert with the ancient *stachelschütze* (Medieval crossbow)—plays for village dances on the green.

Coming into St. Johann-im-Pongau, I stopped beside the Arlbach to walk through one of Nature's most fantastic gestures, an overabundance of serrated rocks and crashing water forming the Liechtenstein Gorge. A wooden railed-in bridge traverses a misty causeway. Towering hundreds of feet on either side, the cliffs open onto a mélange of ferngrown tumbled rocks where copper-red and yellow-green waters, colored by the stains from mineral deposits, churn and thunder, overwhelming to the eye, and to the ear an inferno. The Arlbach screamed in rebellion, as it drenched me with cold spray. The rising and drifting mist steals from the sun thousands of rainbows that would have mightily pleased Ludwig II of Bavaria who, for his pleasure, loved to imitate "Eternity and Infinity." When I came out of the gorge, the silence itself seemed deafening.

My winding way led through Hinterthal and Dienten, a hidden village of dreaming melancholy, famous for tall, black timber houses. The window boxes, fashioned from moss-encrusted fir tree bark, blaze with plants of the intense violet-blue *Wulfenia*, the "mysterious blue eye of the Llama," a horticultural marvel, for no one can explain how this native of the Himalayan snows came to the Salzkammergut though unknown to any other part of Europe.

Piercing the robin's-egg blue sky rises the "spire" of the Hochkönig (2,906 ft.). A popular summer and winter resort lies in the Mühlbach Valley. All is sweeping panorama and whispered legend here. Behind Hochkönig towers a misty waste of rock, Mitterbergalp. On the way up the mountain I passed the ruins of three old castles of murderous memory. Once each was held by a "mountain baron," all bandits of awesome repute, rebellious enemies of the powerful Babenberg overlords.

The best-preserved castle is the Arthursburg near Arthurhaus Hotel,

73

a ski-lift center. The mountaineers will tell you, "The burg is still alive." Haunted, they mean. One sun- and wind-blackened old forester said to me, "I am on the crags at night. I see moving lights and shadows within those walls and hear drunken laughter. I hung two rhebok up to a timber cross to mellow." He nodded sagely, plucking at his upper lip. "When I came back the bucks were gone. I followed the trail of dried blood right to the castle gate, but it was barred by a fallen tree." I believed him—that a *geist* from the castle had pilfered his "hung" game to roast it for a midnight carouse. Sitting on a jutting rock in front of the forester's *hütte* I had a bird's-eye view of St. Johann, the twin towers of the "Cathedral of Pongau," and its attendant clustered houses like white-robed acolytes wearing red-tasseled black caps, all kneeling facing the nave as if at prayer.

I ruminated upon this curious full-bodied word *Salzkammergut*. The word has a sound of strength, of legendary color. When you have uttered Salzkammergut with the accent on "kammer" you have definitely said a word of import. Signifying this world-renowned lake district, the word is derived from a natural resource which was discovered about 3000 B.C. by a prehistoric tribe that used tools of stone. In the Middle Ages, salt mining was a privilege of the overlord (*kammergut*), and to the present time has remained a state monopoly.

The Austrian skiing season lasts seven months, providing a magnificent world of snow and ice, virgin white and icy blue, startlingly punctuated with stands of agate-green conifers all under a blazing sun. What a pleasure world of dreamy Alpine villages, sophisticated winter sports resorts, and "sunset suppers" taken around a fire of pine cones, dripping amber resin, in some mountain-crest ski *hütte!* It is during this long winter solstice that the festivals take place. During Austrian Carnival time *fasching* customs and costumes are many and varied.

I have listened to tall tales concerning the origin of the winter festivals, the *Perchenlauf* ("away with Winter's ghost," is a rough translation) peculiar to St. Johann-im-Pongau. To begin with, the first known legends which form the basis of a great many of the festivals are the joyful celebration of King Winter's demise and the expulsion of his ghost from whatever community.

74

END OF WINTER
FESTIVAL.
ST. JOHANN-IM-PONGAU
SALZBURG.

The masks worn in St. Johann-im-Pongau for Perchtenlauf are often hundreds of years old. The grotesques, like the Glöckner-Perchten-Schemen-Schellen and Döllner dancers and the extraordinary Lucifer mask (18th century) in the Landsmuseum, Salzburg, are painted faces grimacing in combined horror and humor, fascinating in their originality. These masks as well as the costumes symbolize the good and evil forces, spirits which are able, among these superstitious country folks, to rouse mysterious forces and to banish the "monsters and ghosts of winter."

The steps of the dancers follow ancient patterns deriving from pagan cults. They have never been written down but have been passed along from one generation to the next. In the village square at St. Johann-im-Pongau, men in forester dress of green with tremendous headdresses embroidered and painted with stars and mystic symbols, some cut from colored glass, carry torches. Young boys, dressed in costumes composed of evergreen tassels cut directly from the bough, leap about in demented antic steps. (Later these costumes are tossed on the bonfire to crackle away in ashes). The masks worn are the horned, bearded faces of "green devils," the evil children of King Winter. In the center of the dancers, a tall man in a silver cape daubed with cotton snow walks erect, his delta-shaped headdress an "aviary" for stuffed singing and game birds. The whole contraption spouts a fountain of red fox tails and improbably long feathers from the tails of pheasants and the aggressive *auerhahn* (mountain cock), iridescent as jewels. This plumage quivers like sparks of sky-rockets in the flickering light. There are numerous festivals in spring and summer, too, but save for the beauty and richness of detail in the traditional costumes worn by the women, to me, the flare and drama of the "Death of King Winter" carnivals is lacking.

I lunched at the Fuschlsee, a small, bright-blue eye of water reflecting high rock ridges fringed in conifers in contrast to entirely wooded sugar-loaf mountains, famous for deer and feathered game. Indeed as I swung into the long driveway leading downhill to Schloss Fuschl, erstwhile hunting castle of the prince-archbishops of Salzburg and later the residence of the Ribbentrop family, the surrounding hills echoed to the sound of gunfire—some hunter out shooting to "fill the pot."

A tall, square tower rises above the lake with a long wing extending along the water's edge above a terrace where one dines. Pale yellow in color, the castle lends decoration to the landscape by its red and white chevron-striped shutters. Conforming to the old Austrian custom, the armorial colors of the owners. The castle is now run agreeably as a hotel.

Next I stopped in the mellowing old village of Werfen. Even on a day of brilliant sunlight this village is in semishadow from the towering ramparts of the sheer Tennengebirge. Honeycombed by immense ice caves called Eisriesenwelt, here is a vast, echoing fairyland world of ice frozen hard as marble. The narrow passages and wider "corridors" traverse some thirty miles. Glittering ice, oddly dry to one's touch, covers an area of 260,000 square feet. In the great halls where the roofs are beyond the reach of the most powerful electric torch, frozen water deals in the dazzlingly fantastic. Massive chandeliers formed of ice hang at impossible angles. Swags of ice resemble looped curtains caught up with tassels of ice-drip. Gargoyles of ice shapes stare from eyes that are cavernous holes or seem to cavort in hobgoblin attitudes. On a high, pine-clad escarpment rising from the valley floor between the great divide of Salzach Gorge, the Castle of Hohenwerfen affronts the sky. This vaulting pile of masonry testifies that long, long ago, roughly in the year 1000, when the Salzburg bishops had to wear armor under their priests' robes, they clanged-to a great bolt across the door leading from the valley into the plain. This bolt was the Castle of Hohenwerfen, a masterpiece of fortress construction, as its clamorous history has proved.

Numerous features distinguish it far above the ordinary. Two great bastions rise, the lower one hewn straight from the living rock. This ramp, whereon winds the road to the barbican gateway, supports another ramp on which stands the castle proper, bristling with all the battlements and towers that are expected of a legendary castle.

The hoary gray walls are painted with armorial shields of half the families famous down the centuries in Austrian history. The castle has never been taken by storm nor its garrison reduced by protracted siege, as was the fate of so many Austrian fortresses of the Early Middle Ages. In the stone evidence of its activities and might lies the definition of early castle construction. Early in history Hohenwerfen with its long, narrow, black-timber-beamed "saals," its vast frescoed "Knights' Hall," the windows, little more than apertures, commanding a sweeping view up and down the valley, was called by Maximilian I, who sojourned there on his protracted wedding journey to Salzburg, "a plume of heraldry radiant against the sky."

Persons who have never been to Salzburg before are astonished that the surrounding terrain is not *all* towering mountains but is characterized by undulating green hills dotted with white-walled farmhouses, the meadows in spring and summer painted in great swathes of purple scabiosa (*Scabiosa Lucida*) and cerulean-blue enzian (*Gentiana Acaulis*) reminiscent of Scottish moors awash with heather. Indeed, I have often thought of Scotland when wandering through this moorland scene around Wallersee, with its sloping emerald- and bronze-green meadows and sub-Alpine vegetation, which subtly merges into watery moors and marshes spiky with their reeds and rushes, irises and pink mallow, a nesting place for myriads of water fowl.

I drove out of a stand of pine and spruce trees where the gently upgrade road from Fuschl to Salzburg makes a wide sweep into the open and there I had an uninterrupted view of Salzburg, lying spread out like an opened fan on both sides of the swiftly rushing Salzach. It was almost twilight when I topped the rise; lights were just appearing in the city. The sun had nearly spent its gold in a last blaze before slipping out of sight below the horizon, yet a crescent moon was visible in the fading light of an almost matrix-green sky. Salzburg, as befits a proud archbishopric, wears a triple tiara of appellations—City of the Prince-Bishops, Florence of the North, The Festival City, and The Golden City of High Baroque. All these titles are apt, each one alluring and more, for on no count does Salzburg let its visitors down. The once powerful principality no longer has a voice in world affairs. But at one time its importance echoed to all parts of the world, from its origin as a Roman trading center called Juvavum to its resounding

Christian story when St. Rupert founded a hermitage shrine and monastery at Salzburg in 777. After being ordained as a bishopric in 798, so important yet so arrogant was the rule of the bishops that the city became known as the "German Rome." For centuries it was acknowldeged far and wide as one of the most beautiful and luxuri-

BAROQUE
SALZBURG

ously appointed cities in the world, a city built to satisfy a lavish taste for living as envisaged by powerful and wealthy princes of the church. Many of these prelates evinced the tastes of antique sybarites, having been born to wealth in aristocratic families. However, one of the first bishops, Virgilius by his Latin name, actually an Irishman called O'Farrell, apparently an individualist of the first water, lived simply but thought "right out loud," and in a voice said to have reverberated through the ambulatories like mountain thunder, proclaimed that the world was *not* flat but *round*. Virgilius lived over a century before Columbus demonstrated the same theory. Like Columbus, Virgilius, at whom fellow ecclesiastics hooted in derision, stood an abortive trial for impeachment. But individualism continued to flourish from many sources.

Today, besides being a city that is synonymous with culture, music and art, we are regaled everywhere in the streets by the original architectural expression both in the ecclesiastical buildings and in the less opulent but equally arresting houses of the townspeople. "*Petits palais*" in Rainerstrasse, in the Mirabell quarter, shopkeepers' houses where the owners live on the premises, and public offices in the numerous church squares all bear the stamp of Wolf Dietrich von Raitenau's extravagant taste. Very rightly he was widely hailed as the father of High Baroque in Salzburg.

Here in fact is a signal case of "admirer takes admired by the hand," for it was Fischer von Erlach, the most noted and facile Austrian architect of the time, who carried out to, and far beyond, the letter, the designs conceived by Wolf Dietrich, "the Medici prince-bishop who preached in stone."

Perhaps the most perfect view of Salzburg is to be seen on a late spring or midsummer morning when the light shimmers on the fields and woodland dressing of the Kapuzinerberg, the saffron-yellow Capuchin monastery rising above the foaming icy-green river at its feet. When cumuli, those silver-gilt summer cloud edifices, pile up in opulent Baroque scrolls and volutes behind the bulk of Hohensalzburg, they seem an integral part of the extravagant tiaraed frontages, pillared colonnades, slender spires and airy domes. All this is so much a theatre setting that operas, such as Mozart's *Magic Flute* and *Don Giovanni,* are performed out of doors with no other scenery necessary than the façades of the buildings themselves. When alight at night Salzburg magnifies herself like a reflected image. I know of none lovelier.

I walked under the Sautter Archway, the ancient Porta Romana where chariots once passed along Linzerstrasse, the immemorial trade route from Radstadt, a pass for riches from the East, narrow and dangerous, across the once bandit-ridden Tauern Mountains. The sight from the archway is one of tower after tower, a symphony of styles, the finial of each tower a solid gold filigree cross, or in one instance, the burnished branches of a thorn-tree cross supporting a rusted iron crown of thorns. It is a veritable forest of towers and spires seeming somehow to illuminate the fortress in its huge simplicity, majestic beyond all telling, resting high above the city on its dais of green woods.

It is remarkable how many fine buildings and monuments this comparatively small country of Austria possesses and how many famous art collections are housed in churches, monasteries, castles, museums, and even small private collections to be found in the most remote communities. Salzburg is the repository for a surprising amount of this treasure. A great deal of credit must be given to the generous patronage of Imperial rulers down many centuries, and to princes of the church who collected widely and with marked discrimination to beautify their palaces, for in the last analysis the story of Salzburg is the story of its princely archbishops.

Driving in a one-horse fiacre, or a rare two-horse open barouche to be found in the Mozartplatz, complete with a bewhiskered old coachman and younger footman on the box, both in rather threadbare but still dashing livery, is a nostalgic way to savor the widespread quarters of the town. Drive along the Marcus Sitticusstrasse to the Kurhaus and Kurgarten. Take a leisurely coffee at a chestnut-tree-shaded table in the Kurgarten. Sample the delectable pastries, such as *preiselbeere torten*. Buy bouquets of the fragrant arbutuslike cranberry blossoms clustering on the sprig with a few of the ruby berries for, like the orange or lemon, this exquisite shrub flowers and fruits at the same time.

Bismarckstrasse and Schwarzstrasse will presently lead you to one of the chief sights of Salzburg, Schloss Mirabell and its spacious gardens that were, I was informed by one of the gardeners, laid out "in person" by Wolf Dietrich von Raitenau. In this pursuit his Medici blood asserted itself, for all members of this renowned Florentine

81

family were garden lovers, Lorenzo being recognized as the leading horticulturist of his time.

I like to walk slowly along the Auerspergstrasse, to arrive not too suddenly at the wrought-iron gates, as delicately scrolled as altar garniture lace, letting into the Mirabell Gardens. Now we enter the alleys and the grottoes, vistas and bosks where I am persuaded the spirits of Wolf Dietrich von Raitenau and his beloved Salome Alt walk hand in hand in the fountain-tinkling shade of lime trees, ilex and silver beeches, their trunks huge of girth and sheathed in immemorial moss. Letters written by Salome Alt to her mother signify that these two spent idyllic hours in the gracefully stuccoed, gilded and painted rooms of the palace (at that time called Schloss Altenau) and loitering among the flowers borders which now, as then, trace in all reds and pink blossoms the entwined S and W, initials of the two lovers.

Immediately Wolf Dietrich was elevated to the miter he engaged Venetian and Paduan architects and began building a series of supremely beautiful buildings, each one a palatial house to please Salome Alt. Eager to grant her greatest desire, to reign as a chatelaine, in 1606 he built Schloss Altenau. The name Mirabell was later bestowed on the house to "silence a shrew," the mistress of another archbishop, Count Paris Lodron. The gardens describe the form of an S, laid out in three broad terraces and a *tapis vert* stretching away for half a mile to the very foot, it seems, of Festung Hohensalzburg, which like the Acropolis above Athens is usually lightly veiled in violet mist.

Seeking quiet, I walked in my favorite part of Mirabell Gardens, a beech-shaded circular *plaisaunce* called the Dwarf's Garden. In leafy niches cut out from high clipped ilex hedges stand grotesque statues carved from granite, amazingly frank portraits of a band of twelve "Danubian" dwarfs which were presented to the archbishop by the Landgrave of Göttweig. All the dwarfs were accomplished minstrels, "proficient in the dance, dextrous with musical instruments, knowledgeable in mimicry of high-placed personages, impertinent in displaying tricks of astonishment and lewdery," advises an old chronicle. I carefully examined the little monsters in stone. These are really of the essence of dwarfdom. The heads are all hewn disproportionately large.

The limbs are squat and elephantine. The lips are thick and as protruding as a Nubian's. Three of the dwarfs have throats bloated with goiter. The costumes are as zany in design and ornament as buffoonery dictates.

'PUTTI' STAIRCASE
SCHLOSS MIRABELL
SALZBURG

Another of Salzburg's great houses, Leopoldskron (now lived in by the celebrated Austrian actress Helene Thimig, widow of Max Reinhardt) presents an oddly diffident approach. *A castle of reverie:* the King of Bavaria who once owned Leopoldskron caused those words to be engraved in gold on his elegant powder-blue stationery. He came here to dream and read in solitude, a retreat within a wood. The once palest hyacinth-blue Baroque façade is now sun-bleached to the stark paper white of the thousands of poet's narcissi that in spring fringe the reed-grown lake, whiter than the creamy petals of the shy water lilies that float on its surface. The villa designed by Fischer von Erlach, he of the spacious mind, displays twelve pedimented windows graduating in height, piercing the frontage. At sunset the tiers of windows leap vibrantly to life. Red, gold and yellow light blazes on the panes as if Leopoldskron hurled articulate defiance at the dark cavernous windows of old Hohensalzburg which have stared unwinking at the Baroque *schloss* ever since it was built. At sunset the view of Leopoldskron from the terraces of Mönchsberg Hotel, near Hohensalzburg, is superb. By the same token I favor, perhaps above all other hotels in Salzburg, this beautifully situated and agreeably run hostelry. Either this hotel, where the rooms are proverbially cool even when Salzburg in summer is just as proverbially hot, or Hotel Park Kaiserhof, situated a short way out of the city. This hotel, under the excellent management of Herr Anton Kittl, is a large country house once the residence of a noble family. Meals are served with style by Maître d'Hotel Strasse, in fine weather, out of doors on a stone-paved terrace or under a pillared loggia; if inclement, tables are laid in a series of white and gold dining rooms appointed with uncommon charm.

The park of the Kaiserhof is a lovely place, inviting one to wander. I passed out of a tall iron gateway right onto the three-mile avenue of ancient lime and chestnut trees so tall, the branches so spreading, that they form an unbroken canopy overhead. Twenty minutes' walk and one is in the gardens of Hellbrun, an early Renaissance castle painted bright citron yellow in contrast to the dark burnished ilex trees and fifteen-foot-high clipped lignum vitae hedges, a distinguishing feature of the park. In front of the castle spreads an immense pond, the Baroque stone rim shaped like a nine-pointed star. Arrogant carp of ancient lineage and a formidable collection of goldfish of great size inhabit this water-world in constant enmity. Here too nearly everyone, by the screams of surprise, derives great fun from getting thoroughly soaked by spray from the water toys in the renowned water gardens. Archbishop Marcus Sitticus, who built the castle, took purest delight in seating his unwary guests at a stone table set out for a repast. Suddenly bells rang and water spurted from every direction. Again, if one starts to mount a flight of steps to an enchanting fern-grown grotto the better to see the Pegasus Lagoon, the treads of the steps explode with myriad jets of water. These "drolleries" go on for as long as the visitors can stand it.

In the old river quarter of Salzburg the wide, winding tunnels or passages built under houses for pedestrians to short-cut from one thoroughfare to another are often lined with small shops—ironmongers, bakeries, cobblers—or reveal a small courtyard, the houses facing three sides with outside timber stairways and long gallerylike balconies. On these galleries, it would seem, a small farm is maintained. Thrifty folk these Salzburgers. I noticed vegetables grown in huge wooden boxes, and hens astir on hay-filled crates, dementedly cackling to announce the creation of an egg.

A city within a city, never a square inch of space is allowed to lie fallow. Mozart's house of birth stands at the junction of Haffnergasse, noted for fine jewelry shops, and the narrowest street in town, delightful Getreidegasse. This is the old merchants' quarter, the Everyman Street. In this ancient *gasse* or lane, the high, narrow houses present a gay, luminous appearance, the fronts washed with light green, tawny, or rusty pink. As a background for the airy canopy of black ironwork filigree and scroll signs which hang like chandeliers from the shop fronts, the houses crowd like soldiers standing in stiff ranks, shoulder to shoulder. Each sign centers within its lacy grillwork an insignia denoting such premises as a butcher shop, indicated by a huge boar's head painted blue, the classic "blue boar" of legend the world over, his lethal tusks burnished gold. At the end of this relatively short street, where looms the Gstättentor, an ancient structure, half port of entrance through tunneled rock and half guardroom barracks (now converted into apartments), a sign advertises a hotel—the Goldener Hirsch (golden stag)—by a leaping beast with gilded antlers flashing wildly against the pale blue sky.

I am extremely partial to the Aicher Marionette Theatre, an establishment unique in this age. The facility with which the fluidly manipulated marionettes play their roles, engagingly tricked-out in tin armor, silks, satins and tinsel fringes, is a marvel. This is a company with an historical reputation. The season in Salzburg extends from

85

early May to late autumn. The marionettes tour Europe regularly in winter presenting such pieces as *The Magic Flute* and *Casperl, Adventures of the Merry Peasant*, a winning character in Austrian folklore.

Then I have witnessed four different performances of *Everyman* given in the Cathedral at sunset in as many different years. As twilight lowers, dark shadows mantle the walls; I always stiffen at that spine-tingling moment when the voluptuous banquet is at its height and the awesome faraway voice of Death floats from the tower, calling "Jedermann—Jedermann—Jed-er-*mann*."

The Summer Riding School is a stunning example of an archbishop's princely prodigality in opening wide his apparently bottomless purse and suggesting an idea to exhaust the imagination of an architect. Earlier the Romans are said to have "carved a theatre from rock to attract the world." So Wolf Dietrich too must carve such a curiosity. The riding school is hewn from solid rock, part of the Mönchsberg forming the immense cliff that overhangs the Sigmundplatz. Ninety-seven boxes are cut out of the rock to form three ascending tiers. The Lipizzaner stallions from the Spanish Riding School in Vienna used to be shown here in their extraordinary exhibitions of *haute école*. Now the "theatre" is used for some of the festival performances each summer.

On the Domplatz, Wolf Dietrich erected in 1628, to stand aloof in solitary grandeur, Salzburg Cathedral. It was his dream to build a counterpart to St. Peter's in Rome, no less. There is in fact a distinct resemblance to St. Peter's though considerably modified in scale. The Residenzplatz sweeps into the parade-ground vastness of the Domplatz to lend desired perspective to anyone viewing the superbly proportioned Archiepiscopal Palace. This admirably placed residence reminds me more of the grand Renaissance *palazzi* in Rome than any other Italianate building in Austria. Its façade is a high, wide elevation tinted in Nile-green, white and gold, the curvilinear pediments above its tall windows pacing a rhythm as undulant as waves gently breaking upon a lonely shore.

I find it interesting to note that just as Rome is a city of fountains, relics of centuries of papal aggrandizement, so is Salzburg, because of the largesse of the prince-bishops from Leonard von Keutschach, called "The Sharp of Mind and Profile," to Wolf Dietrich right down the line. Marcus Sitticus and Paris Lodron erected fountains and the motif is the horse, either the aquatic merhorse, webbed of hoof, or the Lipizzaner stallion. It would appear that each archbishop, whatever his other pursuits may have been, was inordinately fond of fine horses and voluptuous mistresses. The Court Fountain in Kapitalplatz was built in 1733, its four merhorses, manes streaming like waves of a storm-tossed sea, splashing water twenty feet in the air. It was designed by Raphael Donner. In the Fountain of Neptune, once upon a time, the archbishop's horses bathed while Neptune, his feet firmly planted on the backs of two marble equines, looked on. When this vast expanse of bone-white marble, faintly veined in gray and rose-red, is floodlit, the illumination of the castle on its hill behind the basin merges with the illumination below, to cause a wholly sublime effect of radiance.

At the western end of the Court Stables, marking its entrance, is the Pferdeschwemme (horse pond), its frescoed colonnade nearly screening the Neutor, the entrance to a tunnel under the Mönchsberg. The pond itself is wide and deep, surrounded by a sturdy yet graceful balustrade. It is said that twenty horses at once could thrash about to their hearts' content. In the center of the pond, backed by a frescoed screen thirty feet high and set on an elaborately scrolled pedestal, a marble Bellerophon tames Pegasus.

But depicted on the screen is Pegasus with strong pinioned wings, flashing in sunlight to dramatize the grand "transformation scene." This occupies a pedimented niche between ten panels that portray Lipizzaner horses in furious action, the colors of their coats ranging from chestnut, roan, black, white and gray-dappled, to bisque, tawny, and the classic, unblemished frost white. The central panel portrays the antique myth of Bellerophon, who coming suddenly upon the mysterious winged creature drinking from a spring on the Island of Crete, tamed the horse to do his bidding. Daily the two soared into the empyrean. Finally, overborne by arrogance, believing he too was a god, Bellerophon set his mount to spread his wings as never before, to climb the sky toward cloud-hidden Olympus, throne of the Immortal Gods. Zeus looked over the rim of the clouds. What was this? This was blasphemy, intolerable. Forthwith he hurled a jagged bolt of lightning, striking the presumptuous youth from the back of the winged horse. This story is all there, painted with richly imagined *brio*, the sun-gold body of the youth plunging earthward, Pegasus continuing on into the hyacinth-blue realm of Father Zeus beyond the clouds.

The rambling and to many persons grim hulk of the fortress that dominates the city was built in 1077 in an age when impregnable walls for defense were the main concern of the builders. But if the castle walls are dull, the interior makes up in rich array. Twisting corridors upstairs and down lead to great halls, gilded chambers, huge glistening tile stoves and windowless dungeons galore. The Princes Hall, even on a dark day, seems aglow with sunlight from gold carving, gilded leather walls and golden tile stoves. Red marble reigns supreme for columns and floors. A curiosity beyond compare is known as the "Hornwerk," a musical apparatus consisting of 200 pipes—the so-called "Bull of Salzburg" that thunders like the Bull of Bashan to wake the dead, or, in turn, temperamentally squeaks like a trapped field mouse.

The room where Wolf Dietrich—"the cavalier who brought Italy to Salzburg"—ended his career in deep disgrace contains austere dark oak furniture which he must have hated.

Cafés, beerhalls, *weinstuben* and restaurants abound from which to choose. I dined late one night at what I consider the finest restaurant in the city, the Stiftskeller, perhaps because its Prälaten wine is as exceptional as its famous cheese soufflé. Then I walked down Hofstallgasse to the Sigmundplatz to see the Pferdeschwemme once more, luminous by subtly managed floodlights. After that I walked across the river by the Staatsbrücke to open a bottle of wine at Café Bazaar with its delightful terrace abreast the Salzach.

Next morning I left Salzburg for St. Gilgen, St. Wolfgang, Ischl, and Bad Gastein. On the way I kept a luncheon engagement at Schloss Sighartstein where some American friends were stopping. In beautifully wooded country, with sweeping views of the Alps and distant, blue-rippled Wallersee, stands the castle which for five hundred years

88

SPIRES - PINNACLES and CASTLE
OF SALZBURG

has been in the possession of the same noble family of Überacker, now receiving a limited number of guests. The interior of the castle contains an unusually interesting collection of armor, some of the finest stucco ceilings in Austria, and immense paintings of stirring moments from Austrian history. The staircase hall is enriched by silk banners embroidered and painted, trophies from wars in which sons of the family have fought. The drawing room is mellow in red and gold, with a pearl-white porcelain Rococo stove. The large dining room, hung with paintings of the chase, is reminiscent of many good hunting banquets.

On the way to St. Wolfgang, I made a detour over mountain roads. The sunny Mondsee, its waters so brilliant in the sun of morning, is darkly shadowed at evening by the menacing Drachenwand, a mountain which the lake dwellers stoutly contend is still the haunt of the last dragon in Austria. Indeed, I was told that the pair of red lights seen after dark glowing near the mountain's pointed peak are the eyes of the dragon watching for morning to come, for this creature out of fable never sleeps, fearing that another Siegfried will come one day to finish him off. Villas, chalets, pensions and two good hotels, greatly frequented by yachtsmen who sail in the Mondsee regattas, are nearly hidden from view behind the thick swathes of fir trees that are cut away at intervals so that walking enthusiasts may mount upward by paths to gather the Alpine flora and breathe the eddying fragrance of the pine forests.

St. Wolfgang, a painted village reflected in a painted sea, is pure theatre, rising steeply from the Wolfgangsee, known to the natives as the Abersee. The White Horse Inn here was used literally as locale for a theatre piece, an operetta which won world-wide fame, and the village has never for an instant forgotten it.

It is on the shores of Wolfgangsee that the *"Jodler"* songs of multiple comic verses are heard sung from boats on the lake in the night hours, accompanied by the music of shepherds' pipes, zither and accordion. Every time one hears the songs sung, it is a blind to cover the eternal poaching at that moment going on stealthily in the dark wooded slopes.

The flat, dun-gray wall of the dreaded Totes Gebirge (cradle of cold winds), called the Dead Mountains, where eons ago all plant life was petrified into strange stone shapes, looms on the skyline. Behind the peaks the beautiful, glistening, silver Schafberg rises, unfortunately too often wreathed in cloud mist. There the shepherds say that "the wind howls down the ravines like a funeral dirge."

A sense of celestial glory seems embodied in the unsurpassed Gothic altarpiece by wood carver Michael Pacher (1471), set under the altar nave in St. Wolfgang Church. Beyond the shadow of a doubt this altarpiece is one of the foremost treasures in Austria. To me it is a wonder of the world of art. The subtlety with which color and gilt have been rubbed into the surface—in no way hiding the delicate grain of the cypress wood—is like the memory of color once seen. A central panel shows the Virgin kneeling, receiving anointment from the Son of God, mantled and diademed in carving so delicate that the folds of her silk robe seem to rustle in a breeze, and surrounded by a choir of angels, cherubim and tiny seraphim. Christ and St. Florian, St. Wolfgang the Hermit, and St. George, flanked by four smaller panels which are actually the leaves of two doors designed to enclose the carving, seem to me not to have been carved by mortal hands. So vitally alive is this Heavenly throng that I seem to hear the angels and cherubim sing the notes as clear and far away as the song of nightingales, when those elusive birds of twilight follow the moonbeams to the heart of a shadowy wood.

St. Gilgen at the extreme end of Wolfgangsee attracts a villa colony where lassitude reigns supreme. In startling contrast to the secluded villa life is a constantly visited pale-green provincial farmhouse situated on the main street. In this house once lived Anna Maria Walpurga Perti, the mother of Mozart.

Hotel Excelsior, where I consider the food to be exceptional for the savory, herb-strewn Salzkammergut dishes, has large balconies as spacious as a drawing room. From here one looks up the length of the lake to St. Wolfgang on one shore, and Strobl, greatly favored by sailing enthusiasts, at the farthest end.

The Attersee is the largest lake in the Salzkammergut region. It stretches its waters, unruffled even under storm, for ten miles. An old castle on an island at Kammer dignifies the town, which is so old and so quiet that life centers around men fishing, women baking the blackest buckwheat-flour bread, and young and old kneeling on the cold, damp church floor. In winter the stone floor is heated from below by a crude device, a stone funnel fed with logs.

Nearby Bad Ischl is a charmer—gay, smart today as when it charmed the lovely sportswoman Empress Elizabeth of Austria to the point where Franz Josef gave her a hunting lodge in a woodland glade at the foot of the heavily wooded and rock-templed Weissenbachtal and Rettenkogl—haunt of game both hoofed and winged, soaring into the clouds above Nussensee. In its simplicity the Kaiservilla is one of the most enchanting of all the imperial residences in Austria, spacious but not too grand, friendly and unostentatiously elegant. There is something peculiarly characteristic of the Austrian temperament to like best their chalet retreats in pine woods, beside a lake, in the secluded hunting lodges in forested mountains and manor farms set in flower-scattered meadows. Never was this, the urge for country life, better demonstrated than in this small neo-Classic hunting lodge at Ischl. For the Empress came here with her children (there are scores of photographs of Habsburgs of all ages in country attire at Kaiservilla) to spend long weeks of happy country pursuits. In the last heavily overcast days of the Dual Monarchy it was to his hunting lodge in the forest that sadly beset Emperor Franz Josef came to rove the woods. Here he puzzled his brain to find a solution to save his empire.

The rooms on the second floor of Kaiserville include a yellow and green sitting room under the portico, and a small boudoir at the back overlooking the gardens, where the Empress hung the primrose-yellow walls (all shades of yellow were her favorite color, a stunning foil to her raven-haired beauty) with paintings of her Irish hunters which she had acquired at Summerhill Stud in Ireland. I painted in water color an interior "conversation piece" of this room, the horses in conversation in this case. It was on a sunny day and I remember that as I painted the room glowed with an intriguing, curiously disturbing radiance. Was it the inherently sensitive presence of the Empress, looking over my shoulder to be sure that I did not put a brush stroke awry as I painted the strong hocks and pasterns of her celebrated hunter Apollo? I shall always believe it was the Empress' shade that challenged me, for the picture remains one of the most evocative of the grand, wide days that I have ever painted.

I wandered in the gardens left *au naturel* save for shadowy, winding paths leading to bronze fountains of sea urchins astride dolphins. There is a statue here that haunts the mind. The Emperor in shooting dress, his face, even in bronze, careworn, as if the hollow eyes saw the word *finis* written in tangled pine branches against the sky.

There is a large elliptical pond in front of the villa to reflect the gracefully scaled portico. Six slender columns with lotus-petal caps support a corniced pediment in the delta of which is sculptured a rather witty representation of wild life. On a mountain peak an arrogantly male buck chamois holds court, surrounded by the does of his harem, some standing or crouching on knees, others lying down, fully relaxed.

The hotel situation in Bad Ischl is indifferent. Hotels here should be on a par with the splendid Kurhaus where one takes the several brine cures in agreeable surroundings. Hotel Post is the best one, but primitive in appointments. Restaurants are few, but the characteristic Salzburg cuisine I find uniformly good. Zauner's affords a bewildering array of pastries. The Zitron Torte (orange, lime or lemon filling) are prepared, I am convinced, by a recipe tossed down from Olympus to the original Zauner pastry cook.

Although the Dachstein Glacier, one of the undisputed wonders of Creation, lies in what is known as the Styrian Salzkammergut, I must give it a salute from afar. As I write, I see it from the balcony of my room at Hotel Am See in Altaussee. The sun is shattering its rays into showers of sparks, as diverse in color as the spectrum entire, on the icy wastes which for millions of years have clothed the heights of Dachstein. This titan of the snows is a spectacle that under the sun or the moon should be witnessed from a great distance, as I now see it. Its immensity needs the darkling waters of Altaussee to cradle this improbable gesture of Nature in its depths.

93

It was not by design but owing to pure chance that I arrived at night on the road climbing to the ridge above Bad Gastein just when a sky-shattering display of fireworks was bursting in full splendor. The spa, called "a valley village," is conspicuously elevated itself, occupying a natural amphitheatre 3,000 feet above sea level. The houses set out in ascending terraces were lighted by the glare of red and green fire from rockets and set pieces. Again and again the rockets rose, putting the stars to flight, spreading jets of color hurled into the air above the Gasteiner Ache, the river that becomes a mighty waterfall as it roars plunging down the gorge which, like the sword of Lucifer falling to earth, bisects the town. The night was clamorous with fountains of light erupting in livid tendrils which, writhing in turn, burst into flower petals that swayed and toppled into showers of golden sparks. As a finale, the sky, now a blaze of red and purple flecked by golden motes, found its reflection in the foaming river beneath. Suddenly profound silence, a Stygian darkness, and as the stars reappeared, a dog barked down in the meadows and the lights of Bad Gastein were lighted once again. Curiously, the flicker of gold seems ever apparent in this pre-eminently fashionable thermal springs scene. Over two thousand years ago it was not thermal springs which drew the first settlers to the Gastein Valley, but gold. In the flourishing Middle Ages when the sunset blazed gold on ripening grain in the "golden valley," it was the fabulously wealthy gold masters of Hofgastein and Bad Gastein who sat on the balconies of their handsome houses regarding the sunset gleam on their fertile farms, rubbing their hands together happily, their eyes wandering from the sinking golden sun to the golden seals and carved gold ornaments hanging from their neck chains and broad, red leather girdles. Little by little the supply of gold worked out. It was then that the merchants turned to look for a more lasting source of income.

Silver gilt this time. The treasure of silver water with its faint golden tinge, the thermal springs steaming under the land. Today in the luxurious shops that line the thoroughfares of Bad Gastein (and luxury in shops, hotels, restaurants and pastimes is the shield and buckler of the spa) one may purchase all manner of gold articles, from golden jewelry hammered out as thin as the gold tissue of ancient Egyptian collars and arm bands, to the Medieval red leather belts inlaid with gold wire scrolls, some of them hung with gold coins from the reign of Empress Maria Theresia.

While the accent is on luxury in living, or in trying to regain one's health to go on living, there are endless simple pleasures to be enjoyed. Paths lead through miles of forest to typical Gastein farmhouses, the long, second-story balconies dripping with fuchsia and petunias, where one may take lunch or afternoon coffee with home-baked bread and pastries. Bellevue Alm boasts an Alpine meadow swimming pool; a cable car and three chair lifts ascend every hour to Graukogl summit. From here spreads a sweeping panorama of the glaciers. One may hire a victoria from in front of any hotel, drawn by a team of white horses, their red harnesses "philharmonic with bells." Drive along the Grüner Baum, the lovely flower-decked farmlands that "step up" to the pine-crested heights behind the town. Here again from the balcony of a farmstead you will see the lovely solitudes of Reedsee, the moss-green and copper-tinged water that mirrors Tischler Glacier.

There is a path leading to the ancient gold mines at Nassfeld, where the mine caves disappear into the waters of tiny, dark, romantic lakes. As the moon rises thousands of tiny silver fish leap, to turn the lake waters to a mist of silver sequins. Perhaps the most diversified scenery of all is along the Alpinestrasse leading to Hofgastein, a simpler, gentler, devout sister of worldly Bad Gastein, who, as some say, "has taken the veil." In winter Hofgastein is a famed winter sports center, not so given to pleasures of gambling, dancing, concerts and the night life at smart casinos and night clubs. The accent at Hofgastein is more on *gemütlichkeit*, nearly impossible to translate into English—roughly it means good-humor, well-being and abounding friendliness.

In Bad Gastein, shopping thoroughfares and the long winding forest walks are called by such nostalgic names as Kaiser Wilhelm Promenade, Empress Elizabeth Promenade, and King Carol Promenade. There are twelve luxury hotels, ten of first-class rating, and scores of pensions. Grand Hotel de l'Europe is de luxe. The Edwardian Kaiserhof presents a charming face, florid and smiling, and there is no limit to its comforts. It has that indefinable charm of "character" and its furnishings are as winning as museum pieces, yet ones you like to live with. I hold that dining on its broad terrace overhanging the valley farms is sheer delight. The menu is varied, the food excellently prepared.

On the terrace I sat long over coffee, Espresso black and strong, as I like it. There was no moon, but I could hardly see the indigo canopy of sky for its encrusting stars. I could hear the distant roar of the waterfall, and somewhere in one of the lighted farms below a zither was being played in spirited rhythm. Slap—slap—slap—slap of the palm on leather and bare flesh, the scrape of heavy boots on stone pavings. *Schuhplattl* was being danced with what Salzkammergut peasant vitality I could perfectly imagine.

Chapter 5

INFINITE VARIETY OF LANDSCAPE
ENCIRCLES THE ANCIENT DUCAL
TOWNS OF BAVARIA

AMONG my letters received on my last day in Bad Gastein was an
invitation to join a pheasant shoot in Bavaria, at a hunting lodge
situated not too far from Lindau. I enjoyed four days of excellent
sport and decided then to drive farther into Bavaria.

Whoever goes from Lindau toward the Bavarian Alps experiences
all the possible changes and gradations of terrain for which this agreeable and varied countryside is noted. Passing through Immenstadt, an
ancient market town, the high, step-gable houses frowned down upon
by a surly, earth-brown castle, I glanced upward to see the pointed
bars of its yawning portcullis forbidding as the fangs of a jungle beast.
The road narrows and undulates, winds through farmlands to Kemp-
ten. This town is purported by some historians to be the oldest existing
town in Germany, in origin a Celtic settlement before it was a Roman
trading post designed to traffic in skins and tanned hides used by
Roman legions for military purposes. Certainly an ancient air rides
the town in nearly sunless alley-narrow cobbled byways. These defiles
which are by courtesy called *gassen* (streets) lead to ancient stone-tub
tanneries dating back to Roman days, odorous with animal urine
anciently and presently used in the curing of hides.

Beginning with the first azure-misted sight of far-off mountains as
far as Garmisch, Mittenwald, Reichenhall or Berchtesgaden, the rising
horizon compels the eye; then among sloping meadows and richly

green, sun-dappled or densely shaded forests, the first surging wave of hills begins.

The Bavarian peasants are utterly simple, superstitious, legend-ridden. However devoutly Catholic, they still retain a deep-lying, fiercely nurtured pagan strain. Any number of times, in some remote village—Heising or Günzach, for example—I have been admonished furtively by the innkeeper, "Do not go near Sforzenspitze Pass tonight. It is the night Wotan sets his snares." Perhaps if the murmurous East Wind stirs the treetops restlessly while a hot, golden sun drenches the forest glades, the warning given by a *fräulein* in charming pink and green dirndl, bringing me my morning coffee, will be, "Do not go into the forest today. Sieglinde chooses this day." The *fräulein* stops to listen to the rustling trees, nods, pointing to the hanging forest above. "This is the day she roams the forests seeking leaves of the bloodwort to cure sword cuts, and a mortal must not behold her." So it goes. Local legend comes alive. The man and the girl believe it implicitly, and so do I.

The mountains Hochkalter and Untersberg, pale silvery-violet, stone capped in snow, are a beautiful and impressive sight. But this is also a sterile land scarcely able to support the mountain people who live on it. Notice carefully the faces of the old people whom you see—perhaps a man and woman kneeling before a vitally carved yet crudely painted *marterl*, or a couple standing motionless, calmly regarding you from a hillock of newly scythed grass. The faces of these mountain pasture harvesters are as wrinkled as the serrated stone flanks of the mountains among which they live. But loving this land above all others, they staunchly carry on the customs and traditions of their strong, embattled forefathers which made it theirs. Natives of the Bavarian countryside are a fresh, healthy people, lively, generous to the visitor, smiling, deeply religious, who nevertheless play every bit as hard as they work. In their litany of days, work comes first. But festivals are plentiful, for a large gallery of saints must be honored annually.

In Bavaria it is the male who daily wears the traditional dress of his native region. Save for the ubiquitous dirndl of colored sprigged gingham or cotton stripe, the women of Bavaria prefer to save their costly heirloom dresses, their holiday finery redundant with flower corsage and chanking silver chains, to parade to church on Sunday. Later in the day they may gather at some linden-shaded village *platz* to dance the old-style, swiftly patterned dances to the music of a peasant "wind" band.

At Wesselwang near "the twenty lakes of Seeg," a series of sky-blue waters strung together by a rushing river like the aquamarine necklace of a giantess, I saw a holiday revel. A monument to pastoral pleasures as gay as the painted façade of Gasthaus Goldener Taube, depicting immense yellow and purple "princess pigeons" wearing golden crowns (legendary bewitched maidens) pursued by ardent young swains in beribboned festival dress. All windows of the *gasthaus* facing the village square sprouted balconies of elaborate wood carving identical to the double galleries which hung suspended on three sides of the building. The musicians and men dancers were particularly gala, wearing their best *unstained* lederhosen of black suede, ingeniously embroidered in designs of wild game, acorns, fern fronds, or eagles in brilliant green or sharp butter-yellow silk. Waistcoats were of flower-patterned brocade, their richness nearly obscured by impressive collections of silver coins hung as fobs on silver chains. The hats for these occasions vary widely from a trusty, faded old shooting hat encrusted with carved bone and silver badges proclaiming the wearer's nimrod prowess, to rather fanciful, yet traditional, creations of green silk cart wheels, or rakishly tilted black, tawny, silver-gray or dark forest-green velour fedoras decked elegantly with a variety of wild bird plumage or a posy of *alpenrosen*.

Cruising about the foothill roads I was constantly reminded of the deeply inherent Bavarian feeling for the fine arts, for forms and colors to pleasure the eye. This urge is fostered in the lovely, traditional costumes of the women, many of them, as in the Tegernsee and Berchtesgadener Land, of astonishing elegance; in their wooden-carved crucifixes and statues of the martyrs; and in their lonely, lost little churches set like solitary painted altars in the midst of a wheat-sown field, or seemingly inaccessible on a rocky crag. Great architecture rises in monasteries, masterpieces of Baroque art, and in the Rococo ducal hunting lodges often pendant to castles and country manor houses. The pleasure of creating something alive and changing can be observed in the numerous little village peasant theatres where folkplays, comic and often starkly dramatic in the presentation of gory legends of the old gods, are performed as they have been for centuries, without an iota of change. Undoubtedly the most renowned of the peasant theatres in Bavaria is at Oberammergau, that beautifully articulated structure, a tawny golden temple, the woodwork dovetailed and polished to simulate marble, the proscenium pediment lightly carved.

Driving through the dramatically walled valley of Anger near Bad Reichenhall, I saw two significant expressions of native art. One was an immense *marterl*, the largest, the most violently conceived I can remember ever having seen. The sun beat down hotly on the moss-encrusted gable that acted as a peaked-roof rain guard above the head of Christ. A beautifully carved, lean ivory body, the head of infinite virile beauty, the tightly curled locks of dark auburn encircled with an iron crown of thorns, the points causing a rain of gleaming drops of blood over the face. What gave this poignant figure a touch of immediacy in a weariness of suffering was a wreath of Alpine roses and meadow bluebells, fast fading, superimposed by some energetic devotee upon the rusted thorns of the iron crown.

The other arresting example of native art was a small Baroque church in the same valley. Set amidst a kind of natural rock garden surrounded by acres of meadow flowers, the convex walls of the church were painted in greater than life size saints and sinners. On one wall golden-bearded saints in rainbow-hued raiment airily ascending heavenward. On another wall skeletal, gape-mouth, naked sinners, their raddled hides already scalded lobster red from sulphurous fumes, are shown plunging into a hell of seething flames. Over all this pointed symbolism of man's destiny rises a finger-slender octagonal tower, its onion-shaped cupola vigorously stippled to ape *verde antico* marble. All this exuberance in decoration is isolated, clearly etched against a background of the stupendous icy white heights of the Predigtstuhl.

BAROQUE
MADONNA
TEGERNSEE
BAVARIA—

The favored region of Füssen is alive with legends of the handsome young King Ludwig II of Bavaria, prince of the ancient ruling House of Wittelsbach. His vaulting imagination led him to conceive and build lonely mountain castles from out the realms of fable, where among surroundings brazenly sumptuous he might indulge to the hilt his passion for seclusion—a passion so intense that he became known to his people as "The Royal Recluse."

The approach to Ludwig's Castle of Hohenschwangau is through a ravine, the rock walls covered with immemorial moss as if hung with heavy folds of velvet. Suddenly, in all the density of rock and mountain foliage, appears a gap. I looked upward. *Hohenschwangau.* What a splendid German name, I thought.

High over the forest stands the old lake castle, a mighty fortress of far-off, forgotten days. From the craggy eminence whereon it has stood these many hundreds of years its rose-ochre bastions stand out as if painted on the greenery of the forest rising behind the towers. Here sang the silver-throated Minnesinger Hiltbold of Heaven's Grace. Here the most beautiful women in German legend were gathered as a Court of Love during tourney. Immediately Ludwig had ascended the throne he prepared to decorate the castle of Hohenschwangau according to his extraordinarily individual taste. His favorite birds were the swan, the regal peacock, the eagle. His cousin, Empress Elizabeth of Austria, the sole person in his life who understood his every variation of mood, stoutly maintained to his accusers that "My Eagle," as she addressed Ludwig in her letters, was no madman but a genius.

His first favorite of all birds was the swan. In his decorations at Hohenschwangau are to be found dozens of representations of swans in every conceivable size and material. The muralist Kaulbach painted a series of panels to decorate Schwanenrittersaal (Swan Knight's Hall), the first alteration in a scheme to scrap the old, stuffy trappings of early Wittelsbach splendors at Hohenschwangau.

There is a historic connection between the castle and Lohengrin, the Swan Knight, because of a swan displayed on the crest of the Lords of Schwangau. One panel in the Knight's Hall shows Lohengrin's departure in a swan-boat on the waters of the rippling Alpsee. When Richard Wagner, whom Ludwig moved heaven and earth to rescue from musical obscurity, first visited Hohenschwangau in November of 1865, ten oboists played relevant themes from Wagner's *Lohengrin* from the towers of the castle as a morning greeting. The last evening of Wagner's visit he was surprised by "the arrival of the Swan Knight on the Alpsee." It is supposed that the knight in magnificent silver armor ornamented with a cabochon swan motif in crystal and white enamel, visor of swan-crested helmet lowered, standing erect in a swan-shaped boat, was the King himself. The swan motif from the Edda and Middle High German poetry appears in the early wall paintings decorating the ancient part of the castle.

During his solitary sojourns Ludwig would often stand at his study window at Hohenschwangau, staring out into the darkness of midnight across mountain gorges toward the indigo-black forests in whose deeps the Alpsee, restless in the riffling night winds, lay hidden save for the intermittent glint of submerged stars. Ludwig would search the heavens for Jupiter, the symbol of human wisdom. On a clear night the star shone out huge in brilliance. It was then, as the King wrote in his diary: "I thought upon the cry in Schiller's *Wallenstein*, '*Nacht muss es sein, wo Friedlands Stern leuchten!*' [The night must come, then shines my guiding star]." The long nights of stars, the moon and gilding dawn—this was the very litany of Ludwig of Bavaria's life.

I first sighted the castle of Neuschwanstein on a soft September night when a hunter's moon rode the sky in clearest radiance. A picture of silence in stone, brooding in the beauty of Romanesque towers and spired turrets. I knew, of course, that this was no Medieval pile riven with memories of tourney and siege. Rather, the fulfillment of a dream imagined to the last corbel by a poet-architect of a royal line who had fought an adamant cabinet devoid of any spark of imagination to obtain the appropriation of necessary money.

In a kind of inspired frenzy the King borrowed huge sums right and left. He turned every thought to his greatest dream of all, to construct a "Castle of the Grail." He had long been fascinated by the ruin of immensely ancient Falkenstein Castle on its sheer overhanging rock, the keep set even higher than cloud-borne Neuschwanstein. He asked for a further appropriation of millions. It was then that the cabinet "of dull burghers with peasant minds," as he wrote his cousin, Empress Elizabeth, pronounced King Ludwig II of Bavaria insane and ordered him put away in damp, dreary Schloss Berg on the shallow, reed-choked Lake of Starnberg. Here he was to be kept incommunicado, this time a recluse against his wishes.

Ludwig had often said to his few intimates, "My two reasons for existing are to assist Richard Wagner to present his operas to the world, and to build my dream castles to beautify Bavaria." His first reason was an accomplished fact. If he could no longer build, he wished to die. One dismal, rainy evening he was allowed to take a walk attended only by his physician. Ludwig walked out into the quicksand of Starnbergersee, pulling his hated Dr. Gudden with him.

At Neuschwanstein I felt an atmosphere of unease as I stood in the Minstrel's Hall, copied from the Wartburg near Eisenach. When Ludwig visited the ancient and fabulous Wartburg in 1867 he vowed to present himself one day with a replica of the legendary Contest of the Minstrels, only possible if he first built a castle to contain it. Here the theme is boldly painted scenes from the Holy Grail, the lives of Gamuret and Gawain. In the main hall the story of Parsifal comes to a climax above the minstrel's dais, where Parsifal is honored as King of the Grail; while on the other side his son Lohengrin, a luminous figure in crimson and silver, is seen setting out from the Castle of the Grail. The great staircase leading to the gallery is dominated by two scaly dragons in alabaster, foaming jaws agape, spiked tails uncoiling, which form the balustrades. Each vaulted hall or retiring room at Neuschwanstein glows with rich Byzantine color. A private sitting room in the tower gleams in white marble, gold leaf and sapphire blue. The chair cushions are embroidered in silver Madonna lilies and swans. The royal bedchamber, where one's eyes focus on a Gobelin tapestry depicting "Tristan's Farewell," is paneled in silvery mountain ash and hung with cerulean blue and silver damask. The bed is a perfect forest of tiny Gothic spires, curtained in blue velvet.

The view from windows in the tower rooms and from the hanging terraces is unrivaled in Europe. On a clear day I saw the profound gorge of Bellat, the falls of Bellat and the graceful Marienbrücke, the bridge that spans them. Set like cameos of dark lapis lazuli amid a world of mountains are four lakes: Alpsee; Hopfensee; Bannwaldsee; and, beyond the golden-green larch forests of the Hochwald, Plunsee, called, because of an old folklore curse on fishermen, the Lake of Salamanders. The River Lech winds a serpentine course past the proud old town of Füssen dominated by its Schloss impressively crowning a steep cliff.

I suggest stopping in Füssen while making excursions out to see the Ludwigian castles. For a taste of Schwabian high spirits, or if you would witness racial customs and see traditional costumes as they should be worn, go after dinner to Bräustüberl, a highly decorated and hallowed hall, the tap room of Füssen brewery in the Rupprecht-strasse.

All about Füssen steep mountain slopes are clothed in forests. This is wild game country. Hunters range the mountain forests daily, for Bavarians dearly love the rich game pastries and ragouts they prepare so perfectly from "meat of the wild." Scattered among the Ammergau Alps, winter sports centers abound. Reitweg is the ski pass following past Ahornhütte (4,472 ft.) built by Ludwig II. Arriving at Tegel-berghäuser at 5,600 feet, there is a good inn open for summer Alpinists and winter skiers.

Reutte on the Lech is an ancient, tiny market town, the handsome old houses as brightly patterned with religious frescoes as a Medieval altarpiece. Surrounded by lofty mountains, unique in their marbleized, plum-purple clay stratas, Reutte, a summer and winter sports center, is capital of the Tyrolese district of Ausserfern, northern extremity of Fern Pass, the famous hikers' paradise.

On the way to Oberammergau one should pay a visit to Ettal and light a plain wax or a gilt filigree candle before the wonder-working Virgin of Marienmünster. A papal basilica, the church was originally a Gothic dodecagonal "central" structure, consecrated in 1370 "by an hundred bishops from an hundred principalities," so runs an old chronicle. Josef Schmuzer, the peer of Bavarian Rococo ecclesiastical architects, altered the entire edifice save the early central nave in 1744-52.

As I drove through the gates of the outer park with its inspiring view across a natural lagoon of wind-rush green water to the silvery Laberbergs, I thought the Rococo sweep of the façade as welcoming as any building of similar style that I know. Standing inside the church there seems to be no break in the rhythmical sweep of line which so gracefully distinguishes the long, curving frontage I had admired reflecting in the lagoon. The scheme of decoration is white plaster, burnished silver-gilt, combining pilasters of faintest azure, hyacinth and rose marble. The tabernacle resting on the rose marble High Altar contains the wonder-working image of the Virgin, an Italian marble statuette contemporary with the founding of the Abbey in the 14th century. Times without number this quiet figure, eyelids lowered in repose, has been credited with performing her "miracles" by curing persons afflicted with incipient blindness. She is therefore deeply revered as the "Madonna of Light." The first Sunday in June there is a "Festival of Lilies" when women don long white cloaks and deck the altar with water lilies.

The roads leading into Dorf Ammergau, world famous as Oberammergau, Village of the Passion Play, are as numerous as the spokes of a cart wheel. Indeed, to this wheel the village is a redundantly painted hub. No villagers on earth are so given to decorating in colors of the most florid, and meticulously painted detail, the fronts of their houses and often side and back walls as well.

The Lang family, whose ramifications are practically the village entire, have vied with each other since the 16th century to display on the walls of their houses brilliantly imaginative conceptions of lurid Biblical events, the chase, or the somber traditional festivals of Corpus Christi and Epiphany contrasted with the sumptuous paganism of rituals appropriate to Sowing and Harvest. Standing back from the street in a tree-embowered garden, the Haus der Familie Lang com-

EASTER SUNDAY
The Lily MASS - ETTAL BAVARIA

pels the eye. A kind of informal museum for wood carving, connected with the school for apprentice wood carvers, the white plaster front shadowed by the wide eaves of the spaciously spreading roof serves as background to a lively set piece of pure theatre. Pastoral scenes of fete and frolic are arranged as appliqués between the windows, the figures acting as attendant courtiers to focus attention on the enthroned Madonna and Child. The Virgin is painted seated, the Christ Child on her knee, in full *"glorioso"* wearing an imperial crown and ermine-lined mantle of royal purple and surrounded by a blastingly brilliant radiation of golden rays.

The painter was the same Franz Zwink (1748-1792) of Ammergau, 18th century *lüftmaler* (or ariel painter, as these exterior fresco artists are called), who painted the famous fresco on the façade of the Pilatus Haus. Certainly it elevates a simple farmhouse structure to the palatial.

Above the simple wooden entrance door, its environment enriched by a marbleized russet and green pillared porch, sits a magnificently caparisoned Pontius Pilate enthroned on Eastern silks under a richly tasseled canopy draped from the arches of a marble pavilion. In the distance, between parted crimson curtains, his Roman Legions are grouped in the ruins of a pagan temple to Artemis. At his feet crouches Christ under the scourge.

The actual Passion Play as enacted today was the result of a vow made in 1633 by the population for surcease from the plague. This we know for an historical fact. But long before that time the families Lang and Zwink had written, designed and produced miracle plays, pastoral masques and divertisements for the entertainment of Swabian rulers. It is generally admitted that all Bavarians are delightfully natural actors.

Since fulfillment of the vow, the Passion Play has been presented with little alteration and few interruptions every ten years. All the players must be natives of Oberammergau. Twelve hundred persons, adults and children from five to fifteen years, take part in the play. The theatre is huge, accommodating in comfort an audience of six thousand persons. The auditorium is covered. The open-air stage employs the green hillsides of the Ammer Valley as a natural background lending tremendous depth to the tableau. The acoustic conditions are so perfect that a listener does not miss the lightest word spoken upon the stage. I saw the Passion Play in 1950, when over 300,000 persons, more than three-quarters of them foreigners, witnessed the performances. The spectacle consists of sixteen parts. Each part is preceded by a tableau, an incident from the Old and New Testaments. The color is strong, the line of costumes sweeping. The immobility of the actors is imposing. But above all, the spiritual mood is sustained to cause wonder and contemplation long after the stage has emptied and the lights have closed down.

I hired a carriage, a kind of rural hansom cab drawn by a team of tawny, flaxen maned Swabian half-bred horses, to pay my respects to Wieskirche, a pilgrimage church near Steingaden close to Oberammergau. Across meadows spread thickly with Queen Anne's lace, late poppies, blue gentian and darker purple lupin, I caught my first glimpse of Wies looking, with its tall, slender steeple mast, like a white ship marooned in waves of ripening corn. This church of High Bavarian Baroque persuasion, lovely and lost, stands remote between the plain of the Bavarian Alps and the Swabian Allgäu. It silhouettes against the soaring Trauchberge, green at the base, icy blue at the summit, to present a perfectly proportioned monument to mature Baroque art. There is a curious gleam to the plain white walls which appear almost iridescent, reflecting on sunny days the colors of the meadow flowers, the green and gold of grain in which it stands. Peasants sow and harvest about its walls. The church, so plain on the outside, is a living mass of shapes and ornaments within.

The chancel glows in luminous color—celestial blue, silver-gilt, a soft peach-pink with a touch of sapphire-blue to point up a deep fringe or flick the embroidered hem of a saint's robe. This highly unusual touch lends character, an air of extreme vitality, to the sculptured figures of Cardinal Jerome and Pope Gregory the Great (surely the most elegant fashion plates I know of in all the ecclesiastical hierarchy), which are poised in attitudes of arrested motion on pedestals of exquisite blue, white and gold Meissen porcelain.

The aerial pulpit carved to represent a cloud formation was designed by Dominikus Zimmermann, as was the whole church. The radiant clarity of blue, gold and white spaces delicately scrolled show his characteristic arrangement of embrasured windows in calyx form. The chancel pillars are masterpieces of rose and azure stucco workmanship. A passing strange and lovely carved group crowning a side altar depicts the souls of the Just in Abraham's bosom, the *Just* being infant souls. Abraham himself is immensely *chic* (in the French sense of "grand style") in billowing robes, the folds arranged like the wings of an eagle, his hyacinthian gold locks crowned by a towering Persian miter-turban. Behind apertures cut out of the upper part of the chancel are arranged interesting stucco detail to form elegant little "listening" balconies.

Perhaps the most remarkable of all the stucco work in Wieskirche is in the Prelates Hall, the spirited capitals of which surmount columns painted to imitate lapis lazuli. Wies was until the first World War the summer residence of the Abbots of Steingaden. Here they entertained princes and prelates from the outside world on a lavish scale.

The road to Garmisch-Partenkirchen over the Karwendel stamps itself forever memorably in one's mind by the dominance of the Zugspitze, surely one of the marvels of the world for beauty of rock formation. As one approaches the "Twin Villages in the Wank Valley," a wide green basin at the foot of the highest mountain in Germany, Zugspitze seems to expand in shimmering silver splendor until it blots out the sky and dominates one's immediate world.

I wandered into Floriansplatz in Partenkirchen. At the fountain two teams of tawny oxen, bedecked like Tribal chieftains in collars and headpieces of brass-studded deer hide, were drinking long gulps of cold crystal water from the mountains.

Toward Garmisch loom the long jagged battlements of Dreitorspitze. Mountaineers call these serrated peaks, which present a withdrawn air, *Grünesirene* (the "green seductress"), for the white snows are nearly hidden by mounting regiments of black pine and darkling green spruce covering grottoes and deep crevasselike ravines. The "beckoning green lady of the snows" sings her murmurous, seductive song: "Come, hunter, come. Here is game by day and rest on my breast by night." Alas, many a young hunter has heeded this alluring song, never more to return to his valley hearth.

The Husarhof is a spacious old structure. The hotel was built as a hunting lodge for the Counts of Werdenfels in 1611. The façade is one of the most ornately frescoed in this "valley of painted houses." The scheme is of extreme elegance. A cobalt-blue and gold simulation of a Renaissance hunting lodge, the kind of canvas pavilion that was often erected at night by lackeys to house a visiting potentate, to be

PRIZE BULL

CATTLE FAIR PARTENKIRCHEN

taken down and moved on to another mountain site as the hunting party sought new coverts.

At Husarhof game in all guises is the specialty, supplemented by solid peasant dishes that one finds in such succulent abundance on the tables of Bavarian farmers.

I passed the Olympic Ski Jump on my way to Eibsee. In summer this best-known winter holiday center in the German Alps seems asleep in greenery, just another tree-guarded Alpine ride cut through the forest. It needs all the panoply of ice and snow-laden slopes, flaunting snow-feathered pine branches, to justify its réclame. At midnight on New Year's Eve a procession of young men from the surrounding villages meets at the ski hotel, Adolf-Zöppritz Haus, to form a procession known as The Singers to the Stars. Garbed in brilliant crimson and silver Medieval costume, each youth bears a lighted lantern in the shape of a star. The night becomes articulate with song as the singers perform intricate figures of *slalom* on the slopes.

Eibsee lies mountain-locked, causing the water to lie forever still as in a death sleep. Locally it is often called the Lake of the Dead. Legends concerning maidens drowning themselves in the dark purple waters for "the very depths of love unrequited" are legion. But today when I stood far above Eibsee on the heights of Höllental, its waters were onyx black, and at its heart the reflected chalk-white peak of Zugspitze glowed like the flame of white light that burns in the heart of a star sapphire.

Garmisch has its own personal magic. I went into Frühlingstrasse, the ancient Roman Spring Street, where every house has a well fed by mountain springs which in turn keep horse troughs and a wide, oblong "washing well," its timbers soggy with moss, full to brimming.

Walking leisurely through the old streets of Garmisch, one is almost immediately in the outskirts or *baüernland*, so peculiar to these Bavarian towns, where each white plaster and sepia-brown timber house, the pine-bark shingles of the roof held down by massive stones, is a self-contained farm settled in the midst of vegetable and flower gardens and pasturage for the golden-hide cattle. I thought upon the antiquity of the village. Its recorded history begins with the Romans at the birth of Christ. They called it Parthanum. A Rhaetian tribe of outlaws is known to have settled here, or close by, attracted by the wide, lonely forests so plentifully stocked with a large variety of game, as well as the numerous springs in full flow all the year round. The Rhaetians built altars for sacrifice to their woodland gods, traces of which can still be seen.

On their march of victory the Romans crossed the Alps and started on a frantic career of road building. From Upper Italy they opened a road through the Etsch Valley on through the Brenner Pass to

Innsbruck. From there, engineers threw a wide road over the Seefelder Pass to Mittenwald and on to Partenkirchen, thence to Augsburg. By that time the Roman generals had fulfilled their aim to occupy all of Bavaria. It is over these same Roman roads that I traveled.

There are streets in Garmisch, such as the Kreuzerstrasse, only a five-minute walk from the humming cafés of the Kurpark, which harbor some of the most entrancing old houses in all Bavaria. Built in the 16th and 17th centuries of white plaster and timber, they contrast with tall, wide-faced dwellings of Baroque order where an entire Biblical story is painted in high bravura, perhaps by the peripatetic, prolific and fanciful Franz Zwink. No matter how many houses of this painted-front variety I see, the simple, the grand, or the utterly palatial (such as the House of Pontius Pilate in Oberammergau), whether painted by Zwink, Büller, Baptist Zimmerman, or an anonymous painter, no two are ever the same and rarely is the subject dull or the color bad. It is the natural, racial instinct to decorate for him who runs to see that is strongly emphasized in the Bavarian and Austrian character.

Particularly memorable is Gasthaus Almenrausch und Edelweiss, a high, wide-fronted house rising six stories to a point under the eaves occupied by a stern-visaged stag's head, whereon is painted a great hunt in full cry in the fastness of the Alpspitz. Mounted hunters in 18th-century dress crash through the trees. Hounds pursue wild boars, foxes, chamois, stags, rhebok, a mélange of wild game never before seen together at one time in any locality. But all is action, painted with verve in a wide range of brilliant colors.

The Old Church, with its Alt Deutsch pointed tower, has had an interesting, even vivid, history. According to tradition it was once a pagan temple to Hercules. The nave was built by Romans over a sacrificial altar. Later, an Italianate campanile was erected separately, as was the custom, detached from the Romanesque church. In 1826 the Old Church was dedicated to the Virgin Mary, and her gentle presence seems to mitigate the violent 14th-century Passion pictures, lurid and grotesque, hung on the northern wall.

Hotels in Garmisch are for the most part big and more or less Victorian in character. Alpenhof-Parkhotel is my choice. It has spacious rooms, excellent food and a dining terrace overlooking the Kurpark. It also has a charming colonnade in which are situated smart shops of a sort the French so aptly term *boîte de luxe*.

Chapter 6

THE FOREST ROAD TO MUNICH,
SPLENDID HERRENCHIEMSEE, THE
CASTLES OF DONAULAND

A LONG the Kehlstein Road, heavily shadowed for miles even on a bright day by the fortresslike crags of the Hoher Göll, it is mountains, mountains everywhere. But there is no monotony of picture. In the near foreground the serrated flanks are striped in bronze-red clay deposits. Battalions of firs march right up to the timber line and march right down again. Then appear like side-wing cut-outs on a theatre stage layer after layer of mountain peaks, purple, dark-cobalt or the soft blue of powder smoke fading off to the horizon. As my eyes sweep the farthest reaches toward Mittenwald, there, like clusters of gigantic star-petal edelweiss, rise the stark white striated bastions of Karwendel, called by the poet Rupert Brooke, possibly because of the prismatic play of light on their summits, "more sensitively alive than any mountains in Europe."

Coming from the direction of Garmisch, from afar off an ornate red Baroque tower, silhouetted against the prevailing silver of the mighty Karwendel range, compels attention. The importance of Rotekirche in Mittenwald is manifest immediately as one enters the long, undulating high street. The tower stands four square in the center of the town as would the delta in a river, causing traffic to branch off at either side to flow into lesser streets and lanes. In effect the tower is the host of Mittenwald. Follow the divergent lanes and you will properly see the town.

Small and quiet, the village on the silent, deeply flowing Isar treasures its reputation for being perhaps the most festive in appearance of all the ancient frescoed towns in the Bavarian Alps. The houses in the 14th-century part of the village, called Im Gries, display subjects starkly religious—saints, martyrs in agony of torture, and Dolorosa Madonnas enthroned or clutching at their hearts stabbed with myriad swords. On some of the houses I passed the figures had been misted over with a patina of age until only the ghost of color remains. The Rotekirche tower, arresting in design, rather more harsh in strong reds, blues and golden Baroque personages regally attired, stands sentinel to more than traffic. In fact, it nearly hides from the passer-by the most characteristic market square, ancient, but still in use. Here the houses of 15th- and 16th-century origin are crudely decorated, but interpret with stunning vitality the given subject.

One house belongs to the leading *lüftlmaler* (aerial painter). With apprentice assistants he decorates the exterior walls of most of the new houses that are built in the valley. The over-all effect of this house is the intense blue of celestial regions. Painted diagonally across the front from doorstep to upper window is a flight of golden stairs. The theme might well be "Oh, dem Golden Slippers."

I do not know whom the figures in this great parade from Earth to Heaven represent, but that does not signify. The fresco is undated. It was painted by an "unknown artist." Judging by the costumes depicted and the sweeping line employed to project the attenuated anatomy of the throng, I place the date roughly around 1450. All conditions of privilege and servitude are represented here. Shepherds mount the stairs, their rustic crooks garlanded with field flowers. One of the shepherds has slung a pink-nosed lamb across his brown shoulders. Goose girls with unnaturally thick ankles either braid luxuriant flaxen tresses or stoutly clutch a brace of protesting geese to their breasts. Burghers, fat, cadaverous, or stooped with years, dangle huge red seals of office bearing the arms of Mittenwald. Some bow to let pass noble ladies, heavy-lidded eyes haughty under shaven brows. The tall, steeple hennins so admired by beauties of the period reach grotesque proportions here. The ladies wear pearl diapered velvet or particolored silk gowns. One extravagantly slender lady fetches her singing linnet heavenwards in his willow-withe cage. Noblemen arrayed in crimson, gold and purple brocades or "dress" armor are attended by youthful squires holding aloft elaborately beplumed helmets.

The cream of the jest is this: everyone in this parade is *barefoot*, and many a face is wreathed in a broad grin, in anticipation, I expect, of virtuous reward. At the top of the golden stairs, awaiting the throng, stands a radiant figure whom I presume to be the Archangel Gabriel, not, this time, wielding his Flaming Sword, but carrying in either hand more pairs of dagger-point-toe golden slippers than I could count. These slippers are all in the height of court fashion of the Moyen Age. Quite possibly to be shod in gold is the reward for this heterogeneous crowd of humanity for traipsing barefoot up the steep stairs to Heaven's Gate. In any case, this uncommonly entertaining picture of pomp and circumstance is touched with wit as well as unbridled pageantry.

The streets of Mittenwald reward the stroller. In Hochstrasse, take lunch in the lovely secluded garden of the Hotel Post, built in 1660. A hostelry with a long, enviable lineage, a reputation for satisfying travelers at all seasons of the year. Tables are set out in latticed grottoes from which one has an uninterrupted view of the saw-tooth crags, Tiefkarspitze and Kranzberg, the latter a famous ski-lift resort in winter.

To fully savor the singularly personal quality of Mittenwald as against other Bavarian towns, I suggest a leisurely walk up or down Hochstrasse or Marktplatz. At every turn a different tableau unrolls.

Bavarians say, "The sky at Mittenwald is full of fiddles." You will see *fiddles* in legion form in shop windows, from the genuine article to charming lapel brooches. Violins fashioned of tortoise shell, smoked pearl, moss agate, or amber, the violin strings in gold or silver. In gardens at the back or sides of houses along Hochstrasse and Bahnhof-strasse violins are hung out on long lines to "air," much as a wise housewife hangs out the family wardrobe to soak up the sun. I notice that invariably there are swarms of honey bees buzzing contentedly, if a bit uncertain on their wings, around these violins, for the bees become intoxicated by sipping the sweet varnish applied to preserve the delicate, paper-thin veneer.

Adolf Baader's shop is an unofficial museum, a mecca for musicians as well as the interested layman. Every sort of violin is to be seen being worked upon by apprentices. The majority of these violins are destined to be sent out to world markets.

Mathias Klotz (1653-1743) was born in Mittenwald. At the age of thirty-five, having been a pupil for ten years of Nicola Amati, the celebrated Italian violin maker, he became the most renowned craftsman in Germany. In 1683 Klotz introduced the craft of making violins, guitars, accordions, zithers, oboes and so on, to Mittenwald craftsmen. It is still a flourishing industry. One may visit a state school of violin making founded in 1858. Klotz' statue in bronze, placed at the foot of the red tower of the church, shows an extremely handsome man with curling hair and beard, the classic straight line from brow to tip of nose imparting to his face the look of an antique Zeus. In Obermarkt Number 7, to the left of Hotel Post, is the Museum of Violin Making and Local Antiquities.

Neunerhaus in the Hochstrasse, directly across from the entrance to the Post Hotel, is a huge, five-story structure, originally built in the 17th century as the town "palace" of the Imperial Counts of Werdenfels, to whom Mittenwald belonged until 1803. Its muted grays, mauve, russet, sepia and tawny yellows elevate it to a high plane of aristocratic elegance. The whole range of color is exceptional in conception of design in chiaroscuro, the epitome of Italian Baroque style. Here is seen the plaster surface of a house front, actually flat as the palm of your hand, the placing of doors and windows carefully considered. Depth is achieved by vistas of perspective, the windy reaches of columns, colonnades, broken pediments, urns, scrolls, volutes, the whole order of Palladian Baroque architectural forms *in profondo*. Such grandeur of ornament as one sees in the permanent stage setting at Andrea Palladio's masterpiece Teatro Olimpico in Vicenza.

One may conceivably wonder why this small town—Mittenwald has never been a large community although in the Middle Ages it was

THE BETHROTHED,
BOUQUET COSTUMES
MITTENWALD

a trading center—almost secreted in the valley basin under the vaulting Karwendel range, has about it so much of a Venetian Late Renaissance air. It was situated on the trade route from Augsburg, once the richest city of the Prince-Bishops of Bavaria, to Venice. Rafts and flatboats plied the Isar. Augsburg brought a wealth of traffic to Mittenwald in ancient times. The goods were reloaded here, either to be put on rafts and flatboats on the Isar or to be transported by mule and horse pack on the Rott Road to Walchensee and the north. Salt, spices, silks, wine, wool, carved wood for churches and palaces, the fine burnished gold wood so greatly prized by princes—in richness of commodities it was a kind of Aladdin's Caravan Route to and from Venice, "the portal of the storied East." Many Venetian noblemen came to their villas in Mittenwald to escape the steaming miasma of a Venice summer. It is at these times that many of the frescoes on the houses were originated, some of them by Italian artists following in the train of wealthy Venetians. Because of these frescoes, Goethe, who spent some time in the so-called Goethehaus in 1738, called Mittenwald "a luring picture book."

I crossed the darkling Wildsee by a lone rowboat, to a wooded stretch of beach at the spot on the lake where, I had been told, the red deer come down from the mountains to water at midday. I found a secluded spot, a pavilion of greenery under the low, sweeping boughs of a mountain larch. Presently there was a stir, a susurrus of movement among the branches that masked a path down from the heights of Seefelder Sattel. Stags, their horns furred "in velvet" of curious sunlight-green the color of Benedictine, a harem of does and three tiny fawns stepped out delicately into the clearing, as only creatures of the wild can do. I tossed a slice of rye bread into the path as a stag raised one cloven hoof in the classic listening posture. He sprang back, but he could not see me, and as the wind blew in my direction, the deer could not scent me. Although all heads turned my way and ears pricked, there was no alarm, no stampede. Oddly, it was an infinitesimal buck fawn, as softly colored as powdered snuff, that trotted delicately over, sniffed at the bread, picked it up in his teeth, deposited it at the feet of a doe, bowed as if to say, "There, mamma, see what

I brought you," and in one leap was down at the lake brink quenching his thirst.

Later I wove through miles of forest glades. Red deer skirtled through the forest rides at either side of the road, sudden flashes of flame to crash away in the brake. This is famous game country, the hunters supplying the great demand in Munich for game of the wild. Then I came out into the Royal Park of Linderhof to see sunlight flashing again, this time on the fountain waters that jet into the air for a hundred feet to fall back, eternally laving the voluptuous gilded flanks of the Goddess Flora, hewn in marble and far larger than life size. Flora, attended by cavorting cherubs, looks away across her great circle of water as if directing one's attention to the Fountain of Neptune which falls in foaming green cascades down the mountain-side behind Linderhof Palace. It was partly King Ludwig's eternal search for solitude, partly the elemental beauty of virgin forest, that prompted him to choose Linderhof, an old mountain farm site, whereon to build this Rococo fantasy in white marble, in the shade of a three-hundred-year-old lime tree. The venerable tree that stood at one side of the spacious old brown timber farmhouse was left intact. Indeed, Ludwig duly honored "Alt Lind" by having the words painted in gold and green on his menu whenever he dined at the table he had caused to be constructed in the branches of the tree where he sat on a bench cushioned in dark claret velvet.

Blue and white or palest lilac are the colors of all the flowers in the gardens. Lupins, gentians, iris, clematis, all in their seasons. Tall Canary Island lilies rise in sculptured marble urns. The clipped borders, edging like a wide band of velvet the parterres of dusty miller and saxifrage, are all blue and white rock flowers.

Inside Linderhof Palace every room is a welter of ornamentation, a frenzy of French Rococo on walls, ceilings and doors. Rococo gilt and colored enamel tracery ape the highly individual Bavarian Rococo of Zimmermann and Feuchtmayer. It is as purely Bavarian in taste as Nymphenburg porcelain. In the Vestibule the walls of white, cool gray and blue marble offer a pleasing background for a copy in bronze of the Versailles equestrian statue of King Louis XIV of France. Louis is garbed as a Roman conqueror, save that he sports an elaborately curled full-bottom wig. His prancing mount is caparisoned in leopard skins and heavy gold fringes.

The Lilac Cabinet is one of four horseshoe-shaped salons. The walls are hung with exquisitely delicate Ottoman silk of palest lilac hue. There is an identical salon in rose color.

In the Yellow Salon the lightly carved wood filigree of grasses, birds and musical instrument trophies is silver instead of the prevailing gilt. It is a curious circumstance that Venus, the Goddess of Love, who played no part in Ludwig's temperamental journey through life, should recur again and again as a leitmotiv both in exterior and interior decorations of Linderhof Castle.

We are told that as the years of Ludwig's reign advanced towards its grim close he spent more and more time quite alone in the solitude of his mountain castles. It was his wont to retire after an early dinner and arise at midnight. He then habitually rode out alone on one of his white horses, attended only by one groom who was instructed to ride far behind; in winter he used his fantastically ornate gold sleigh with its octette of Lipizzaners harnessed in gold and blue. This equipage and accouterment of white plumed bridles, with silver and blue liveries for the postilions, may be seen in the Museum of Nymphenburg Palace in Munich.

In the immediate vicinity of Linderhof, or lying not too many miles away, remain, in varying conditions of repair, a dozen or more of the curiosities in architecture devised by Ludwig in his long reveries during the night watches when his imagination really soared—*cottages ornés*, sham castles, fantasies in hunting lodges perched precariously atop wild wind-swept gorges, to which, although a notoriously bad shot, the king was addicted. Or the true flowers of his fancy, Eastern pavilions composed of perishable mosaics and alabaster fretwork. The king purchased a Moorish kiosk at the Paris Exhibition in 1867. He had this prim little white building with its sparkling gold dome, its interior splashing fountain modulated to brush with crystal drops the stalactite vault of the cupola, its blazing green, blue and topaz "peacock throne," set up in the larch-tree-encircled garden at Linderhof. This conceit was furnished with Eastern divans, hookahs, and chandeliers of blue, green and purple glass globes.

Schachen is the earliest, most remotely situated, yet the roomiest of Ludwig's retreats in Oriental style, a composite of rooms from two great Turkish palaces of the period, Beylerbey and Yildiz. Plans and sketches in wash drawings of these castles were found among the King's papers. Exteriorly the castle is undistinguished, brutish and ugly in proportion. On the ground floor the plainly furnished rooms are very like those found in any Bavarian village *gasthaus*. But mount the stairs! Here stretches to windows on four sides the marvel of its time in Bavaria: the famous Moorish Hall, immense in scale, furnished in turgid, smoldering, throbbing Oriental colors, from blood-red carved cedar wood screens to the padded-silk arras and coverlets from Isfahan. Some find this Bavarian-Moorish pleasure dome an anomaly in this landscape. The magnificent austerity of the Bavarian Alps could, with less forestation, be the Atlas Mountains, or the indigo and amber vistas of the mountains of Asia Minor. The windows in the great room reveal the Steilenfällen, the "magic" waterfalls that legend says are haunted by Luta, the last of the river nymphs of pagan days, who caught her foot under a rock as she was fleeing the scene at the final thunder roll of the gods. Unable to release herself, she sways in the plunge of the falls. Her eternal moaning is the eerie sound that characterizes this exquisite torrent of mountain water.

The way to Munich leads through forest roads, mountain gorges, dark and dripping damp, where monstrous ferns grow pallid as ghosts of flora for the lack of sun. Then suddenly the road swerves and dips into farmlands, the orchards heavy with fruit, the solemn black and white Holstein cattle grazing knee-deep in fragrant, juicy grass. This is a smiling land of farmsteads. Not the painted variety, but the old Bavarian white plaster, dark-brown timber and chestnut bark, shingle-roof type. The spreading roofs shelter man, beast and the harvest of fruits of the earth alike. On the whitewashed walls, usually above the door, hangs a large crucifix flanked by antlers and skulls of wild beasts, trophies of the chase, which means that great feasts for returned hunters have taken place within these walls.

I came at high noon into the ancient town of Grünwald. This large village is set high on the hills above the Isar. The tower of the Jagdschloss (hunting castle) bears striking frescoes of boar hunts on the upper walls.

The road along the Isar turns into a long alley, a forest ride. Fifteen miles of greenwood, a pleasure park that nearly surrounds Munich. The village of "München," first mentioned in the year 1102, was a monkish settlement laid out on the left bank of the Isar; hence its name. The monks from Tegernsee became powerful under Reinald of Schäftlarn, a dwarf monk, in memory of whom the figure of a small monk, the *Münchner Kindl*, is displayed as the city's coat-of-arms. Its first importance came under the Guelphic Duke Henry the Lion, who fortified the constantly embattled river crossing, and established under his "pleasure" a market and mint privileges. In a devastating siege in 1180 the Lion lost his possessions to Otto of Wittelsbach, the "Mighty" Count Palatine. Later Munich came to be the permanent residence of the House of Wittelsbach under Duke Louis the Severe (1253-94), of whom it was said that "he would bite off his tongue rather than utter a kind word." Munich steadily rose in power as a trading center under Maximilian I (1597-1651), who became the first Bavarian Elector. In 1623 he built the magnificent royal Alt Residenz and from then on the Wittelsbach kings became, next to "The Bourbon Builder," Louis XIV, the greatest builders of parks and esplanades, libraries, churches, museums and palaces in Europe, thereby elevating Munich as an art city of importance as well as an acknowledged center of German culture.

From afar off in the countryside the twin dark-red brick towers of Frauenkirche, with her two round cupolas, the acknowledged landmark of Munich, stand up against the sky like exclamation points. Sharply etched against the farther horizon on the south, the radiant white-silver tiara of the Alps may be seen on clear days. The interior of the church is devoid of all ornament. White, white upon white. Bone white, pearl white, an illusive white that becomes amythestine in the vast upper reaches of the nave, act as an almost articulate foil to set off a piteously emaciated Christ upon the Cross, immense in scale, that appears to hang suspended between heaven and earth mid-way in the nave. The black cross, and the sallow ivory flesh of the Saviour tinged with runneling rust of blood from the thorns of his crown, viewed against the white vaulting holds one's attention far more than all the gilded chapels, marble-enriched columns or sculp-tured altars in Christendom could do.

At all times there is a curious kind of ominous reverberation in this church. It is footsteps echoing along the cold white aisles of stone. I noticed that no matter whether it was the footsteps of a thinly shod, sad-faced old woman in frayed black garments, her trembling hands, even while walking, steepled in silent prayer, or the hobnailed boots of some wind-browned young mountaineer, come shyly into the church to say a paternoster before he talks the priest into posting the banns announcing his coming marriage, light or heavy tread, it is the same, a clatter that resounds like gunfire.

The lovely Madonna, Our Lady of Munich, crown, mantle, lily-staff in her hands all in gold, the tips of her gilded feet lightly resting on a crescent moon so large that it more resembles a Venetian gondola, is tenderly beloved by every Münchener, who carries her image some-where about his person at all times.

The Neues Rathaus, the "new" town hall (1867) in Marienplatz, is an excessively ornate building, but the truest example in all Bavaria of Hoch Deutsch Gothic. Too, the Spieltor (town crier's tower) of the Rathaus is the repository for a well-nigh magical clock, where, on an apron stage-set in a brilliantly painted "theatre," dancing figures and jousting knights, cap-a-pie, mounted on richly caparisoned chargers, play their parts to entertain a crowned king and queen and anyone else who can crowd into the square below at eleven o'clock every morning. The Eagle Knight rides forth to combat his dark-habited adversary. Behind him leaps the red and green particolored jester, prancing and grimacing to make the loosely jointed king and queen, in the painted gallery above him, hold their sides in mirth.

In the beautifully foliaged environs of Munich lie the Nymphen-burg Palace and the Amalienburg. Schloss Nymphenburg is a superbly proportioned Baroque palace, once the summer residence of the Electors and Kings of Bavaria. The five-story central block was completed for the wedding of the Elector's daughter in 1669, in the style of a Palladian villa that one might come upon in the salubrious reaches of the Brenta Canal not far from Venice. The arcaded galleries that one walks in today and the pavilions on either side of the villa were added

HIGH NOON
NÜRNBERG

in 1704. Besides the famous Nymphenburg collection of Meissen porcelain urns, the galleries and walls of the *Festsaal*, or ballroom, are hung with a calculatedly varied assortment of large paintings, romantic views of Bavarian palaces and ancient mountain castles. The South Pavilion, "Gallery of Beauties," contains twenty-four portraits painted by Josef Stieler for Ludwig I. The long flight of marble steps rising behind the palace commands a sweeping view of the Grosses Parterre and of the lagoon decorated with elegantly graceful Italian statues, a "Tableau of Nymphs" from which the palace derives its name.

Now we come to the Amalienburg dreaming away the days, secluded among silver beeches and chestnut groves. A one-story hunting lodge, it is my favorite of any domicile of its persuasion anywhere. Too, I believe this pavilion, designed by the dextrous François Cuvilliés in 1736, to be the most original, certainly the most suave, finished gesture of a princely *rendezvous de chasse* in the Rococo taste. The complete destruction of the Reichen Zimmer, Cuvilliés' masterpiece in the Residenz, has left Amalienburg almost without a rival as an illustration of the sophisticated elegance of this style.

The exterior is fluid in line, of palest ivory marmora (stone treated with a wash of marble crystals), iridescent under gilding sun or the frosty stars. The pedimented entrance door, reached by a broad low flight of blue slate steps, is flanked by flat pilasters separating panels depicting carved trophies of the hunt, in compliment to Diana Huntress, her image posed airily amid stags and pine branches above the door. A shallow dome encircled by an exquisitely wrought bronze-doré balustrade surmounts the pediment. Save for the *Spiegelsaal*, a mirrored entrance hall nearly circular in form, the rooms letting out of it, called Salons of the Four Seasons, are rather small. They appear spacious, however, due to Cuvilliés' ingenuity in employing subtle proportions in scale, the lightest possible touch in coloring the lacquer walls and in tracing the panel and molding detail through the house in burnished silver.

The ground color of the walls in the hall is in a shade of blue so illusive that I must be wary of my descriptive adjectives. Possibly the Chinese would call it Celadon blue after a glaze used on rare Imperial porcelains. I identify it as palest turquoise-matrix, for there is an underlying hint of the limpid green that I have so often seen in the shadows at the heart of ice. Crystal, icy-blue and silver walls are reflected in the high polish of magnificent, deep honey-color, lattice-pattern parquet floors which the architect so wisely used in all the rooms. Placed about the walls under the mirrors, white and gold banquettes, graceful of frame, are covered in palest primrose silk damask. When the doors to the salons are left open, unending vistas of lacquered walls, yellow and deep rose, of silver sheaves of wheat, waving fronds of fern and bursting chestnut burrs, and motifs of the chase gleam softly in the sparkle of cascading crystal prisms pendant from delicately articulated chandeliers.

I linger to evoke the life of this forest retreat in the days of languorous, poetic Queen Amalia. Princely huntsmen returning at twilight, tossing to lackeys in powdered wigs and silver-laced white liveries their dusty hunt-coats—claret, plum-color, sapphire-blue, citron, black or forest-green—laced in scarlet and gold, for in those days as we see in paintings on the yellow and silver walls of the Hunting Room, where banquets were served after a hunt, correctness in the matter of turnout for the chase was ruled by the wearer's own individuality of taste. During the day when the hunt was out, the Queen and her ladies would relax. Informality in dress was the rule. Again, for the purpose of evoking past days, there are a series of paintings of the Wittelsbach family hanging in the marigold yellow and silver bedchamber. The Queen herself is portrayed in simple muslin country attire with her favorite Venetian grayhound Zobeide. Maria Amalia is portrayed inspecting designs by Clemens von Zimmermann for the stucco work burnished in silver to be used in the Mirror Hall in this loveliest of villas, the gift of her husband and designed expressly for her by Karl Albrecht. Even today in the summer stillness of disuse hovers the romantic mood, the environment of luxurious seclusion in which the poetess queen who loved beauty in every form preferred to spend her days surrounded by admiring sycophants. I stood in the mirrored hall sparkling with sunlight streaming in from the park through the open front door. The house has a lilting air of striped muslins, chip straw hats garlanded with roses, heliotrope and mignonette, and little pages in parrot plumage liveries scurrying in and out of the kitchen, lined with delft tiles, serving endless cups of chocolate to the ladies.

Set on the fringe of a small water-lily-starred lake not far from the Amalienburg is another pavilion pleasure house built with a distinct purpose in mind. The Badenburg, the Elector's bathhouse, was designed by Josef Effner, the architect, who paid particular attention to the sumptuous and lofty bathroom with its sunken Roman tub. The Elector, it is said, took his bathing seriously, if not too often. When the spirit moved him, he submerged to spend the whole day soaking as he leisurely quaffed the rarest vintage Moselle wine. In the Garden Room the painted ceiling—in warm russet, grape-purple, all reds and forest-green, from the exuberant brush of Amigoni—represents the Four Winds, in full strength, surprising Venus and her attendant nymphs at her bath. A short walk through the gardens the path skirts the Marble Cascade, a series of notably beautiful marble basins dispensing a fall of water to the Pagodenburg, a retreat in Chinese taste situated at the end of the lake. The interior contains salons, bedchambers and a breakfast room, each scheme of decoration a suave expression of the art known as Chinoiserie.

The Chinese-red, gold, and black bedchamber, the wall panels painted in pomegranate trees and white Manchu peonies, is a room one will long remember. Emblematic of living gracefully among the beauties of nature, the park and gardens of Nymphenburg Palace with their luxurious little pavilions bring a past age to life.

Dreifaltigkeitskirche (Holy Trinity), with its lively Baroque front designed by the versatile Italian winebibber Giovanni Antonio Viscardi (who asked only to be paid for his art in casks of wine), has the remarkable distinction of having been the only church in Central Munich that has escaped bomb damage. A kind of resurgence of vital color spreads across the magnificent vault ceiling painted by Cosmas Damian Asam.

No visitor can say they have seen Munich before the war or presently without having gone "down Platzl Am Kosttor" to drink a stein of beer in the *Schwemme*, the vast downstairs beer hall of the Hofbräuhaus, or taken "bratwurst and sauerkraut" under the barrel-roof *festsaal* on the second floor among the happy, unblushingly lusty frescoes and painted silk banners representing the provinces of Bavaria. Hofbräuhaus is visited by all classes and all ages, from infants in arms to old gaffers—a place for recreation for all, unique in the world. Founded in 1589, it is the principal house of the originally ducal, later royal, brewery. I was told with smiling pride by Otto, the gigantic *braumeister*, his vast paunch swathed in a leather apron foam-stained from dispensing brimming steins of beer, that the milling crowd served daily averages 16,000 "throats." "But," his features saddened, "once in 1935, during a convention of brewers from all parts of Germany and Austria numbering 75,000, the beer *gave out.*" He shook his several chins in mourning. The memory of this treachery of the beer vats still haunts him.

Bierkellers—large public houses—in such as Bürgerbräu in Kaufingerstrasse, or Augustinerkeller nearby, invariably serve good food in their large gardens while brass bands play all the old German airs. The rousing Bavarian dance *schuhplattl* is danced to the slapping of bare brawny thighs of the young men and the swirling skirts, displaying even sturdier hips, of their blond *fräulein* partners.

I went in for a few minutes to Asamkirche (St. John Nepomuk) a notably fanciful creation in South Bavarian Rococo. This façade was designed to harmonize with ornate stucco swags and statues of the Muses decorating the residence of the brothers Cosmas Damian Asam and Egid Quirin Asam, worker in stucco and painter-sculptor respectively, who built the church at their own expense as a gesture of humility for the vast successes they had enjoyed from their artistic careers.

The interior of white, soft pink and gold appears to me as if Titania had wielded her wand to its utmost to create a fairylike effect of gilded angels' wings spread in the act of flying heavenward from the niches and timpani above the altar, defying every law of gravity. This vibrating activity of gilding, sculpture and painted canvas, and the lighting effects achieved by an oval window above the cornices diffusing light to burnish the wealth of gold embellishment, are uncommonly striking.

For centuries Munich has held high carnival, called *Fasching*, from January 7 to Shrove Tuesday. While various festival performances are held in the Deutsches Theater, with music and dancing in some of the hotels and *redouten* or masquerade balls in the beerhouses (*bräuen*), it is the fancy dress of strollers in the streets that daily and nightly take over the festival, ending with a magnificent procession advertised as "the last draught [beer presumably] before Lent." I am always struck by the originality displayed in the wonderful carved *fasching* masks. Many of these are traditional, of Medieval origin, and are not only of great artistic worth in themselves but have become collectors' items highly valued by foreign connoisseurs. At the end of September begins Oktoberfest, the biggest popular festival for the country people who throng into Munich to enjoy the sights for a whole fortnight. There are side shows, beer tents, open furnaces for roasting venison, oxen, chicken or any game that a man happens to have shot or acquired by barter. On the second Sunday a procession of traditional costumes from the provinces takes place. Prime feature of the shows are the beer wagons drawn by four or six hugely muscled draught horses, their luxuriant manes braided with spangled ribbons, red leather harness chiming with bells.

Feldherrenhalle (Hall of Generals) in Ludwigstrasse, a freely translated copy of Loggia dei Lanzi at Florence (1376), is an attraction for visitors because of its hugely scaled frescoes of ferocious battle scenes. For the well-known hotels, Bayerischer Hof, with its agreeable Königshof terrace restaurant on the first floor, and the smart Hotel Vier Jahreszeiten, its Walterspiel restaurant world-acclaimed, it is wise to book hotel accommodations far in advance of arrival.

Munich has always been notable for every class and condition of restaurant, for Bavarians en masse are great trenchermen. Most restaurants seem to me to be in as fine fettle as ever I remember them. For lunch a Munich specialty such as *Schinkenknödelsuppe*, a clear, strong chicken broth enriched by dumplings of rye-flour dough mixed with shredded ham or bacon; or for dinner a bounteous dish for the truly hungry, *Kalbsnierenbraten* composed of choice cuts of roast veal with kidney, fried red-cabbage pancakes and roasted potatoes, accompanied by a *"grosser"* stein of Märzenbier, a refreshing beer brewed in March for late summer and autumn and stored for some time in casks of beechwood before being drawn. My long-time favorite Munich restaurant, Schwarzwälder in Hartmannstrasse, is a *weinhaus* of notable repute. No beer is served here—in Munich a sufficiently unusual fact in itself—but every classic vintage of wine may be ordered, even some of the great names in winedom being served "open" or by the glass.

In a downpour of heroic proportions I took myself on a Friday morning to stay at the Schloss Hotel on the island in Chiemsee where stands the Palace of Herrenchiemsee. This vast structure, set in the middle of the island, almost hidden from view amid its park of oaks, linden trees and silver beeches, save for one long vista caught on the move as the launch passes an allée cut from the reedy water's edge straight up to the long, deep-ivory stone frontage, is the king's finest gesture. Ludwig fondly hoped this palace was a more felicitous example of the Baroque-Rococo period than Louis XIV's Versailles, to which many windowed frontage, "a monument to monotony," according to spiteful Voltaire, it bears a distinct resemblance.

I purposely came to the island of Herrenchiemsee on a Friday afternoon to stay the night at Schloss Hotel so that I might have ample time to explore the gardens and visit the palace in leisurely manner. Some time during Saturday I would take a boat across the lake to Fraueninsel (Frauenchiemsee), the Benedictine convent of most ancient lineage founded in 782, before attending in the evening one of the concerts of chamber music which had been arranged by Herr Volkhardt, owner of the Bayerischer Hof in Munich. He instigated these concerts to bring the palace to life after years of romantic solitude. Every Saturday evening from May until September four thousand wax candles are lighted for three hours in the palace. (It takes six men two hours to lower the chandeliers and light the candles and to arrange them in the *torchères* and sconces placed on marble pilasters between the mirrors.) After entering the palace and passing through the Grand Staircase Hall, one comes to the Hall of Mirrors, one of the great sights of the world, far exceeding both in size and in decorative beauty the famous Galerie des Glaces at Versailles. Twenty-seven high arched windows form one side of the gallery while a corresponding number of tall mirrors cover the opposite wall. "Eternity and Infinity" was what Ludwig said he wished to express. He loved to place mirrors with the greatest exactitude opposite each other, their surfaces vertical, each reflecting its opposite in never-ending repetition until the eye does indeed seem to reach infinity. This unending vista is immeasurably aided by the smoldering reds, emerald, sapphire and purple of the powerfully painted coved ceiling. There are three rows each of eleven vast crystal chandeliers and two rows of standing gold candelabra hung with crystals, the whole collection, when lighted, embracing a dazzling array of twenty-three hundred candles. On entering the castle to attend these concerts an impression of stately splendor is immediately created by the white marble staircase richly embellished with burnished gold ornament, its walls hung with apparently acres of immense pictures symbolic of the nation's life. Each painting is flanked by figures in frost-white marble by the sculptor Perron, presenting Apollo, Ceres, Minerva, Mercury, Flora, and many other of the pagan gods. For the concerts, nearly two thousand candles are lighted in this hall, timed to burn brightly for three hours.

The State Bedchamber baffles description. It surpasses magnificence. The great four-post bed raised as on an altar is surrounded by a heavily carved golden balustrade, an "impassable" barrier. The bed stands on a purple velvet carpet embroidered with great *brio*, in a pattern of golden sunbeams. The curtains weigh three tons, so heavy is the padded velvet ablaze with gold thread embroidery. Frau Jörres, an embroideress with twenty women to assist her, worked for nine years on the embroidered bed curtains and spread alone.

While Herrenchiemsee is a dream of surpassing richness that literally stuns the mind, it is a dream of its creator that was never completely realized. Only one-half of the interior was ever finished, as Ludwig planned it. But inside and out the palace persuades one with the quality of a dream fulfilled. Anyone who has spent any appreciable time on the island knows that at the close of a summer's day the setting sun casts long, delicate shadows from trees and classic statues across the *tapis vert* leading to the lake shore. Burnished bronze-gold, the Latona Fountain rises, the severe-browed goddess guarded by her ring of fifty frogs, the once sportive peasants whom Latona turned into frogs as punishment for their incessant gambling. Twilight draws a gossamer veil of rising evening mist across the lake. Sun rays gild the sails of yachts and fishing boats impartially. Nightingales sing, the cuckoo calls his sad, tremulous note. It is of this essence—a summer night, the song of birds, the music of harp and violin—that poets write.

For three days the weather had jockeyed untiringly between downpour in volume, electrical storms of great aerial beauty but inconvenient to travel through, and latent breezes drifting under sparkling

HOCHGRAT
BAVARIA

BEE HIVE BOY—
WOODEN FIGURES AS
BEE HIVES.

sunshine. It was during this latter phase of weather that I set out from Schloss Hotel bound for Tegernsee, a lake of so deep a blue it reminds me of Mediterranean waters reflecting the steep massifs of Sardinia. I passed acres of the feathery green marsh cattails encircling the dreaming silence of Fraueninsel Convent and took lunch at the island castle of Seeon, a residence of Bavarian nobility turned into a hotel. A castle of the Dukes of Leuchtenberg combining a Benedictine monastery once famous for brewing a clover-blossom liqueur, the hotel is a delightful arrangement of vaulted rooms, hanging terraces, simple but well-prepared food, and grandly sweeping views of lake and mountain scenery. Traunstein is majestically situated on an eminence around which flows the Traun. This town of proud old burgher houses, always "in wealth" from the salt trade, on Easter Monday holds a festival, *Georgiritt*, which features a sword dance.

The oldest Bavarian health resorts, the flower-decked villages of Tegernsee, Bad Wiesee and Rottach-Egern at the southern end of the lake, are prepared to receive visitors from the wide world now as they have done with notable hospitality for centuries. Bells ring out from the brilliantly frescoed churches and tiny chapels romantically placed on wooded knolls. Their slender spires are quiveringly reflected in the ripples of the lake. Swimming is a great pastime in these pellucid waters, acknowledged to be warmer than the water of most Bavarian mountain lakes.

In Rottach-Egern, lunch or dine, or stay as many days as you can manage at Hotel Bachmire. The oak-raftered lounges are inviting, fragrant with a wealth of garden flowers. From the terrace dining room and garden fronting the lake, to the gaily painted little chalet with its peasant Madonna and Child hanging on the outside walls, where Frau Bachmire arranges urns of fresh flowers to be set about the hotel, the grace and well-being of living is everywhere apparent. Be sure to visit the shop of the handsome and friendly Fräulein Luise Greif where she will personally show you her collection of pure silks in every hue of the spectrum, used in creating the true dirndl. She will be wearing one of these creations herself.

I am of the mind that nowhere is the dirndl seen in such elegance of cut and variety of material as in Rottach-Egern. A generous bouquet of flowers is tucked into the low-cut bodice, above which is worn a beautiful dog collar of gold or pearl beads, clasped at the front with a brooch carved from jasper, malachite or rose quartz in the profile of Aphrodite, about whom there is a beguiling legend here. The tale runs that one hot day the restless goddess was floating leisurely over the earth. She looked down and noted a rippling, sun-spangled, intensely blue lake. It appeared cool and inviting, no doubt irresistible, for after all the goddess was born of wave-crested water. She drifted down and swam about for a while. Preparing to rise again, refreshed, to Olympus, Aphrodite spied a stalwart young fisherman standing knee-deep in the shallows, pulling in his nets. The legend continues that the goddess tarried for a while in dalliance. The youth fashioned for his alluring companion a crown from the bronze-dusted ferns, growing to improbable size, that plume the edges of Tegernsee. And so, even today, the maidens from the lake villages often deck their wide-brimmed hats with fern leaves. This panache is called "The Plumes of Venus."

To the east, on the border of the Salzkammergut, Berchtesgaden with its satellite communities, Mitterbach, Falkenstein and Königsee, fills a wide mountain-girt valley. The parklike scenery of the valley basin is dotted with farms, interspersed with classic-pillared villas like Ramsau and Bischofswiesen. All are dominated by the rocky horns of the Watzmann, called because of its color the "Ivory Tower" mountain. When the sun rises over the mountains, white mists cover the valleys. Bright snows and ice-filled crevasses gleam on the summit of Watzmann. The villages, their gable points and chimneys alone visible, seem to float in a magical middle-mist. In a deep cleft between the steep rock flanks lies the Königsee, dark as a polished shield of indigo-matrix. I suggest an early morning pilgrimage to St. Bartholomäus, the exquisite "peninsula" church with its oddly appealing arrangement of circular chapels topped with onion-shaped turrets grouped around three more towers similarly capped, which rise to different heights like the ascending notes of the Italian organ that plays for early morning service. One wing of the chapel is a hunting lodge of 18th century Rococo, built for the Wittelsbachs, now a forester's house and restaurant. Before reaching St. Bartholomäus the boatman blows on a ram's horn. Six loud blasts, one for each chapel tower, "to waken the saint," he says. The echoes are deafening as the notes reverberate many times, diminishing in volume through the mountain gorges.

At Obersee in the cheese dairy take afternoon coffee and *käsekuchen*, the nutmeg-dusted cheese cake of the region. From here you will see the lovely silver threads of the Rothwand waterfall descending 1600 meters.

Through the fertile farmlands of the Lech Valley I drove to Wiblingen on the Danube, planning to follow that storied stream to ancient Passau rising as a mighty fortress, secular and spiritual, from a confluence of waters where the Danube crosses the Austrian frontier.

Driving inland, I came to Dinkelsbühl, a smiling red and gold Medieval town in the grassy plains of the Wörnitz. The ancient brown and gray stone house walls were painted in red and gold to celebrate the termination of the Thirty Years' War, during which the town had withstood eight sieges.

In the Weinmarkt stands a timber frame building with rich ornamentation in carving by Hans Schäufelein, a famed 16th-century craftsman who carved the "miraculous" Pietà in the Ziegler family chapel in Nordlingen. This resplendent house acts as a foil to the long, simple stone *kornschranne* or corn market.

Ulm on the Donau presents herself to the eye of an approaching traveler with clamor. The spire of Ulm Cathedral, a solitary pinnacle of mauve-gray filigree stone lace is said to be the highest (528 ft.) stone structure in the world, soaring fifteen feet higher than the towers of Cologne Cathedral. The Dom Hotel is small but comfortably appointed and good restaurants are numerous.

Rotenburg is the one "picture town" of the Danubian region that was scarcely touched by the war. The "old town" precincts are surrounded, as in Dinkelsbühl and Nordlingen, by an ancient wall topped with a timber-pillared and -roofed covered way.

I swung round a turn of the river at Eichstätt. I have always felt that the marvelously preserved ancient Bishops' Palace at Eichstätt is too little known. The oriel and ogival windows are still filtering light through the original glass painted in every conceivable hue of the spectrum by the greatest artists of the Early Middle Ages. All here is considered immensity to impress the beholder. The massive columns that support the vaulted roof of the Great Hall are hewn in semblance of folds of cloth, the spirals so distinct that it seems as if the clenched hands of a titan had wrung and twisted them into shape, reminding me of the writhing forms of Majorcan olive trees.

Regensburg (Roman Radisbona) is known in the history of Napoleonic wars as Ratisbon. It is the chief city of rich and royal Oberpfalz, Upper Palatinate. Walls rise from the Danube, and the Regen River joins the city at its northernmost point. Goethe wrote, "This situation was bound to attract a city." The Eselsturm (Ass's Tower) has a spiral inclined plane gouged in chevron ridges instead of steps, so that an ass loaded with sacks of wheat could mount. This relic is all that exists of the original Romanesque monastery-church.

Park Hotel and Weidenhof are excellent. Many of the restaurants, such as Von der Tann, Bischofshof and Steinerne Brücke, agreeable little *wursthaus* for grilled pork and parsley sausages and delicately wine-flavored sauerkraut, have gardens in which to dine and watch the ever-changing picture of river life. The Alter Kornmarkt presents a pile of curiously intriguing stone buildings comprising Romanesque arches, tile-hooded market booths and an ambulatory, a relic of the former vast palace precincts of the Carolingian emperors.

At the romantic gorge of Kelheim the Danube makes a gigantic sweep, a hairpin bend, nearly turning back upon itself. On a wooded delta sprawls the Benedictine Monastery of Weltenburg, built and adorned in their most exuberant style by the Munich brothers Asam. It is here that St. George, clad in golden armor, mounted upon a golden steed and bathed in golden light, seems to be riding straight from heaven into the nave of the church.

From here we follow another turn of the river and behold Passau, once a fortified settlement of the Celtic Boii known as Boiodurum.

The stately old fortress and see of the Prince-Bishops of Passau lies atop a plateau on a long, narrow peninsula at the junction of three rivers, the Inn, the Ilz, and the Danube. The rarest feature of this mingling of river waters is the fact that for a distance of five miles the differently colored waters, slate-blue Danube, gray-bronze Ilz, and tawny-yellow Inn, flow eastward in broad stripes, each river maintaining its own identity until relaxing to intermingle, finally slipping into a flat yellow-green Danube River watering the meadows of

PASSAU -
LANDSKNECHTE
MEDIEVAL
GUARDS
AUTUMN FESTIVAL
JRa

Engelhartzell. Passau presents an air of antiquity appropriate to its emblazoned history. The Altstadt or older part of the city is dominated by the Cathedral. Old houses cluster around a fortified hill from which perilously crooked cobbled streets wind down in shallow steps to the more spacious squares bordering the Inn or the Danube. Here rise richly carved and frescoed old town houses or "palaces" of the nobility who once "sat in audience and intrigue, the double face of court and piety," at the sumptuous court maintained by a long line of succeeding prince-bishops. The houses of the burghers are often joined together by Medieval buttresses, or by colonnades of pointed arches, the roofs of the houses hidden by tall, pinnacled parapets. The shops for carvings in wood or stone, for leather work tooled or etched in gold of fine quality, and porcelains, particularly breakfast and dinner services delicately decorated, attract many buyers. Hotels are few but restaurants many.

Hotel Passauer Wolf stands in the lovely frescoed Bahnhofstrasse called "Street of the Blue Madonnas." Ratskeller Garten on the river promenade is a most attractive place on a fine starry night to eat the Passau specialty, a large white fleshy Danube fish rather like sea bass, poached in white wine, served with paper-thin sliced cucumbers in sour cream.

Stiftsschenke-zum-Heiligen Geist (the Holy Ghost) also has a garden. Here the great dish is broiled *oxfleisch* (rump steak) garnished with a satisfying array of Danube Valley vegetables. Of course all the classic wines are served in tall, slim-throated bottles covered with dust, cobwebs and romance, as well as the good "open wines" by the glass.

Chapter 7

STYRIA, THE BAZAAR OF AUSTRIA, OFFERS A BEWILDERING ASSORTMENT OF WARES

A s I ENTERED Styria (Steiermark) I thought it would be difficult to find in any land a province offering a visitor terrain more variegated, where the natural scenery, allied with man-created monuments, is so full of color and ancient conceits. The over-all panoramic view of the region seen from the summit of the plateau of Ramsau (3,000 meters), highest mountain in the province, reminds me of a gigantic patchwork quilt.

Styria lies on the northern fringe of Austria against which the Kalkalpen stand like gleaming walls. Into Styria, between the passes of the Wechsl and the Radle, empties the Lower Tauern, whose sources, legion rock-angered torrents and deep pine-shadowed rivers, flow from forests and rocky fastnesses formed in the remote Ice Age of Time. This Styrian land indulges in acrobatics. At one moment I was traversing a roadway leading through a dank crevasse from which rust-red tendrils of iron-impregnated mineral drip from the walls in fernlike fronds. Then with no warning I suddenly emerged from this hobgoblin demesne into uplands presenting a vista of broad valleys of plowland and gently sloping vineyards. Near Trieben, set in a world of stunted conifers covering the ledges of the Ennstaleralpen, roam herds of wild deer; the stags, huge in build and gloriously antlered, dashed across my path, crashing through the underbrush headlong, hell-bent for destruction it would seem.

Red squirrels inhabit the spreading branches of oaks and beeches in the gentle woodlands around Schloss Wölzerberg and its moss-grown stone buttresses stoutly shouldering the ancient stone walls. Drowsy with antiquity, the towers and castle terraces of Oberwölz are infested with colonies of squirrels numbering thousands, chattering away in deafening volume while they scramble for acorns and beech-nuts. For centuries pelts of long-hair softness and of a particularly dark shade of red have been used to "dress" the garments of peasant and noble alike in ingenious as well as obvious ways. In the Tauern region this garniture usually takes the form of cuffs and collars, lining and bordering for greatcoats and circular capes. For winter wear there are ulsters, cut wide and roomy, fashioned of dark-green cloth fully lined and generously collared in red squirrel fur. When the garment is worn with the broad, roll-brim, high-crowned Styrian hat made of either larch-green felt or corded silk, ornamented with a band of black velvet encircling the crown and a cockade of two long, curled black and white tail feathers of the black cock, this rusty red and green coat achieves a most swagger appearance.

Styria is called "The Green March," due to the vast stretches of forest motherland climbing the mountain flanks to great heights and offering, between rocky summits and lowland vineyards, cool coverts for furred and feathered wild life. Styria is also frequently referred to as "The Iron Province." To understand why, one has only to wander in the Armory in Graz, a repository unique in our time for every sort of body armor and lethal weapon forged by famous armorers and used down the centuries by these warrior frontiersmen of Styrian Salzkammergut.

In all the world I am sure there is no sight to compare with the open-face, terraced iron mines of Erzberg. To me, this flight of gargantuan steps that reflect the prismatic color of sun and moonlight is every bit as stunning as the ice fields of mighty Dachstein Glacier.

The Gesäuse is a forest valley where the Enns runs riot, roistering in whirlpools and torrents through the chalk cliffs it has carved out down the centuries. From time immemorial the Erzberg (Ore Mountain) near Eisenerz has yielded its valuable iron ore. The entire mountain, which rises to a height of 3,000 feet, is composed of pure iron. To remove the ore, no mining operations, as such, are necessary. The Erzberg alone is enough to make Styria a rich province. No matter that, since the Late Stone Age, men have constantly been shredding the long, tongue-shaped shards of ore from the rust-bronze flanks of Erzberg. What appear to be scales of molten color dripping down the rises of cyclopean steps defies description. When I started to paint the scene from a high shelflike escarpment across from the Erzberg (no one is allowed to visit the actual scene of mining operations), I found that although my painting gear is well-stacked with tubes of color to meet every requirement, I had not nearly the proper range necessary to mix these brazen reds, hot and cold browns, earthy yellows, tawny orange glowing with a sheen of gold, purple-blacks muted to silver-gray, and every iridescent green that rimes the corroding rust of centuries. Because this pure iron has been so long exposed to the extremities of sun, rain and frost, the iron has become armored in such colors as no Byzantine knight in armor, overlaid with enameled kingfisher feathers, could ever hope to outshine.

Miners worked on the ore terraces wearing coveralls of a curious ivory-yellow denim. From across the gorge I watched them. Here was perpetual motion. Like thousands of puppets manipulated by an expert puppeteer, all were busily hacking away at the mountain. Remembering that gold was found in the gorges of the Enns and that silver had once been mined in these mountains, I thought again of a legend that was once told me in Graz about a distraught little merman and his "treasure mountain."

In ancient days a merman became fouled in the net of a fisherman trawling the Leopoldsteinersee. The man put in for shore and called a number of his neighbors to see his curious catch. He was about to wring the merman's neck, for the fisherman thought the scaly green creature to be an evil omen, when the merman began pleading for his life. In return he offered treasure from the mountains as his ransom. "I will give you a choice of *three* treasures," he said. "Gold to last one year, silver to last for ten years, or—iron to last *forever*." The throng of men chose iron, and now the market town of Eisenerz rejoices in its inexhaustible iron riches. It prides itself as well on numerous old inns built as townhouses by the early "ore-rich" burghers. Schicht-turm, the Medieval bell tower, is shingled in thin scales of rusted iron, uncommonly glowing in the setting sun.

Solitary, aloof from the marketplace of Eisenerz, bulks a fortified church, St. Oswald. As a relic of remote antiquity it compels attention. A religious house such as this—a sanctuary and a fortress all under one massive, strongly buttressed tower—is rare today in Europe. Its origin is obscure. Old documents testify that in 1100 a "dungeon keep" stood on this elevation. In contrast to the rough-hewn masonry of the walls, scaly, encrusted with rock-plant growth lending a latent softness to the tower, the interior comprises a curiously narrow nave, gaunt and echoing, and as cold as only ancient stone can be cold. Few worship-ers save the old come here now. But profoundly moving in this soli-tude is the immense iron crucifix, the larger than life-size figure of Christ running rivulets of crusted rust from a hundred wounds.

The region called Salzkammergut is shaped roughly like a three-petal clover leaf. The two petals flanking the stem extend, one into the Province of Styria, the other into Upper Austria. The third petal is Land-Salzburg.

On the lake shores of the Grundlsee, where it straddles the Salzburg-Styria border, lie, according to an old song, *"Die Schwestern Aussees"* —Alt Aussee, older in years, and Bad Aussee, much larger, a sister spa of repute but considered by the stern-visaged, thrifty, fanatically re-ligious inhabitants of Alt Aussee to be flighty.

In what period of its history Bad Aussee gained a reputation for "flightiness" I cannot seem to discover. Certainly walking in its narrow streets lined with dignified, unpretentious old houses, its quiet gardens bordering the swiftly rushing river, the town presents an atmosphere of decorum. This very air of respectability, the simplicity of the daily round, endeared Bad Aussee to Archduke Johann of Styria, the princely friend of country people, and in particular the ancient, hardy, gentle-mannered stock of this forested spur of the Alps. Not only did the prince rescue the province from economic and mental decay to the extent that evidences of his reforms and improvements exist today, but he gave proof of his love for Styria by an impressive gesture endearing him to his countrymen beyond the ordinary. To the utmost surprise of the Bad Aussee postmaster, the archduke asked him for the hand of his daughter, Anna Plöchl, in marriage. This romance is a typically Austrian story.

Alt Aussee is a small, tree-embowered village, the old white-plaster and timber houses strung like beads on a chain along a roadway that leads from the center of the village to Hotel Am See, set within a garden above the lake. The waters of the lake below form a shimmering path to a valley between the forested mountains. Seemingly far, far away on some days, so close on others that I felt I could reach out my hand and touch the prismatic beauty of the ice fields, soar the forever glistening peaks of Dachstein Glacier. In the setting sun, evening clouds form a curious pattern of purple-black shadows against the sun-gilded flanks of Dachstein.

In the twilight I walked down to the village and dined at Hotel Kitzer where the proprietor always appears at evening to greet his guests attired in gray and forest-green hunting garb so immaculate, so beautifully pressed, that I am sure it is reserved for "dress" alone and never saw a hunt in trappy mountain fastnesses. He is the supreme host, ever concerned for one's comfort, and he sets a remarkably good table. A specialty of the house is Emmenthaler *gebäcke*. Thick slabs of Emmenthaler cheese are dipped in egg batter and fried in deep fat. This is a dish that must be served immediately, smoking hot, crisp and golden on the outside but creamy tender within. While I was dining in the garden under the chestnut trees we had a sudden, trumped-up sort of shower. But so thick are the leaves of the trees forming a continuous canopy overhead that not even a spatter of raindrops fell upon my food. I feared for the moon showing tonight, but by the time I had finished my coffee the rain had ceased and there was a glint of moonlight. This, I may add, is true Salzkammergut weather during the summer months. As I walked back to the hotel ragged clouds raced across the sky, badgering the moon. By the time I was again seated on my balcony the heavy black cloud rack hanging over the glacier had parted to form a proscenium. As a prelude, a phenomenon of nature took place. Steam clouds, caused by the hot sun beating on the ice floe all day, rose wavering, darting like white cobras. A mountain wind soon drove the reptiles of mist away. It was then that the glacier, pulsing like white fire under the full moon, flashed to me a story of Creation learned millions of years ago.

Castles, some dating from the 10th century, were elevated to command the plains and valleys. The Rutgerersburg, built in 1360, is supported by a kind of Gibraltar of rock, its arrogant splendor of interior greatly magnified by a Baroness von Wechsler of astoundingly picturesque memory who, among her vagaries, caused her vast catafalque of a bed, to whose comfort she was notoriously addicted, to be placed on wheels. By this method she was pushed by serfs about the countryside. On pontoons placed under the bed the baroness was able to glide about the lake waters. In winter, runners were attached when she toured the countryside and bestowed largesse at Christmastime among the villagers.

The immensely long, low hulk of Castle Riegersburg looms more like the Ark stranded on Ararat than a fortress. Its seven gateways of approach lead through tunnels of basalt rock and wrought-iron grills to an inner courtyard, vast and windy as a *champ de Mars*.

But to me, the most nostalgic of the grand days of Styrian chivalry were the "tourney lists" within the town walls of Fürstenfeld, built by the Dukes of Styria. The Knights of Malta who, it seems, still maintain property rights in the province, claim "revenues" from the parish church built in 1232.

The ancient Monastery of the Prebendaries at Vorau rises from a massif of mauve-blue rock. Built in the 12th century, it was fortified in the 14th century because of constant attacks by foes envious of its nearly impregnable position and its reputation as the wealthiest religious house in Austria. Now, the monastery-castle-church embodies a seat of learning, far famed in Europe for young men entering such universities of highest standing as the euphoniously named Stella Matutina, the ancient university at Feldkirch.

The church raises heavenward, as if in exaltation, two German Gothic towers. Inside, however, the Baroque order takes over in redundant vitality of scroll and volute, like the clouds of a rising storm, in hugely scaled stuccowork, particularly joyful wall panels, and ceiling paintings in the nave. Dazzling light emanates from twenty immense crystal chandeliers ingeniously contrived to ape a woodland glade in which birds, winging among grapevines, are intermingled with the sun's rays, giving the effect of a sun-warmed vineyard encased in frost. The pendants hung from the painted ceilings reflect in their gleaming crystal depths all the reds, purples, greens, and gold vigorously brushed in the coffered dome above.

Johann Hackhofer painted the sacristy in an almost Spanish profundity of smoldering color and taut draftsmanship, choosing such dramatic subjects as Judgment Day and The Last Supper. The afternoon I visited the church it was hot, and for Austria, strangely humid. An air of suspended action hung over the entire monastery. A heat haze mantled the somnolent edifice. All the monks and students were at prayer or resting. Alone in the church, I was gazing up at the deep, throbbing reds, the flowing robes of the Disciples in the Last Supper painting. Quiet supreme reigned. I was startled out of reverie to hear the faint warbling notes of a bird. I took it to be the throaty song of a meadow lark. Then I perceived a stir of movement. At the place where Hackhofer had painted the goblet from which Christ drank wine at this fatal repast, a bird had built a temporary nest from a few bits of straw. Two or three larks from the meadows surrounding the monastery had taken it into their small heads to become part of the decoration, choosing the cool, shaded area at the right hand of the Saviour.

Now, by long winding roads, I traversed fields of wheat, the bearded golden spears—nearly ripe for harvesting—bending to a susurrus of latent breeze, the sun-drenched distances quivering in the hot red of the buckwheat blossoms, sown later than wheat hereabouts by wise farmers who husband these fertile valleys to secure two harvests instead of one. A surprising sight are the rocks—jagged, conical as a witch's hat, or as "ax-head" sharp as the prow of a Roman trireme— which jut haphazardly above the fruitful plain. Here is castleland with a vengeance. Atop each escarpment, sharply etched against the sky, a castle preens its memories of great days as a falcon constantly preens its feathers. Indeed, the roughly plastered stone walls resemble ruffled plumage.

The mighty dungeon fortress of Ober-Voitsberg is as much a princely residence as a fortress. With walled gardens and terraced *plaisances*, it was greatly favored around 1368 by Friedrich the

ANCIENT FESTIVAL
HOLIDAY OF THE STRAWMEN
SCHLOSS FREISTADT.

Handsome, designated by a score of sobriquets as an indefatigable and accomplished philanderer.

During the excessively hot and dry summer of 1529 the Turks harassed this part of East Styria, burning the peasant houses. For centuries the farmers have laden the roofs of their houses with sheaves of wheat laid four foot thick on a covering of straw thatch, "to attract wild pigeons," they say. This traditional roofing was the perfect, inflammable target for Turkish *huzerits* or bowmen, who rushed out of the Hungarian prairie solitudes at night to set afire the plains around Radkersburg and Pollau.

Defenses against marauding Turks from the East, thought up by the Styrian farmers, took curiously inventive turns. One sees ample evidences of such today. In an old stone vaulted wine cellar at Hartberg are hung a series of carved wood panels depicting the neighboring peasants spreading grapevines massed with bunches of fruit hidden under a covering of grass on the roads and fields leading to the town. The unsuspecting Turkish cavalry, riding breakneck speed, and the archers on foot would, treading upon the grape clusters, slip on the juice and pile up in writhing heaps to be slaughtered with ease by the aroused peasantry, as the carvings so vividly portray.

The savagery of Turkish invaders wherever they penetrated into Austria is proverbial. Only Vienna, fortified by four circles of walls, stood between the Turkish armies of Sultan Suleiman the Magnificent and his conquest of Central Europe. The defense of the city was assumed successfully by Nikolas, Count Salm, and left such a deep impression in the minds of Styrian peasantry that they have since 1683, following the defeat of the Sublime Porte at Kahlenberg, erected at the apex of their straw-roof farmhouses effigies of Turkish Janizaries, "the infidel spearmen." Usually carved from wood and gaudily painted, these figures appear in various state of mutilation, head nearly severed from trunk, or dangling by a rope around the neck. I even saw, wired above the ridgepole of a spacious farm roof near Pollau, the image of an infidel painted in red, black and pink, a spear thrust through his fat belly, being borne skyward in the talons of an eagle ingeniously made of straw.

Styria from her "bazaar" of natural curiosities offers one which I feel would be hard to duplicate anywhere in the world—the Land of the Seven Valleys. This panorama spread out fanwise I observed standing at the highest point of the road over the once volcanic Gleichenberg, a plum-colored rock pass leading to Bad Gleichenberg. The site of these valleys, lying between the rivers Raab and Mur, appear to have been furrowed into the soft earth by a giant plowman named Ice Age. Each valley is separated from its fellow by strangely distorted rock formations, crested like some tropical bird with dark conifers. These trees partially shadow the valleys to the blackness of jet, stratas of which are found in Gleichenberg and darken the streams that flow silently through the valleys past white villages. The inhabitants are grave of visage, living with their legends. The shutters on all houses are cut to the shape of an armorial shield and are painted grass green, displaying the white leopard with a flaming tongue that is the coat-of-arms of the province.

Vineyards thrive on the sun-warmed slopes and I saw small secluded white churches surrounded by alder groves and trees that bear edible chestnuts. After these nuts are dried in the sun, the meat is ground to flour and kneaded into dough for the rich golden bread of Mureck, the best bread I know of to eat with cheese.

Mureck is frowned down upon by the ducal Castle of Oberradkersburg. The floors in the stables are a curiosity surely, made from the hoofs of red deer, chamois and stag, shot in the forest and laid in a pattern of squares, triangles and circles in unimaginable numbers. The bone hoofs are imbedded in red mortar, leveled off (the old oak leveling planks can still be seen), then polished through the years by the thick felt soles of hostlers' boots.

And then I came to Admont Monastery. From afar off I caught sight of the twin towers of this lovely, mellowing Baroque edifice, the daringly scrolled cupolas rising like plinths cut from mother-of-pearl out of the light mist now drifting downvalley, giving way to the importunities of a blazing sun. Hot and pulsing, the sun's rays broke forth in full brilliance as I drove along the banks of the Enns, where it emerges a flashing emerald torrent to encircle the alder groves surrounding Admont—"Whispering leaves never still, never hushed," as the poet Schiller wrote.

I like to approach a great gesture in architecture on foot or, if a riparian edifice across water by boat, so for a while I followed the Enns. The name Admont is of Illyrian origin. Centuries ago Armonus Camus, a pilgrim monk from Illyria who possessed not one iota of worldly goods, came to a riverside settlement of fishermen, hunters and woodsmen. He repaired to a cave beside the river where fish, charcoal and game were brought to the holy man. He set up a rock-hewn altar and a cross fashioned from two sapling alder trees. In the Illyrian tongue he called the spot Admont—"region of plentiful water." Somewhere around the year 1000 Archbishop Eberhard received "pouches of gold goodly in number," contributed by St. Hemma of Gurk, to build a monastery on the site of the rock cave hermitage. When monks from St. Peter's in Salzburg came here in 1049 they were amazed to find in so remote a place a flourishing center of worship where agriculture and forestry, closely allied with the studies of art, the classic poets, and science, were the prime pursuits of the monks. And so down to the present day, this has ever been the pattern of life at Admont.

Admont's most famous treasure is the Baroque library. Through a great chestnut doorway one enters a noble apartment rising four stories to a gallery that embraces four hexagonal rooms connected one with the other by semicircular alcoves formed by engaged columns of Istrian marble, pure white, faintly veined in illusive azure blue, the Corinthian capitals of burnished silver-gilt. The floor of the library is tessellated in sepia and palest "Venetian" pink marble, the tessellations laid in the form of chevrons. Bookshelves of ivory and gold gessoed wood contain books bound in all shades of red leather and parchment tooled in gold. The parchment has aged to the tone of luminous, nautilus-shell white. Above these bookcases rise two more tiers of books bound in red and green Cordovan leather. These are reached by a balcony, the balustrade composed of bronze-doré grill-work forged in the monastery ateliers. In this superbly conceived room, wedding the exquisite colors of gold-tooled leather, diverse marbles and gilded wood, it is the richly painted ceiling by Altomonte that proclaims the apotheosis of the monastery's history.

In the center alcove of the library are arranged four groups of figures the size of life, artfully posed between the Corinthian columns and tall, pedimented bookcases. There is one uncommonly bizarre duo in bronze. In painting and sculpture I have seen the figure of

Death portrayed in many ways. Indeed, artists in Latin countries from Early Medieval times, through the Renaissance and Baroque periods, have been obsessed with a mania for portraying Death and his various macabre demon satellites. As funerary embellishment the figure of Death is considered an essential ornament.

At Admont, Death is portrayed as a skeletal, winged figure, hooded in grave cerements and suspended above the head of a monk purported to be Armonus Camus. The monk, leaning on his pilgrim's staff, draws away from Death, who carries in one hand the broken arrow of life. The other hand, raised on high, holds an hour glass, the sand having run its allotted hour. Modeled in tremendously vital style reminiscent of Bernini, this macabre duo is set under a wall entablature representation of a muse, her heavy breasts voluptuously pointed, her sullen brow shaded by a diadem of wheat and flowers. Written in Latin underneath the bust I read *Sibylla Lyrica*. At least, I thought, Armonus Camus, in answering the whisper of Death, was bidden farewell by the lyric muse.

Anyone visiting Admont should be sure to go into the colonnaded courtyard and watch the ironsmiths at their anvils, hammering long "snakes" of iron or bronze into patterns of red-gold or black cobweb lace. On the white plaster, vaulted wall hang scores of "patterns"— wrought-iron gates, fragments of balustrades, weather vanes and every conceivable hardware for doors.

As I left the cool, dim cloister of Admont and came out into the garden the only sound was the drowsy murmur of bees disappearing or emerging from the calyx of Madonna lilies arranged in serpentine flower beds. I thought of what Epictetus once wrote: "No great thing is created suddenly. Everything grows. A tree, a house, a school of thought, a nation, a religion, a way of life. And why are they great? Their growth is more leisurely. These ask not for generations, but for centuries."

Klosterkogel cradles in her lap a tiny black and white village and proudly bears upon her crag excessively turreted Rötelstein Castle, considered the finest expression of Baroque-Rococo architecture in Styria. The walls bristle with hundreds of stag antlers painted white.

Each year, in celebration of the Nativity, these are lit by Christmas tree candles in glass globes. I happened to see these pronged natural chandeliers, illuminated by electric bulbs of bright color, upon the occasion of a wedding festivity.

In the 12th century the village of Hall-in-the-Valley leapt into sudden prominence when salt was crystallized out of the waters. Today it lies quiet, "all passion spent." The Nordic-fair inhabitants devoted themselves to grinding Turkish wheat and buckwheat in its thatch-roofed mills, baking the flour into cart-wheel loaves.

Moving on to the northeast, if one is so fortunate as to traverse the road from Weichselboden to Mariazell on a day when the air affords vistas of far horizons, the memory of the Hochschwab region will remain always vivid in the mind. This range covers an area of some four hundred square miles. One hundred peaks attain a complexity of shape, color and ancient Styrian names comparable to no other single mountain range I know. Locally these peaks are called "the Magician's Mountains," the haunt of Faust, or Satan. From disparate points along this highway one can see the Danube, glistening like a silver serpent, and the Dachstein, up to its tricks of glancing off white light. To the south I could see as far as the Grossglockner.

All the way to Mariazell my eyes were constantly drawn to the ivory-white strata of alabaster, and the rose-red veins of quartz that seem like arteries tracing the mighty body of Hochschwab, commanding the Styrian world. Remember that Austria, above all else, is the land of magic mountains and, in happy consequence, of equally magical lakes to reflect them.

The Maria-Zell, a huge church though comparatively simple as to its exterior, is now a shrine for pilgrimage, for the spiritual influence of this Virgin, Magna Mater of Austria, reaches into other lands far beyond the confines of the nation.

The founding of the church goes back to the time of Otto VII, Abbot of Lambach, sometimes called "The Contemplator" or "The Dreamer," a powerful prelate of the 12th century. Otto dreamed he had made a vow to send one of his monks into the wilds of the mountains, which he knew full well were the haunt of outlaw tribes and malcontents "on the run" from the bondage of serfdom to the duchy. Lawlessness was abroad and impiety rampant. The charcoal burners in the depths of the forests caused concern. They were, so Otto wrote, "no better than Egyptians [gypsies] exuding the stench of paganism." The year was 1157 when Otto sent the monk Henzl on his journey, carrying an icon of the Virgin carved from the wood of a lime tree. But after a few weeks Henzl felt himself defeated by the mountains. His path was barred by range after range. Gorge winds buffeted him, snowstorms of blizzard strength covered his frail form. At last he sank down calling on the Virgin for succor. Falling into a deep sleep he roused to hear, as he thought, the crashing of thunder. But it was the walls of unsurmountable rock parting asunder. His prayer to the Virgin had been answered.

Next he chose a salubrious site beside a quiet stream to build himself a hermitage in honor of the Virgin. This is Mariazell, lovely in summer or in winter, a pearl-white town set amidst the silver of water and magnificent reaches of mountain scenery. Its walls and towers the pink of a sunrise sky, the largest pilgrimage church in Styria rises in the center of the town. Architecturally the church fuses the styles of Late German Gothic and Austrian Baroque. Above the entrance portal two square towers flank a higher campanile or belfry. At the rear of the long, white and gold nave is the Chapel of Our Lady. By design this nave is kept devoid of any eye-compelling ornamentation. The plain walls and ceiling point up extravagance of detail in the pillared alcove where stands Maria of Zell, holding the Child. This sumptuous reliquary is a blaze of silver gilt burnished and oiled to the semblance of crystal. The motif of surrounding walls and dome is frost crystals. Centuries ago the Virgin Mary appeared out of the snowy blast in answer to Henzl's prayer. Her robes are fashioned from white watered silk, heavy as papal damask, the folds embroidered in *repoussé* silver Alpine roses and crystal Annunciation lilies. Extending from under her pontifical crown of silver filigree encrusted with diamonds is a lace mantle frosted with crystal. Her smile gentle, her eyelids lowered, the Virgin of the Snows looks down at the Child in her arms who is robed in crystal like herself.

So proud of their province are the Styrians that they erect at cross-roads a tall pole supporting its coat of arms, the flame-tongued silver panther on a green ground, device of a 12th-century Count of Steyr whose deeds of valor were so heroic that Styria takes its name from his House.

Nine hundred years ago and more Graz, the capital of Styria, was a market "wharf" at Mur Bridge for fishermen netting in the waters of the Mur. Part of each day's catch had to be sent "up" to the lord of Castle Rock, of ancient bad repute. Today Graz proudly displays a sign advising visitors that she is a city of a quarter-million inhabitants. As well, Graz is a center of long-established culture and a "patron of industry."

The Diet Hall, a vast palace in German-Italian Renaissance style, contains the famous quadrangle, with an inner courtyard encircled by three tiers of arched colonnades of superbly articulated and sculptured stone. Before returning to Italy, architect Domenico dell'Allio, considering this his masterpiece, cut his initials in stone and the word *L'Ultimo*. The double-spiral stairway, a Gothic contrivance in dovetailed stone of amazing ingenuity, twists and turns in the Rathaus. The Provincial Armory in Landhaus Platz was built in 1640 to house armor of every description, from stirrups wrought like a lion's jaws to the lethal-looking spike-studded oxhide gloves worn by lords of the castles when riding out on their domain. A blow in the face of a rebellious varlet with one of these gloves might well have blinded him for life. Today this armor, arranged with the greatest imagination for design—steel and embroidered saddles, "box" stirrups and heraldically adorned casques for tourney and battlefield, hung so as to form "pictures" on the stone walls—is celebrated as the chief collection of historical armor housed under one roof in Europe. It is estimated sufficient to equip an army of 30,000.

I greatly favor a helm of 14th-century casting worn, as I read on the tag underneath, by Count Heinrich von Halbenrain in 1380 on his marriage to the lady of the House of Babenberg. All in gold, the front quarters of a stag, legs folded at the knees (as the legs of a knight who had gone on crusade were arranged for burial), the hoofs of carved amber falling on either side of the face across the shoulders. A crown is set between the widely branching antlers from which rises a magnificent crest of pheasant feathers. A gorget of gold disks set with rubies encircles the stag's throat. At the back, to hide the absence of hindquarters, falls a mantle of rouge velvet embroidered in gold oak leaves and acorns. So luxuriously ample are the folds that this tabard would surely have spread out across the back of the horse and trailed at least a yard behind its hoofs.

Iron-rich Styria has always been noted for its splendid estates, many of which are celebrated hunting preserves. Hereditary castles that are stone symbols of the power and wealth of the old nobility rise everywhere in the province. Some are turned into hotels or schools, but many are lived in, however sketchily, by members of the original families. The castles spread over the landscape are museums of art, a kind of pageantry of Imperial days embodied in stone. Not far from Graz are two such castles singularly representative of the grandly spacious manner in which their owners lived at a time when it was not thought remarkable to maintain a staff of two hundred or more servants "à la Esterhazy." A whole village might be given to game-keepers under a *Jägermeister* (huntmaster) or head forester, a sort of lord in his own right of all his forest realm. He kept the preserves "open" and well stocked with game for the entertaining of shooting parties.

Schloss Eggenberg, owned by Count Herberstein, is kept in its pristine glory to personify, as perhaps no other great house in Austria, a way of life which, save in rare cases, we will see no more. The castle is set in the midst of a park, as much gentle woodland as horticulturally impressive gardens. The plan of the hugely scaled, pale-saffron house of Late Italian Renaissance order is a three-story hollow square. At the angles four pavilion towers, topped by graceful cupolas, rise above the surrounding oaks and beeches, in turn surrounded by a double ring of ancient chestnut trees defining a bridle path. In the Deer Park, outside this ring, graze mouflon, stag and rhebok, raising their heads and gazing haughtily at any visitor approaching along the carriage drive.

The *festsaal* (ballroom), painted by Alessandro Serenios, depicts Attic myths in color that deepens in richness by contrast to the white stucco and burnished gilding ornamentation on the walls. Perhaps to accent the grand scale with delicacy, rose and violet crystal pendants shimmer from twenty Venetian (Murano) glass chandeliers.

The floor of this apartment is of rose and black marble, so highly polished that when the castle is opened to visitors each one is duly presented with a pair of loose-fitting quilted felt slippers. Everyone dons them for the guided tour of the rooms. This precaution is two-fold, preventing heavy walking boots from scratching the parquet floors inlaid with rare woods, and guarding the uncautious person from taking a header on the glassy surface of the famous marble floor.

In the Hunting Gallery the accent is on La Grande Venerie. Paintings, and accouterments for the chase, range from silver "false" spurs for fighting cocks to toe-stirrups in the form of a slavering fox head cast in silver. This collection is widely acclaimed as the sole museum in Austria devoted exclusively to hunting.

Throughout the house the Austrian Rococo furniture was designed by François Cuvilliés the Younger. Largely painted white, touched with burnished gold, the furniture is conceived *en suite*, the separate pieces produced in multitude.

In September and October the castle comes dramatically to life. Besides the celebrated Hunt Ball, when often guests are to be found from Ireland, England and Virginia, all the traditional hunting ceremonies and festivals of the chase are observed, including the fishing parties at night which stem from the days of that "Compleat Angler," Charlemagne.

When I left the gates of the castle I found that the outlying farms, the grain mills and the sawmills for dressing timber all flourished, mantled in an aura of well-being eddying from the castle. As darkness fell I noticed far off in the sky behind Leoben an orange glow, at first faint, then a burst of sparks rising, dimming, then rising again. I learned this was the nightly pyrotechnics above Donawitz, the foundry city ringed with snow-clad mountains forever stretching out its black arms to receive the ore yield from Erzberg. The distant glow cast a faint patina of gold on the claret-red tiles of the stable roof, and burnished redly the dense foliage of chestnuts and beeches.

I passed through a stand of ancient horse chestnut trees. Then into a grassy clearing. Here rose the urn-topped gate plinths of Schloss Harmannsdorf. The Baroque castle-hunting lodge is nearly hidden in the depths of a *"bois dormant,"* where all that seemed awake were three does and a tiny fawn, ready to disappear instantly into the fern brake. Harmannsdorf is a pavilion, an architectural rarity in Styria. The long, low structure, a single story set above a deep basement, is simply defined, allowing the entrance staircase, arresting in its grand sweep and ornament, to steal the architectural thunder. The wide staircase ascends in four platforms to a spaciously conceived balustraded terrace extending across the pavilion frontage. Due to the extensive length of the staircase, it was possible for the architect to utilize the richly molded stone handrail of the balustrade as a shelf on which to display a collection of immense stone urns—thirty-two in number—all of the same height, set at intervals. No two are alike, yet all are a variation on a single theme. This original idea of ornament lends not only an imposing but a singularly "different" air to the whole entrance façade. In itself each one of the violet-gray stone urns is beautifully sculptured in festoons, masks of Pan, satyrs and forest creatures.

Next I planned to spend three days at the Lipizzaner Stud at Piber. From a roadway breasting a slight rise I looked down across rolling meadowland to the stud at Piber, near Köflach, the present home of the white Lipizzan horses bred for performing the most intricate exercises in the *haute école* of horsemanship. Only stallions of the Lipizzan breed are used for show at the Spanish Riding School in Vienna. The Lipizzaners I saw quietly grazing below me were descendants of a proud race.

The late Queen Mary of England called these horses "the living treasures of Austria." Their lineage is as impressive as the beauty of their noble presence and their remarkable grace in movement. The Iberian horse was famous even in the days of the Romans, greatly sought after and highly prized. "Caesar's snow-white steeds which Hispania did him send" were extolled in song and story all over the antique

LIPIZZANER·MARES
AND FOALS IN PASTURE
PIBER·STYRIA

world. The Carthaginians, great horsemen all, when colonizing on the European continent favored the introduction of Arab blood, thus advancing the improvement of horse breeding on the Pyrenean Peninsula. From this mating developed the celebrated Arab-Barb. And from then on, the rise in beauty of conformation, stamina and intelligence was consistent. The horses were transplanted to Italy where the Polesinian and Neapolitan breeds reached considerable fame. In 1580 Archduke Karl Habsburg founded a stud at Lipizza near Trieste to perpetuate the line, hence the name. At the Danish stud at Friedrichsburg and in the studs of Prince Lippe-Bückeburg the breed was clarified to produce the pure white stallion.

As I looked across the meadows toward the old castle of Piber on its eminence, there grazed a herd of about seventy mares and foals. Foals are born jet-black or dark sepia-brown. Not until their fourth or fifth year do they begin to shed the dark hairs. Then the coat becomes a dun-gray or fawnskin. The dazzling white of such famous stallions as the incomparable Pibero (there are six dynasties today stemming from Danish, Neapolitan, Hungarian, and Arabian sires of the period 1765-1790) is known as the purest white hide in horsedom.

It was quiet on this rise. I was pleasantly shaded from a mortally hot sun. Suddenly I was alerted by the ringing of a deep-toned bell. The sound came from the direction of the tower rising from a long, many windowed building set at right angles to the castle but on lower ground. As if on cue every mare and every foal turned toward the gate leading from the upland pasture to the hilltop stables. The bell had announced dinner time. It was then, watching the parade of horses crossing the lower pasture, flicking in and out of long shadows cast by the tall, dark conifers, that I caught all the shadings of color among the mares.

They were crowding around the two young hostlers at the gate. Their hides varied from pale bisque to golden sorrel. Some were moleskin gray with black manes and tails. Two I picked out were almost purple-roan with flaxen manes and tails. A few were black, others bronze chestnut or honey-golden, strikingly set off by black points. Only a few were cream-color sprinkled with sorrel-red and black spots like pepper and paprika. I saw only two mares of the unblemished white that their little black sons would achieve one day.

The stable was all activity. Two veterinarians were in residence at the castle because two notable stallions were to "serve" mares the next day. I spent the following day roaming the pastures and the stables at Piber Stud, where I witnessed a "mating." A proud Lipizzaner stallion in full "randiness" is a stirring spectacle—passion incarnate—a creature dealing in elementals.

The old Renaissance castle is nearly stripped of furniture. It has the air of an indulgent old "nanny" half asleep though keeping a desultory eye on its famous Lipizzan charges, the least fractious of horses.

I put up at an old manor house, now Pension Alpenhof. The food was plain farmer's fare, abundant and delicious. Freshly baked, crusty buckwheat bread eaten with Zür cheese and washed down with local light beer. The morning I drove away and out of Styria I crested the same hill road where I had sketched on the first day. The horses were grazing there. It was a grand picture entirely, with the quiet, watchful mares and the young Lipizzaners munching the grasses of their breezy Alpine pasture.

Chapter 8

CARINTHIA THE HARMONIOUS

O F ALL provinces in Austria, Carinthia (or Kärnten) remains a world apart, jealously guarding its traditions derived from age-old sources. Carinthians maintain that the fairy Fata Morgana created this province, breathing of the Latin South, expressly for her refuge when the cares of her office weighed too heavily upon her. Villages like St. Jakob, with its herb gardens in the form of a St. Catherine wheel and its ancient saffron-colored houses, are so hidden away in secluded pasture lands and torrent-watered gorges that they do not appear on a map. After I had lost my way a number of times, consulting my detailed map to no avail, I inquired in St. Veit why this was so. The proprietor of Hotel St. Veiterhof raised bristling sandy eyebrows and shrugged. "Foreign visitors seldom go to these little villages," he said. "They all want swimming, jazz bands and dancing in places like Velden on the Wörthersee, or," he smiled, "to get as near to Heaven as possible at Heiligenblut where the air is so mild and refreshing the year round."

The Lessachtal, where the immense sweep of grassy meadow slopes are sown thick with flowers, savors strongly of Italy. The Gail winds a serpentine course into the Lienzer Dolomites, crowding their prodigious bulk right onto the doorstep of Lienz itself, romantically situated town of East Tyrol. When I stand in Schlossplatz and look upward in the direction of the mountain town of Bolzano (erstwhile Austrian Bozen) in Italy, it always seems to me that the Dolomites are raising their alabaster brows to peer down into the center of Lienz, admiring the pale pink and white castle which rears its slender pastiche turrets above walls of stone anciently quarried from their flanks.

On this Italian frontier of Carinthia I again mark a strongly accented point so often resulting from juxtaposition of different races. The buoyant stream of life in daily contact with foreign customs takes color and, in this case, a kind of dreaminess from the allure of distant lands. In golden hair, golden voices, and golden ornaments, there is a hint of the Slavonic East. The delicate perfume of mimosa, the more heady acacia, the haunting scent of flower of orange, derive from the Latin South. Too, I notice the racial characteristics of the people are a fusion of the medium tall, blond, soft-spoken Slovenes, to whom a certain lassitude is handed down from their Celtic ancestors, with the Latin South and Far Eastern type, not so prevalent but still apparent in dark complexion, raven-black hair and gray or dark-amber eyes.

In the 12th and 13th centuries Carinthia was constantly invaded, first by the Mongols, then by Turks, Hungarians and Venetians. The imprint of these races remains today traceable in various characteristics. Yet the old saying, "Carinthia free and undivided," can also be applied to an Austrian-Alpine type known to anthropologists as "Carinthian."

The love of music throughout the province by everyone from the cradle to the grave is remarkable. The taste seems to be flexible, from somber laments to rollicking mountaineer ballads and Italian *romanze*. In the smallest mountain hamlet I heard the shrill or muted notes of a shepherd's pipes played by small boys and old shepherds alike. In Griefenburg and Heiligenblut young boys form "orchestras" and go about the countryside playing shepherd's pipes, violins and zithers. Stalwart young mountaineers from St. Lorenzen in Lessachtal and Iselsberg near the Italian border, carrying accordions of heroic proportions, play old airs with a pagan abandon fit to shake the rafters, or a serenade so dulcet that it would cause a harder heart than mine to melt with ardor.

I stopped one evening at Kötschach in Gailtal to eat the famous dish of the region, *nudel*, a pastry made from soft flour paste with the edges folded over herbs, poppy seeds, sweet peppers and *täfen* (cheese curds). At Gasthaus Kürschner I ate large slices of *nudel* and was regaled with rousing country dance tunes played on a harmonica by a youth with the physique of a Krumpendorf bull. He wore the costume of Oberdrauberg. High boots of soft leaf-brown leather, into the tops of which were tucked his full breeches of dark green *loden* (coarse woolen cloth). A loose jacket of rust-red, home-woven linen was elaborately trimmed with vines and leaves cut out of brilliant green felt. But it was his hat that especially took my eye. An immense cart wheel of rust-red felt, the brim curled up like a breaking wave, it was lined in the green of his jacket trim. Thrust into the cord wrapped around the low crown was a really impressive cockade made from three perfect specimens of red fox tails. A gala note was added by the three-legged wooden stool which the youth sat upon when he played his harmonica. But he scorned to carry it about. So—he had attached the seat to a belt buckled around his waist. When he was walking about, the effect of three wooden legs sticking out at right angles from his broad behind seemed unremarkable to anyone in the room save myself.

Besides music of divers instruments and the voice of song, Carinthia is the chief "costume" province in Austria. By that I mean that each locality wears almost continuously the traditional costumes of its ancestors with scarcely any changes, the design going back to the tourneys and festivals held by pleasure-loving Count Meinhard of the Tyrol in the 14th century.

In Central and Lower Carinthia some costumes have a Roman air from the days when Ottokar ruled. Too, there are many traces of Turkish influence, such as the high turbans, looped with fringed ribbons, worn by the women of the Glan Valley. Of Hungarian derivation are the short, full-pleated skirts displayed over many layers of starched, lace-bordered petticoats, and the vividly embroidered wool stockings, worn by young girls from the Gail Valley villages. The elder men of St. Lorenzen in the Lessach Valley, it would appear, take their costume from those worn by rich Venetian merchants of the Early Renaissance. They wear a long, loosely cut mantle with turnover revers. The wide sleeves are turned back in a flaring cuff. For feast days and ceremonials the scene changes. Now the "robe" is cut from red, olive-green, or pehaps, like the magnificent example I saw in a wedding party, sunset-orange Italian damask.

The young men of St. Lorenzen are no-end dashing. Actually their costume would be most appropriate for a pastoral ballet. A bucolic Romeo, in fawn or violet cloth knee breeches, striped stockings, a swagger jacket of orange, pale green or white cloth frogged in silk cords of a contrasting color. The hugely brimmed, flat-crowned hat is of corded silk, the color optional, with a long scarf embroidered in brilliant floss silk and gold thread.

Carinthian women of any condition in life carry themselves erect, striding the roads with lithe, easy gait. A matron's headdress is of black silk moire ribbon looped, fluted and piled high, like a turban. The jewelry largely consists of heirloom pieces—Baroque pearls, tourmaline or carnelian intricately set in silver or gold filigree. Studying a necklet or bracelet, I am convinced that gold and silver smiths, wielding their tiny mallets in the musk-scented shadows of some bazaar in the indolent East, inspired these parures. It is a signal part of Carinthia's economic history that gold and silver in quantity were mined for centuries in the Tauern Mountains. The traffic of jewels, gold and silver ornaments, tinsel-threaded damasks and velvets from Italy and "the East" brought many Venetian craftsmen, and workers in gold, silver and jewels, to the old ducal towns of St. Veit, Lienz, aristocratic Villach (where the Bishops of Bamberg held sumptuous and licentious court) and Klagenfurt. These gentry, it is said, hailed "out of Turkey and the byways of the Levant," by way of Venice.

Again, as constantly occurs in the history of the Austrian provinces, it was the Princes of the Church, a hierarchy rapacious for riches and the pleasures thereof, that gave the countryside the imprint under the rule of a Medieval aristocracy, by virtue of their numerous castles and country residences called "manor farms."

The huge, square, fortified mansions of the region near the Italian border are chiefly remarkable for bronze-studded chestnut-wood portal gates opening ponderously into hexagonal courtyards awash with tubbed flowering citrus trees and cooled by the spray of fountains. Jets of water, foaming in full spate, rise to improbable heights, fed by rampageous mountain streams. I was told at one house that so strong is the pressure exerted by these torrents, sometimes half a dozen streams converging in one gorge, that the underground tile piping often bursts, requiring constant attention and repair.

In the Gail Valley between Sachsenburg and Flattach the farms are surrounded by wide fields where horses graze knee deep, cropping a particularly juicy blue-tinged grass. Over a large area horse breeding is not only long established but economically important to the people. I walked out into a grazing meadow to look over a group of young geldings, big sorrel-red fellows with black manes. This grass, I thought, must be ambrosia, for as the horses looked up from nibbling, unblinkingly staring me straight in the eye in the odd, unabashed way of equines, I noticed how sleek, how contented, they all appeared. These horses are descended from a breed of Babenberg "destriers" or war horses, the kind of horse that Emperor Charlemagne was wont to send to some knight who had earned a princely gift. A destrier was trained to fight an enemy, man or horse, with his flailing hoofs. The horse's temper was not improved by such tactics.

At the farm I was invited to a really lusty meal, a midday dinner— boiled ham, roast veal and *sterz* (a milk and buckwheat pudding). Food was served in a long, whitewashed *kachelofenstube* (tiled stove room) of the farmhouse. Two chests took up half the long wall opposite the stove. The chests were painted in scenes from life on the farm. Door and side panels depicted the cycle of a horse's life from newborn foal to full-grown horse decked out in bell-hung yellow leather harness, a panache of Alpine roses and wheat ears, for prosperity and fecundity, waving above his forelock, ready to draw the bridal coach.

Copper vessels, circular trays big as cart wheels, and monumental steins and flagons were hung on the walls, radiating fiery rays of light from the bright sun streaming in at deeply embrasured windows. A room of good fellowship, of well-being entire.

As it turned out, the aftermath of this farm meal proved to be the surprise of my stay in Carinthia. During the afternoon the eldest son of the family asked me casually, while showing me around the farm, if I had ever seen the annual festival called *Kufenstechen* (pierce the ring) held in the Gail Valley. It was to be held the next day in Lainach in the Möllthal. I had not seen it, but knew that it derived from the days of tournaments held by the ruling Babenberg princes and later by knights under the banner of the House of Eppenstein.

The following day I arrived at the tree-shaded square in the old village of Lainach. I had been told this was a village bathed in the quiet of the grave, utterly remote in time. The somber Gothic church was shrouded in nearly black ivy. Each leaf set quivering by a rustling breeze seemed to have a life of its own. Extreme agitation reigned, added to which, thousands of starlings darting among the ivy sprigs were twittering like bedlam. People seemed streaming from every lane. This unwonted clamor and frantic activity in sleepy Lainach was due, of course, to the furore caused by the annual festival.

At the edge of town a sort of race course had been roped off. Six riders took part in the ring-spearing, mounted on horses appropriately caparisoned. If not so richly bedizened with gold embroidery and ostrich plumes as mounts in the days of Babenberg supremacy, certainly the painted linen housings for man and beast were as brilliantly diapered in contrasting colors.

The young girls were costumed, a few as Medieval maidens from the castle halls, others in their best traditional costume, which is so nearly like that of the "Castle Lady" of earlier times that the continuity of a Medieval picture was not impaired. Each girl stood on a dais, holding out a wooden hoop, or ring. This must be speared by the "knight" riding a "Babenberg" horse at full gallop. It takes a cool head, a clear eye, and expert horsemanship to spear the ring on the point of a lance.

Next morning I left the atmosphere of hospitality, friendliness and spirited horses at Rossturm Bauern (farm of the horse tower), bound for Spittal. My last glimpse was of a "clutch" of buildings, characteristic of this province, the effigies of galloping horses woven from ripe wheat spears acting as weather vanes atop the towers, glowing like molten gold in the sun. I passed Weissensee, Carinthia's warmest lake, a wildly lovely stretch of water which the troubadours called "Lake of Ten Thousand Lilies." Its dark-green waters, flat as a mirror of polished moss-agate, extend beyond Techendorf. I saw below me a wide gorge cleft by an angry torrent of water churning a deep pool in what appeared to be the bowels of the earth. But this is a region where nature is variable. Gentle valleys, quiet lakes and fantastic rock formations of hobgoblin aspect prevail. I noticed spanning the gorge a narrow timber bridge set on high stilts cut from forest pines, nearly hidden from sight by clouds of spray. Across the ancient bridge three shepherds, cloaked and bearded, one giant wrapped in flowing capes, a veritable "Old Man of the Mountains," drove their herds to a large raft to pole the sheep across the lake to some village market. Here was antiquity come immediate.

The Drau Valley cradles innumerable lakes, remote mirrors of nature. I saw little lakes and tarns which are marked on only the best maps. The gleaming white road to Spittal-on-the-Drau is full of turnings. Sharp curves pierce mountain tunnels on the heights, where I glimpsed, through apertures cut for light into the rock walls, eagles effortlessly circling in the pale blue heavens, wing pinions air-borne, appearing at rest. Eagles of the Carnic-Julian Alps and misty crag pinnacles of Karawanken Range display breast feathers of smoke-blue flecked with black, the strong wing pinions rusty-bronze and green, iridescent as the hackles of any Cochin-China fighting cock. High on an outcrop of rock, I lay back to watch the eagles wheel, and to try to count the attenuated threads of water which laced the rock flanks and fell into pools hidden from my eyes far below. Falling from the glaciers, the cascading streams drop silently for hundreds of yards, suddenly to hit a spur of rocks and shatter into veils of white spray.

Winding down from out the mountains I came to upland meadows. A great swathe of color lay across my path. *Frauenschuh* (*cypripedium calceolus*) lady's slipper, the "toe" of the shoe a clear yellow, the narrow, curled petals, or "laces," that lovely, illusive, haunting shade of raisin-brown with just a hint of crimson. One rarely sees this exact shade any more save perhaps in velvets or damasks, faded, lightly glazed with dust in the incense-tinctured choir lofts of a monastery church or basilica.

The first thing I saw as I entered the ancient ducal town of Spittal, straddling the torrentuous mountain river, was a civic ceremony that had in some manner to do with ancient fishing rights. Decorations were in full strength. Most arresting were the arms of Kärnten displayed beneath the ferociously handsome horned helm of the Princes of Porcia.

Spittal has ever been a flagrantly proud, high-stomached town. In 1560 the powerful family Salamanca-Ortenburg ruled a considerable area of land surrounding the walled town. The horned steel helm in the decorations of Spittal Marktplatz has what is known in armorial terms as a "basket mask," interlaced strips of steel plate rising from a high gorget, or collar. Two tall ox horns, gilded, are mounted on the brow of the casque to rise in the semblance of Apollo's lyre. Branching at right angles from the outside of each horn are gold filigree brackets from which hang fifteen metal badges, three to each bracket, cut in the shape of a heart. Those on the left side are enameled blue; those on the right, blood red. Of the numerous legends concerning this device, one which seems to me quite probable has to do with vows made on a crusade. A prince of Porcia was grievously wounded before the walls of Acre. He prayed to a statue of the Virgin which he carried in his saddle bags. If he might survive his wound, might find a ship to carry him home, he would dedicate a chapel and found an order of nuns, to the Sacred Heart of Mary. His squire offered extravagant sums to captains of feluccas, a craft the Arabs call "swift, white-winged birds of the sea." At last on the fifteenth day the nearly dying man set sail for Italy. Once home, true to his vow, he is said to have erected not only a convent-hospice to receive the sick but fifteen chapels in Carinthia, all dedicated to the Sacred Heart of Mary.

Who was the architect of Porcia Palace? An enigma. Considering the wealth of historical fact, such as substantiated murders to curdle the blood, committed in its cellars, it seems odd to me that so splendid an edifice, ranking in the forefront of Austrian residences in Italian Renaissance style, has not in its archives the identity of the architects who built it. Only one document sustains a flimsy clue—"the Porcia Palace was built in the 16th century by unknown Italian architects." This may mean any one of half a hundred Italian architects who came and went at will, for it was the fashion in Carinthia to build in the Italian Renaissance, later in the Baroque, taste. The origin of the palace is Salamanca-Ortenburg aggrandizement. The massive floriated marble cartouche above the entrance portal embraces twenty quarterings, princely and ducal coronets, two amazons bearing arms, and a Neptune trident. Later the palaces became the property of the princes Porcia, who were responsible for adding many of the richly sculptured architectural features.

The edifice is a hugely scaled square rising four stories, built in the pure Italian manner, featuring a vast inner quadrangle, the *cortile noble* represented at its best in Medician villas in Tuscany. Ornament is restrained, vital in movement yet extremely elegant, as in the marble pargeting (incised and high relief design) carved around the doors and windows. There is a wealth of Italian grotesque in bas-relief both inside and out. Perhaps the finest gesture is the grand staircase leading up to the three-colonnaded galleries that surround the courtyard. Here is a lightness of touch, an airy grace, a sense of sails set for voyaging, heightened by the sea-blue and green wash on the gallery vaultings.

As I mounted the rises of the stairs and took a turn around each gallery, I felt that if someone called "Up anchor" and lifted the huge bronze anchor in the shape of a horned sea monster, which reposes as an ornament near the iron grillwork entrance doors, the palace would sail off to some unknown clime, with myself a most willing passenger.

Biannually in May and September a horse fair is held in Spittal. From miles around come farmers with a few horses of draft-animal type to sell, and important breeders from the Gail Valley with Babenberg breed stallions and mares. Great eating and drinking takes place. Hundreds of horses change hands, and to cap the day the town puts on a spectacular display of fireworks at night. This is the day to see peasant costumes from the villages roundabout. It is a marvel how many variations on the main theme one will see.

Maria-Wörth lies on the idyllic southern shore of Wörthersee. It is one of the larger Carinthian "pleasure lakes" or, as these celebrated lakes are sometimes called, "Fünf Schwesterseen" (Five Sisters), the other four being Millstätter See, Ossiacher See, Faaker See and Weissensee. Maria-Wörth is possibly the quietest village in all Austria. It lies wrapped in a personal brand of enchantment on a curving peninsula heavily embowered in ancient trees across from fashionable Velden, with its great Schloss Hotel. Roadways on this southern side of the lake are too narrow for auto-bus traffic. The lovely church of Maria-Wörth with its childlike peasant Madonna, where baskets of eggs or a newborn baby's shirt are laid at her feet to be blessed, is still a sanctuary for the sorely oppressed. A rope hangs beside the door at the adjacent priest's house to ring the Hunger Bell. No suppliant is ever turned away.

In many parts of Austria, perhaps more in Styria and Carinthia, one continually comes upon the charnel house, adjunct to a church. Sometimes standing sentinel in the midst of a crossroads graveyard, these massively built towers, cylindrical, hexagonal or pyramidal repositories of skulls, are purported to be a legacy of Celtic burial ritual. The oddly fascinating charnel house nearby is a huge stone structure, the walls built on a rocklike pyramid. I saw it first through a forest of black iron-lace crosses in the churchyard, which heightened the macabre atmosphere that hangs like a pall over the interior. I was shown the inside by a sexton. At first the darkness was Stygian. Thousands of skulls of persons from every condition of life down the years, be he mendicant or great nobleman, are piled to the roof, following the pyramidal form of the walls. All is a confused jumble of bones, the sagging ivory craniums bolstered up by a wide pelvis bone, thigh bones and a "cradle" of ribs. It was mortally hot the day I ventured into this anteroom to Hades. The blast of decay, the dry, choking stench of cerements, nearly mowed me down. I turned to speak to the sexton who had ushered me there. In the aqueous light his hairless dome gleamed palely, his eyes were sunk in shadow. It was purely weird. As Ichabod Crane said of his horse, "He's not *alive* but he's standing up."

I drove on to Heiligenblut soon after, highest of the villages lying at the foot of the Grossglockner, the mightiest rock abutment on the Carinthian frontiers. Grossglockner High Alpine Drive is an engineer-

ing marvel with its roots in pre-history, when it was a goat path over the Tauern Range for Celtic shepherds. On the upland plateau a freshening coolness reigned. I felt a lift of the spirit as well, engendered perhaps by everything in Heiligenblut pointing upwards. The village climbs a steep hill. Steep-pointed gables on the white and pastel tinted plaster houses seem about to spread sloping roofs and sail away to the jagged tips of High Tauern. Everything gleams opalescent in moonlight. The valley people still participate in an autumn dance festival, stemming from pagan nature worship, to propitiate "The Mountains of the Moon."

Most noticeable of all in this village is the pilgrimage church. A basilica in miniature, its nave is exceptionally high and narrow. The altar alcove walls form a half octagon. The slender tower is remarked as uncommon. Attenuated as a classic pillar, the spire resembles the blackest exclamation point. The belfry is a landmark, a beacon seen from as far away as the lovely Möll Valley. Here again an ancient nature-worship festival is held in early spring. Oddly, this rite has Christian overtones, for the valley deity to fertility and the Madonna in the Mariakirch are jointly called Our Lady of Abundance.

The Pilgrimage Church of St. Vincent is a quite simple, small Gothic edifice, the original stone walls rough-dressed and coated thickly with countless whitewashings. On entering the nave one is presented with an interior of sweeping simplicity, a vaulted treasure chest. The high altar is Carinthia's most important winged altarpiece. Richly carved *in profondo*, the triptych is burnished gold and matrix-green of a singularly vivid tone, a "burning" green, like the larch trees, each needle shimmering in sunlight, which I could see out the window. Regiments of larches marching up the mountainside right to the church door. The altar carving is by Wolfgang Hasslinger. He signed it "W. H. 1520. *Magnum Opus*."

Night descends suddenly in Heiligenblut. Sharp coolness embraces the plateau, the winds sweeping from the adjacent glacier peaks which one can admire in the primrose-pink Alpine glow—that indescribable, illusive last smile from the setting sun that I find more exquisite from this high vantage point than any other because it reflects the violet-rose sunset glow that deepens to bronze-purple in neighboring Italy.

A warm dining room where one may partake of good hot food is imperative at night in this high altitude. I suggest the far renowned Alpenhotel Franz-Josef-Haus. If the weather holds sunny next day, take lunch on the terrace of Rupertihaus. Try the lake trout, and a special kind of hot potato salad, glowing more golden than any setting sun. This is due to the yolks of raw eggs beaten into the salad dressing of sour cream and lemon.

Mounting the Grossglockner Pass the "curtain goes up" on one stage setting after another for Nature's "Extravaganza," the one theatre piece that runs forever. Looking off among the glaciers to the "Türkische Zeltstadt" (Turkish tent city) I saw a fantastic jumble of peaked, scalloped and apparently roped and tasseled snow tents of giant size. The glacier whirlwinds twang brazenly, flinging sprays of frost particles against an ethereal blue sky. Pasterze, longest glacier in the Eastern Alps, links its flow with that from towering Johannesberg. This great tongue of ice pushes down the valley to feed hundreds of waterfalls and nine valley rivers. Climbing ever upwards along the most modern Alpine highway in Austria, by describing innumerable serpentine bends, the road climbs to 8,216 feet. From the summit I looked into three provinces. Sweeping far, far above me were the indigo-blue granite walls of old Grossglockner himself, his flanks scarred into deep ravines, honeycombed with caves and caverns —"leading down to China," so runs an old mountaineer's song. Great tongues of snow caught in these crags never melt the year round.

And so, the heat having been cooled off by glacial breezes, I kept my tardy appointment with Villach, which lies on the roughly star-shaped delta formed by the junction of two broad rivers, the Drau and the Gail. Many smaller streams flow around the old town. Legion acrothermal springs bubble and spurt like caldrons of witches' brew among its river meadows.

Villach wears a proud Renaissance air. Even a princely one, for Villach has ever "chinked her gold too loudly," say the envious neighbors. "White gold" from the thermal waters and "black gold" from metals, silver and iron. Not in the quantity mined on the Erzberg, but goodly. There are countless songs to be heard in the *weinstubes*, in the parks, where concerts are held nightly. Old songs of great days of the court troubadour or minnesinger. Paragon of them all was Walther von der Vogelweide of the "golden throat." But there was also Carinthia's "princely lark," the less celebrated Zachäus von Himmelberg.

One of these songs is called "Villach's Dwarf," referring to the village of Nötsch. This tiny hamlet is set among weird scenery, fantastic, savage, but of unforgettable beauty. Rock, boulder and shard are flung helter-skelter among grassy knolls. Devastation on an heroic scale stemming from a series of landslides during the Middle Ages. It is said the ancient village of Nötsch was obliterated at least twenty times. But it was always rebuilt on the cairn of its previous existence.

Villach is so close to the Italian frontier that a sense of dreaminess, a *dolce far niente*, rides the town. The starlight nights are murmurous with music. Guitar, mandolin, zither and violin are played with light romantic touch in the parks along the rivers. As Marie Antoinette said to her jailer in the Temple, "I long for Vienna where everybody dances." Everybody dances in Villach with Italian abandon. And nearly everybody speaks Italian as a second tongue.

Parkhotel has a large white and gold ballroom in Italian Rococo style. Dances are held nightly and the food is notable. On the first Saturday and Sunday in August occurs one of the gayest of costume fetes, with torchlight and firework processions and dancing in the streets at night. Costumes are for the most part Rococo in essence, like the *commedia dell' arte* of Venice—Harlequin, Columbine, or the Mad Doctor Nero in voluminous black breeches and scroll-brim hat. He cavorts with his long syringe full of perfume, cognac or *ink*, one never knows what until squirted.

St. Veit-on-the-Glan, where I returned next day, is ducal to the last cobblestone and still plumes itself on having the longest history in Carinthia, fittingly eulogized by Walther von der Vogelweide. Certainly the Romans loved the town. They built temples to whichever deity was fashionable at the moment. A ring of Early Medieval,

Renaissance and Baroque castles surround St. Veit, a kind of jeweled girdle of castles which includes Hochosterwitz, Groppenstein and cathedral-like Petersberg. It is a veritable *"pomp gürtel"* of castellated might, from which derives the girdle worn by feudal knights at the coronation of their sovereign, set with plaques of rubies or sapphires cut intaglio, in the semblance of their castle.

The paramount treasure of St. Veit is a Roman relic of great size and greater worth, the "Cup of the Gods." It was used as a gigantic altar cup in a Roman Temple to Jupiter. It lay buried for 1,500 years. For the last 400 years it has been a public fountain. Shaped like a massive drinking bowl on a pedestal, it is surmounted by the figure of a young Roman patrician drinking from a ram's horn. From the lips of the youth water spills into the basin.

At Hotel Weisses Lamm, a white lamb is painted on the staircase wall—a Pascal Lamb, bearing in the crook of one delicately raised front leg a gilt cross tied with angel-blue ribbons. The food is average, but to those interested in dancing the orchestra is excellent, not always the case in fairly remote Austrian towns. I stayed in a room that could, with ease, have been used as a roller-skating rink. The great bed complemented the room in scale. I have never felt more princely nor been more comfortable.

The roster of pre-eminent Romanesque churches or cathedrals of documented antiquity in Europe contains fewer names than in any other era in architecture. So it is to me purely marvelous to wander in the cloisters of the Cathedral of Gurk, the oldest Romanesque edifice in Austria, to stand beneath the arches carved in mysterious symbols defying translation, supported by columns capped with the rare "tongues of the saints" design. This lappet design resembles reversed armorial shields. On some of these "tongues" are inscribed the "exploits in life, the heroism in death," of knights who lived in the Early Middle Ages. They bear the names of families that have reverberated with the sound of battle-trumpets down the centuries of Carinthian history.

The church was built in 1165, rising unscathed from the battle for power between the archbishops of Gurk and Salzburg. Its treasures are numerous and of highest worth. The wall paintings and the dramatic, lovely, and indescribably poignant Pietà, completed by the gifted sculptor Raphael Donner in 1741 a few days before he died, strike even the most chattery tourist to awed silence. The cathedral is dedicated to St. Hemma of Friesach, who is buried in the porphyry-embellished crypt. A series of carved wood panels as sharply carved as Indian ivory from the Rajputana portray, in the most minute detail, incidents in the life of this saintly woman. To me there is a decidedly Spanish touch in the painted and jeweled veil, depicting a stately pageant of Biblical personages, which conceals the altar. A seated figure of St. Hemma, garbed as a Roman matron, watches over her Aventine marble sarcophagus in the crypt.

This painted veil, depicting the Creation, which partially obscures the High Altar of Gurk from Ash Wednesday to Maundy Thursday, is unique in Austria. It was suggested by the greatest humanist and visionary of his time, Konrad of Friesach, who, being an artist as well, painted the veil himself to immortalize his own vision. The jewels which sprinkle the gauze like a Milky Way of stars were presented by St. Hemma's brother Otto and sewn on the veil by ladies of the most prominent families in Friesach.

The ancient Roman town of Friesach would be a historic monument in any land. It is a walled town that to a great extent still preserves its towers and bastions. Almost concealed from view by wooded knolls, the trade routes pass its gates winding to Klagenfurt and Knittelfeld—roads hewn from the rocky soil by the Celts.

Schloss Lavant lies in the fruit-producing Lavant Valley. An ancient palace, once part defensive bastion, but more a gracious manor house where fruit orchards caught the sun and vineyards, espaliered fruit trees—pear, peach and plum—ripened juicily on the walls. In this house at the end of the 14th century lived the great beauty of Carinthia, weaving her famous tapestries "The Courts of Love" and "singing sweetly at each stitch." She was called Edwiga of the Fair Girdle, she who "died of longing" at her loom.

Many of the old battlements have fallen into the long grasses that lace the dry moat. But about the roofless manor house drifts an air of dreaming melancholy, of "old, unhappy, far-off things." I listened to the evening chirruping of birds in the woodland. Then a songster trilled, perhaps of Edwiga at her loom.

Villach, St. Veit and Klagenfurt. The latter town, capital of Carinthia, is the apex of the ancient "ducal triangle." Klagenfurt, noted for its wrought iron, rises in nearly flat country within sight of once-Roman Virunum. The Landhaus is an imposing structure, the façade a blend of Italian Renaissance (in the manner of the Porcia Palace in Spittal) and strongly pointed-up Austrian Baroque overtones. The two tall towers flanking an arcaded gallery, reached by a long flight of elaborately balustraded stairs, are topped by the most richly curved and graceful copper cupolas I have seen in Austria. Displayed on the walls are gaudily painted representations of the Dragon Fountain, the chief attraction of the town as well as the device for the municipal coat-of-arms. The Lindwurm (dragon) of Lindwurmbrunnnen (Dragon Fountain) centers everyone's attention in the *marktplatz*. This stone dragon rests on a fountain, surrounded by a kind of barricade of superbly wrought ironwork. The immense reptile was carved from a single boulder by a Carinthian sculptor named Ulrich Vogelsang in 1600. He labored for years hewing the beast from fiercely resisting granite. When it was finished at a spot far up on a rock crag where the man had found the thirty-foot boulder, he insisted that it be dragged to its present site by schoolboys, each one named Ulrich. It took 300 sturdy boys named Ulrich to do so. I heard this told by the bartender of Hotel Sandwirt, the best of the hotels in town. Its specialty, the Dragon Scale cocktail, is particularly good.

Now hereby hangs a tale—the version paramount of the dragon legend, the one which every boy born in Klagenfurt implicitly believes. In the heroic days of knight errantry, an overlord hunted wild boar in the mountains. He was chased home by a dragon. He thereupon forebade his young son Ulrich to go near the dragon's cave, which he carefully told the lad was marked by a long funnel-shaped boulder. This was definitely out of bounds. Like all boys living at a time when adventure rode the air like a steady breeze, he disobeyed his father and went lightly armed to "slay the dragon." Instead Ulrich himself was killed. When his body was found his father decreed that henceforth every man-child born within his domain must be named Ulrich. By this means the memory of his son's bravery in trying to rid the region of the fearful dragon would be kept green. The decree still prevails, probably more through habit than anything else, though it must cause utter confusion in a family of ten boys. Today, I venture that if I stood at the foot of the fountain, raised my voice and called "*Ulrich! Ulrich, komm!*" I would, within minutes, have a formidable crowd of youngsters surrounding me.

I have always maintained that in "seating" a castle, position is three-quarters of the battle. Certainly no castle is more gloriously elevated or so aggrandized, in the best sense of the word, as Hochosterwitz. Driving from Velden to Klagenfurt, the countryside is pleasantly undulating. Farmsteads seem to withdraw shyly under groves of alders, limes and beeches. Cattle and horses graze in the flowery meadows from which rises a tremendous cone of rock, densely wooded at the base. It is there for no apparent reason save to present a traveler with a piece of stark theatre he will not see soon again. The soaring height is doubly impressive because of its solitary thrust from relatively flat lands.

Burg Hochosterwitz was first mentioned as "a fortified place" in chronicles of the year 860. Towering as it does above the countryside, it is a symbol of the province. The edifice is generally regarded as the "Carinthian Castle of The Grail." The Lords of Osterwitz, noted for extreme height and fearlessness, were hereditary Royal Cup Bearers. Their "livery," to be seen in the castle armory, was of astonishing richness, crimson and orange in color with ornament in silver and gold. In the year of the Turkish invasion, 1475, the last Graf von Osterwitz died in captivity without leaving an heir. Friedrich III possessed the castle for a while. He added greatly to the splendid carvings and gildings, the frescoes and bronze *doré* interior grills. He called it his "hunting lodge" to which, it is said, he used to bring a hundred guests at a time. Ferdinand I, to whom the castle came "in fief," mortgaged it to a knight, Christoph Khevenhüller. The castle is still owned by the Khevenhüller family.

I ascended the winding road from the "meadow gates" to the portcullis, passing under fourteen gates. A castellated wall on the outer side of the road protects any adventurer. Each gate is different in some respect, just enough not to become monotonous. This system of defense was erected in 1586 "to confound the Turks." Confound them it did. The castle has never, in its long history of attacks and siege, been reduced.

There is an entertaining story told in connection with one of the sieges. The heroine was that monumental, fantastically plain, redoubtable woman Margarete, Countess of Tyrol, a warrior, indeed a "general," of renown. Among other flights of fancy, or temperament, she drove her first husband out penniless in order to marry her stripling first cousin. She was ex-communicated by the Pope in Rome for "seduction and incest amounting to a double sin." About this time she went all out for battle and showed her devious wit. Her garrison was starving. The enemy were so close beneath her walls that she wrote, "I can hear snarling among the men below." Nothing daunted, Meg of the cavernous mouth called an assembly of her forces. She dressed some of her men-at-arms as women. The tall headdresses swathed with veils, fashionable in that period, would show off well from below. From her woefully depleted store of food she had an ox roasted whole. Then she lighted torches and sat her "guests" down to table, arranged on the battlements, high enough for the besiegers to see a banquet in progress with wine, women, and hilarity. Then as a *beau geste* she had the smoking carcass of the ox heaved over the walls to fall among the ranks of an astounded enemy. They departed at dawn, convinced that there was no hope of starving this garrison to surrender.

The rooms at Hochosterwitz are splendidly appointed, the frescoes painted in great vitality and style. There is an armory of battle and tourney gear. Every year in September a costume fete is held in the Knight's Hall of the castle, an occasion for a display of armor and the "habiting" and accouterment that was used in connection with the knightly sport of tourney.

I had lunch in the castle restaurant, which is set in such a position that I looked out across a vast panorama of Carinthia, and I looked down the walls, an avalanche of age-pitted masonry affording me a superb idea of the stupendous natural bastions on which the castle is built. And I remembered that in Styria too it is the high and mighty position that peculiarly identifies the castles of these legend-haunted Austrian provinces.

Chapter 9

UPPER AUSTRIA PRESENTS PROSPERITY, TRANQUILLITY, AND THE TIMELESS BEAUTY OF ANCIENT MASONRY

HOWEVER famed in history the Danube is—"who controls the Danube, controls all Europe" is an ancient proverb—the River Enns enjoys a quiet celebrity, having earned the sobriquet "River of Everlasting Fertility," bestowed by a grateful populace upon this lovely, quietly flowing waterway. Along the Enns are abundantly manifest the two most significant achievements of peasants and townsmen which are Upper Austria's chief claims to fame: bounteous agriculture and glorious castles, abbeys and monasteries. "We lift our eyes to the hill summits where shine the houses built to the greater glory of God"—such is a fragment of a prayer heard in the parish churches of this province.

The "Green Province" Charlemagne called this, in his day a far vaster tract of land comprising what is now both Upper and Lower Austria and Burgenland, anciently much more densely forested than now. Where the Enns flows swiftly northward, with scarcely a murmur of moving waters, to join the Danube, Lower Austria joins Upper Austria at the immensely ancient iron town of Steyr. Here at the juncture of the Enns and the Steyr rivers the mountain ranges, so arrogant and skyward-thrusting heretofore, decline to gently rolling hills and undulant farmlands, fields of grain and orchards heavy with divers fruits, to subside restfully at Steyr. For hundreds of years Steyr has been known as the "Armorers' Town," noted as well for the finest cutlery exported to all parts of the world. For it is here that the iron of the Erzberg is fashioned into implements of war and peace in the huge welding plants rising as would the bastions of an impregnable stronghold from both banks of the two waterways.

There are a number of world-famous industries in Steyr which employ half the population of the large town. The plants are so carefully hidden in groves of trees, surrounded by gardens or, as in the case of Werndl Rifles and Steyr Motor Cars, camouflaged to resemble a towered and pinnacled feudal castle, that many persons entering the town to visit its historic monuments, museums and palaces of the ancient noble families, with which the town is richly endowed, are never conscious that industry reigns supreme.

The name of Michael Blümelhuber stands for an original form of art in metal brought to the peak of excellence in design and craftsmanship during the 18th century. He created objects delicately wrought from iron by steel-cutting, and jewelry so fragile that the faceted beads "outshine the diamond," according to Empress Elizabeth, who added a specimen of each of Blümelhuber's designs to her collections. Although this man tried to impart his skill to apprentices, their work was never of the master's high quality, illusive as gleaming cobweb strands. In the Landesmuseum at Steyr may be seen the finest specimens of Blümelhuber's work. Many pieces of jewelry have been donated privately to a permanent exhibition of "cut-steel."

The marketplace of Steyr enjoys a spacious area once used as a parade ground for troops during the reign of Empress Maria Theresia. The linen shops in Steyr, both for linen by the yard and finished sets of tablecloths or bed linen, uphold the weaving traditions of the valley, considered supreme in Austria since the days when the women wove togas for the Roman residents.

Characteristic of Steyr are the "candle snuffer" cupolas, finials to towers and church steeples, and the "Old Mother Muchabout" (Mother Goose) hooded roofs spreading over the burghers' houses. This is a high, peaked roof, the tip turned down forward, like the pointed brim of a witch's hat. Under this jut may be set a small penthouse, a balcony or an arched loggia. Color is applied to the house fronts with a lavish hand, the whitewash brush being dipped into powdered color—pink, saffron, vivid green, mauve or rust-red. Each house achieves individuality through a contrasting color applied to the fanciful trim of sea shells, pine cones or swags of meadow flowers outlining doors and windows. Black enamel on pale yellow is used with great style to enscroll the façade of the Rathaus. Small iridescent river shells bedew the startling white walls of the Swan Inn. Set on a high stone bastion, the ancient Dominican Church towers above the market place, assuming the stature of a skyscraper. The three Medieval archways, under which pass ramps leading to the castle, display perpendicular panels on which are frescoed immense figures in houppelande, tabard, nobleman's cloak or full armor, and painted in high color, striking imagination and vitality.

Many communities in Austria rise from its winding rivers, great or small, sometimes historically renowned. The riparian towns appear to take on an air of antiquity far more noticeable at first glance than those situated inland. Raftsmen poling logs or ingots of iron downstream see from afar the massed towers of Enns, a town of Celtic origin, later a Roman military depot. One of the oldest towns in Austria, its Landsturm, in the Hauptplatz, surrounded by stately old Baroque houses, is a veritable castle in the air. A sky-riding castle straight out of old German folklore where the corbels and water spouts are cast-iron sea monsters ridden by cast-iron river maidens, possibly a covey of the innumerable daughters of Lorelei of the Rhine.

The castle of Fürstenberg looms above forest trees, its masonry of Swabian granite glittering in moonlight or the sun as though sheeted in isinglass, so veined with crystal is this rare species of dusky rock.

Preserved in the museum of the castle is a curiosity, a replica of the 14th-century chain of iron hoops, each one ten feet in circumference, used to block the river traffic in order that Fürstenberg henchmen might exact toll from all navigators. On each flat iron link is inscribed the words THE ENNS IS FÜRSTENBERG AND FÜRSTENBERG THE ENNS.

More German fairy tales were laid in and around the witch-haunted town of Perg than in any other hamlet I have ever heard of. Once famous for its vast sandstone quarries, the stone running the gamut of all shades from tawny-gold to deep cream color, the town built entirely from these quarries seems eternally bathed in luminous light. Even on a day of leaden rain, scurried by a high wind, the outline of the houses and Baroque church takes on a sheen, a luminosity, as if from an inner light. Orchards spread along both banks of the river. It is the only time I can remember traversing a waterway between miles of apple trees in full fruit. Baumgartenberg thrusts its galleried tower above this orchard density.

The matrons of Baumgarten wear dark, dour-looking woolen or linen gowns girdled in bronze nailhead-studded leather, rather like those of a Medieval abbess. But the young women in search of a husband blossom like the rose. Bright pink linen aprons are trellised in bands of flower-embroidered ribbon, the red, purple, yellow and acid green of petal and foliage silhouetted in sharp detail against the black moire silk ground. High conical flower-embroidered linen turbans act as a kind of base on which to balance immense-brimmed beaver or ribbed-silk cavalier hats. To denote the arrival of spring, the hat brims are scattered with fresh crocuses and narcissi. When summer winds are sultry, poppies, daisies, wheat spears and cornflowers wreath the crowns. Autumn is heralded by vines clustered with amber or purple grapes and red apples.

The festival of the Winter King is characterized by wisps of cotton snow and a powdering of mica, the hat crowns spiky with icicles of isinglass. At this time young men dressed in white, wearing girdles, anklets and wristlets of silver bells, carry on their heads transparent headdresses in the form of an ice ship, a crystal dragon, a river nymph or an aquatic monster. A light is placed inside the transparency so that a group of fifty or more youths winding down a village lane take on the guise of a company of softly glowing legendary creatures riding the frosty night air.

I drove across country now. The roadway wound through miles of orchards—apples, plums and a wide variety of pears. The large, juicy, white-flesh pear called Weisser Glocke (white bells) is a memorable companion to the pungent Edammer cheese. I noticed that the upper-story walls of most farmhouses were trellised in grapes, the lower walls bearing the sprawling design of espaliered apricot trees. This golden-pink fruit is prepared in countless ways here, from the break-fast jam served with the rolls and coffee of "coffee complete" to a light summer drink, "apricot beer," served with spring water. Apricot brandy of compelling fragrance but tremendous potency is drunk with afterdinner coffee.

Gmunden, so prideful for being termed "Gateway to the Salz-kammergut," is, in fact, the "southern gateway," famed as a holiday resort of stature, "one of the seven holidays of creation."

Above the "promenade" town of Gmunden one mounts a series of rising levels, the streets going back into the undulant hills, the least mountainous section of this predominately mountain terrain. This quarter is the Maria Theresia town. The Empress caused the tall Baroque mansions to be built to house families of the members of her retinue when she came to Gmunden to inspect her ceramic works. On all her journeyings a considerable company of retainers and "entertainers" accompanied this energetic, usually good-tempered, "most accomplished royal dinner conversationalist in Europe," as the Spanish ambassador Ildefonso said of her.

The crescent-shaped terrace of the Hotel Schwan overhangs the lake. A specialty of the house, vanilla ice cream molded in the shape of a swan, the open beak fashioned of candied orange peel holding a brandied cherry, is served with great flourish by ash-blond maidens in flower-patterned dirndls.

Gmunden is famed for its open air cafés set on arcaded terraces, all facing the lake. Here one may enjoy at leisure a tremendously stimulating panorama of rippled blue lake dotted with flocks of shim-mering white swans in the hundreds, the whole scene backed by the Traunstein rising to 5,500 feet. Resembling a larger specie of swan, sailboats of every class dart about the lake racing one another or perhaps engaged in a classic Trophy Regatta. White pleasure boats ply the lake from Ebensee at the foot to Gmunden at the head, making numerous stops at fishing villages and bathing resorts along the way. The larger steamers serve meals on board while a brass band plays Strauss waltzes and the sentimental, languishing ballads of the lake fishermen.

A long, tree-shaded avenue called Schwan Promenade describes the serpentine shore of the lake, starting from Schwanenplatz to halt abruptly across from island-borne Schloss Ort. Here one crosses a Medieval timber bridge, erected stoutly, buttressed by interlacing logs intended to support large companies of mounted knights yet fashioned with a certain airiness to enable swift destruction by fire in case of attack. It is said that by actual proof, demonstrated by a "spectacle" in the time of Maria Theresia, the bridge can be burnt to the water's edge in half an hour.

Schloss Ort rises on a small wooded escarpment a few hundred yards from the shore. Dominated by a tall tower surmounted by a black-bronze onion cupola, the castle gleams white as bleached bone, its wooden shutters under red and black tile roofs emblazoned with black Habsburg eagles on a ground of red and yellow.

The walls of the courtyard are frescoed in a most entertaining manner. Scenes from the Bible portraying horrific purging of souls vie in interest with those of the hunt. Long banners painted as if whipped by a high wind describe in *Hoch Deutsch* script the pleasures of the hunt in contrast to the perils of Inferno for the ungodly. Painted in the 16th century, the whole decoration resounds with action and drama in brilliant color undimmed by time or the fractious Traunsee elements.

Gmunden has an eventful history. To the Romans the site meant riches from salt, and the Medieval salt tax made Gmunden one of the richest cities in Austria. It was the Romans who made the Traun River a navigable waterway over which to ship salt to their vast army bases "in the southland" (Styria) and into Italy. This Traun area was a Benedictine stronghold. According to the chronicler Josef Fadinger, the monks "made Christianity popular with the pagan Byjuvares" (a raucous yet resourceful tribe).

Fishing is a major industry on Traunsee. Since pagan days, altars to the God of the Lake, a sort of local lesser Neptune, have endured, partially hidden among the alder, hazel and evergreen foliage that fringes the lake shore, or set back in rocky caves. Even in the present time trout fishermen slit the throat of the prime specimen of the catch and lay it on a hidden altar to propitiate the lake god, a mysterious deity mentioned in hushed voice, who seems to bear no name.

Not far from Gmunden there is the old monastery settlement of Traunkirchen, perched on a steep hill overlooking the lake. A haunt of solitude, worlds away from the present. The Romans called this "The Secret Lake" and set up an Oracle in a cave that one may see today. A great stone seat was hollowed out of living rock under the buttress of the church, the Oracle's Throne of Prophecy. A monastery lies within a secreted garden, a wilderness of ferns and flowers adjacent to the Romanesque church. I sailed to Traunkirchen early one morning when the sun was just climbing above the mountain peaks. The dew had been so heavy, the spiders so busy the night long, that the brilliance of dew-drenched cobwebs covering hedges and low massed trees seemed to shatter the sun's first rays into a trillion shards of light. Early as it was, a small boy out at dawn with hook and line offered me the choice of three lake trout he had caught. I asked him if he knew how to cook the fish if we built a small fire. A shade surprised that I should ask so stupid a question of an obviously exceptional young fisherman, he rather diffidently answered that he did. Swiftly the boy gathered twigs and branches from among rock crevices and the rank grass of the hillside. Deftly he built a small crackling fire. I provided butter and salt and pepper from my knapsack.

Now I have prepared food over a campfire in half the countries of the world. But if I ever tasted anything better than that spanking fresh, crisply browned lake trout served with sliced tomatoes and "black" barley bread on a knoll high above sun-spangled Traunsee at seven o'clock of an August morning, I cannot remember it.

The church at Traunstein is known to be dedicated to fishermen. The Fishermen's Pulpit, entirely of cedar wood, is a show in itself, worth coming many miles to see. Elevated fifteen feet above the red stone and blue slate floor, it is composed of an immense carved and gilded shell shaped like the deeply fluted prow of a ship, afloat on boldly carved waves. Thrown as if nonchalantly over this shell is a delicately carved fish net caught with Neptune's trident. Garlands of seaweed, a heterogeneous collection of shells, strings of pearls and curious finny creatures nestle in the meshes of the fish net. The great folds of the looped net drag for at least a yard on the ground.

Having been abroad with the rising sun, I had spent a long day of wandering. A day of constant surprises which one comes upon in corners of these ancient lakeside and mountain villages. Medieval fish markets; Romanesque churches, the rounded doors so low one has to stoop nearly double to enter; a shipbuilding yard where for seven hundred years descendants, both men and women, of the family Vögelberg have built the long, narrow, rakish boats of tawny waxed pinewood resembling overblown Venetian gondolas, which are the characteristic local "aquatic equipage."

I sat on the terrace of Gmunden's Kurhotel. The sun was setting behind the rocky silhouette of the "Schlafende Griechin." The contour of the mountain forms the quiet profile of the "sleeping" Greek goddess whom the Romans called Demeter because of the extreme fertility of the region. Legend has it that the Roman general, Vespius Callus, Governor of the Province, a victim of insomnia, caused the white opium poppy to be grown, "an opiate flower of silver hue" (from a Homeric hymn). Vespius built a small temple halfway up the mountainside. A vine-grown ruin now, the columns of the portico were anciently painted blood red. Vespius and devotees of the goddess Demeter wore red and black robes at worship, when he poured libations of a "wine" distilled from opium on the porphyry altar. Discount this legend as one will, it is said in all seriousness that no one living on Traunsee ever suffers from sleeplessness.

One of my favorite hotels in Austria is Kurhotel, set high above the harbor on a ledge of rock in the midst of a trellised rose garden. Frau Döppler, with her gracious manner and instant charm, presides over her Kurhotel. She is a person of great enthusiasms, a versatile gardener, and, as I have learned from the special dishes prepared at my request, her knowledge of *haute cuisine* in a number of countries is impressive. Cheese soufflé at Kurhotel, richly flavored, all but floats in the air with lightness. A "schnitzel nature"—tender veal cutlet sautéed in garlic butter or butter flavored with parsley and a pinch of ginger, according to one's desire—is a dish to savor like vintage wine. The fame of Frau Döppler's fresh garden salads of bewildering variety in greens and vegetables, served with a tart French dressing or sour cream and wine vinegar, spiked with crumbled Roquefort cheese, has spread even as far away as food-conscious Salzburg and elegant, slightly finicky Bad Gastein. A leisurely dinner on the terrace at Kurhotel under the stars, with the moon rising over the lake about the time an apricot soufflé appears, and reaching its high-riding zenith over Espresso coffee and liqueur brandy, is my idea of the grace of living.

In the spring Traunsee comes alive for the Corpus Christi Day procession as at no other time during the year. The massive height of the surrounding legend-haunted mountains stirs popular imagination to the point of a sort of controlled frenzy of religious zeal. The core of ancient customs lying dormant during the rest of the year leaps to life. Always at this festival time the general restlessness increases. A rumbling in the bowels of Traunstein, an aloof massif lost in mysterious dreams, is regarded as the stirring in his sleep of a Celtic giant—possibly the nameless God of the Lake. Will he waken to cause landslides? Or will he "roll over and sleep for another year"?

There is a water carnival, a Swan Fete, held in July. At sundown a magnificently impressive flotilla of floats assembles in parade form on the lake. Swan floats vary from rowboat size to a spectacular eighty-foot float I saw bearing a wire swan composed of thousands of white hydrangeas set close together. The long, flat swan beak, from which swung a gilded iron lantern, was composed of orange marigolds. Crimson candles in gold sconces were set about the gunwales and along the bowsprit to light the way across dark water. A keg of beer and a keg of wine were placed in the center of the boat under the guardian wings of the swan, so that no one would become thirsty during the water carnival.

Some of the mountaineers come down to Gmunden only twice in a year's time. Their world is the solitude of the stormy heights. Often clouds wreathing the mountain peaks obscure the entire lake from three to four weeks at a time. The women embroider their garments with wild beasts, forest flowers, the starry firmament and the moon, newly crescent and at full beauty.

Fields of brown coal spread across the region of Wolfsegg, a market town which would be dreary but for the teeming life and color in the Altmarkt, where baskets piled high with fruits, vegetables and lake fish create a gigantic masterpiece of still-life painting. The blaze of color gains a startling clarity in contrast to the background of stern-faced, dun-gray houses, walls and roofs shingled in slate.

As in Attic Greece, so in Austria is Candlemas (early spring) the season for the sowing of the crops, celebrated by any number of festivals conducted in precisely the same manner as in earliest Medieval times. In Upper Austria none is more enjoyed than *Aperschnalzen*. A great cracking of whips takes place at the entrance to sowing fields. The long, oxhide whip-lashes sweep clear the late snow from a symbolic patch where a furrow is dug and seeds are sown. It is a Festival of Fertility in every sense of the word. A baby born at Christmas time is often alluded to as "an *Aperschnalzener*." The girls of the countryside don bright spring-green dirndls and white-lace halo headdresses. Cockades of green ribbon are worn by the stalwart hip-booted farm youths. Even the horses drawing the farm wagons wear elegant bows and streamers of sap-green ribbons on tightly braided manes and tails. Wagonloads of food and kegs of beer are drawn through the farm lanes and the villages so that a wayside banquet may be had by all comers.

Almauftrieb (the driving of cattle up to mountain pastures) is a gala event in the countryside, particularly pleasant because the gaiety is heightened by the revelers' knowledge that in the autumn another phase of the festival will take place, when the flocks, fat from a long summer of cropping mountain grasses, will be driven down to the valley farms. For the up-mountain trek the cattle are decorated with horseshoe-shaped collars artfully woven of bright ribbons and flowers. Crescent headdresses of vines and flowers lend a flirtatious look to the heifers. Frisky little calves sport crowns of flowers set askew between their embryo horns. The leading bull invariably steals the show. The rippling muscles of his neck and his massive withers are covered by a net woven from ropes of wheat. A huge pear-shaped bronze bell hangs pendant from a wide leather collar studded with brass nailheads. Perhaps the design will trace the signs of the Zodiac, a favorite device of the constantly weather-watching farmers, who are well versed in the language of the stars in their courses, the moon, the tides, the winds, all "spasms of the wayward elements" according to Charlemagne, who never started a campaign save at the turning of the tides.

Hallstatt is set on piles in one of the Gosau lakes, the Hallstattersee. An intricate system of intersecting timber ramps, buttresses and ascending terraces like hanging gardens creates an effect of mystery, the eerie beauty of mirage, a village lost in the middle-mist of fable. The mountain flanks rise sheer from the lake, leaving no room for a road. Prehistoric remains found on this site have given the name of the *Hallstatt Culture* to the Iron Age. Thousands of years before the birth of Christ the salt deposits in Hallstatt brought tribes across the mountains to this improbably remote spot from points as far away as the Carpathian Mountains in Romania. From that early time, until the close of the 19th century, the mines have been a bone of contention for "every helmeted dog in Europe to snap at," as the 13th-century Count Rudolf of Habsburg is supposed to have shouted at the Archbishop of Bern. The bishop expressed himself succinctly on the subject of Rudolf: "God on high had better look to His throne or Rudolf will be after it next."

Bronze was cast for warrior implements and a sort of crude scale armor. Fragments of this have been dredged from the lake as well as beautifully shaped vessels of red and purple clay which appear to have been deftly formed without the help of a potter's wheel. The long, slender, six-oared boats presently used for fishing and, to some extent, sightseeing tours of the water-level caves, are said to be constructed identically to those presented by the Celtic tribes as peace offerings to the hardy Byjuvares at the time of their union. The houses crowding one against another seem to take color from the bronze-green lake water. A timeless air broods over one of the most secluded villages in Europe. Sun and shadow are unevenly divided in this mysterious place. Even at the height of summer the sun is tardy at morning, and twilight descends by five o'clock.

A Celtic burial place was discovered built on piles in the center of the lake. The yield of hundreds of Celtic and Byjuvare skeletons, some still sheathed in armor, bearing weapons of bronze, added substantially to data of early life on the lake.

Perhaps because the town is largely built on stilts, the most conspicuous costumes worn by dancers in the Corpus Christi Procession feature stilts. The dances are performed on flat rafts towed behind ingeniously decorated floats. A dragon, ferociously breathing fire, crouches in the arch of a cave. A symbolic creature of Alpine villages pertaining to ancient forest worship, the dragon attracts a flotilla of small boats bearing youths who pelt the dragon with balls of wood, hoping to secure a "bull's-eye"—a shot down his fiery gullet—which will guarantee them a prize.

I walked up the tortuous terraced streets, more a flight of uneven steps than a thoroughfare for other than goats or donkeys, to the slopes of the Salzberg, the mountain at whose foot the Hallstatt crouches. I passed villagers and inhabitants of the curiously humpbacked cottages that are half hidden in bracken and firs. These people are tall, spare of frame, with the rough-hewn features seen on statues of Gothic saints and martyrs surrounding the portals of churches in the Innviertel.

Nature has been extraordinarily prodigal in this remote corner of the Salzkammergut of Upper Austria. As if the Gosau lakes, so deep and rippleless, shadowed green and turquoise from firs and limitless sky, were not beauty enough, she rears the Dachstein Glacier as a background of unimaginable splendor.

Near St. Pantaleon, set in forest clearings and hidden from any long view, are old manor houses of the lesser nobility. Many houses are Medieval in origin, enriched in later times by adding wings in the ebullience of Baroque volutes and fluted columns. Others, like Alverwald, show a spacious primrose-yellow plaster, many-windowed Rococo façade enlivened with trophies of the hunt. The spiky stag antlers placed on painted plaques above and between each window lend to the walls the look of a gigantic pincushion bristling with copper and gold Edwardian hatpins. Above the portal of Alverwald was a painted wooden banner, the yellow and blue paint faded and crackling in the hot sunlight. On it I traced the words AUSTRIA FELIX (Happy Austria).

Narrow rivers wind through the countryside, some to trace a serpentine course so irregular that old houses appear to stand on an island within a moat. Contemplating these drowsy habitations of a shy, reticent gentry from a distance, I recalled that the names of some of the families had resounded in the annals of Austrian history, Mühlhausen, Vogelweide, Reinmar, long before the numerous branches of Habsburg starred the Austrian scene. I thought of a line by Sir Thomas Browne I had but lately read: "Generations pass while some trees stand, and old families last not three oaks."

I went my way through forest roads. These solitary mountain fastnesses are painted in sweeping brush strokes in every conceivable shade of green. The only sound is a sudden whirring of the wings of birds invisible in the upper shadows. At regular intervals I caught the sharp metallic ring of the woodman's axe—"the pure music of the forest aisles," as Goethe called it. A short way farther on I came to another clearing, heralded by wisps of blue smoke from charcoal burners' turfbedded fires. Piles of bundled charcoal, onyx-black, as softly gleaming as deep-pile velvet, were arranged in castellated formation like the bailey of a Medieval keep. But the clearing was deserted.

The lime trees of Schärding are world famous. Not alone for their great age—two hundred years is a comparatively young sprout—or the extraordinary girth of the silver trunks dagged with black points like the ermine tails on an imperial mantle, but for the immense spread of the branches foliaged by a larger than usual leaf, a brilliant emerald veined in gold. These branches cast such welcome shade that every country inn fortunate to have been built near a grove of limes touts its "Linden terrace" as much as its beer and wines, its cider and light perry brewed from the hard tawny-bronze red-cheeked, perry pear. I stopped at Gasthaus Goldener Kreuz (House of the Golden Cross), set in a curve of the town's famous Medieval walls. Here I drank perry served in a huge yellow pottery jar which had been submerged the length of the day in an icy spring fed by a waterfall that I could hear crashing into a rocky gorge off to my left.

In old riverside shipping towns like Obernberg, Mühlheim and Aurolzmünster—the latter distinguished by houses of the rich Medieval burghers, painted in horizontal stripes in every color of the rainbow—everywhere one senses the characteristic *joie de vivre* of the Innviertel, expressed in his passion for vivid festival costume and brightly painted dwelling house, both inside and out. This region of Upper Austria has been called the "Dancing Valley." To that I might add the "Singing Valley," the music of violin, zither, cornet and accordion accompanied by lusty voices, raised in traditional ballads or religious praise, rising ever on the air.

I saw a celebrated castle looming above the fir forest, the mighty keep appearing to rise as a carven pinnacle hewn from living rock. Everything about Kürnwald, this haunt of eagles, seemed unreal. Somnolent blue herons stood motionless on a strip of sand, as if painted on a Chinese screen, until of a sudden a big red-legged fellow let out the strident heron shriek, flapped black-tipped wings and the whole flock of birds rose, painting blue flashes against the rusty red stones of the keep to be swallowed up in the misty-green distances of the Alps.

The castle story concerns the self-imposed "entombment" in the 15th century of a chatelaine, Margravine Swanfreda, a member of the Babenberg family of notoriously wild, passionate disposition. Widowed by a strange turn of fate—a duel to the death with two-handed swords between her husband and her lover—the Margravine was soon bereft of lover too when he was decapitated in her bed by the brother of her murdered lord. She caused the severed head of her paramour to be embalmed with a secret unguent from Egypt. For thirty years the head of the murdered man was kept within a glass case, standing on a table in the Great Hall of the castle. The Margravine lived her days clad in sackcloth, her head swathed in the enveloping coif of a repentant sinner. She lived immolated in semidarkness, her only companion the grisly head of her dead lover.

Near the Bavarian frontier lies the old market town of Engelhartszell. The Marktkirche (market church) dominates the breeze-swept market square. Color is rampant, seen in traditional costumes, in baskets piled with fruits of the earth, and in massed flowers. The flower sellers thrust great bunches of cottage garden flowers into the mesh of willow withes or twists of straw fashioned into pyramids. Danube dwellers are flower conscious. I learned that a large portion of the cultivated flowers—the roses, lilies, petunias, carnations and scented stock that one finds in such profusion in the florist shops in Vienna—are "rafted" down the Danube at night from river villages. The immense rafts called *donauflösser* are a fine sight at any time, doubly so when the raftmen race their floating platforms around such turns in the river as the Schlögener Schlinge, "great bend," a complete hairpin loop where stands the Premonstratensian monastery of Schlögl. This monastic retreat seems the most silent place on earth. Only the gentle whir of flax spinners stirs the air, sounding more like the drone of countless bees that hover over the sweet William flowers planted in variegated masses along the river gardens.

This is blue flax country. Flax is grown, spun and bleached. The paper-white linen is cut, hemmed and sent off to beautify houses all over the world. Now suddenly it becomes windy hop country. Hop vines wave from long poles, the clack-clack-clackity-clack of the green, stiff-petaled hop blossoms sounding like castanets as they toss in the Mühlviertel wind.

The dark, mysterious fastnesses of the Böhmerwald, The Giant's Wood, of old legends, even in bright sunshine seems a dread place of constant shadow, the forest floor beset with "sliding sand" pockets to trap and destroy the unwary walker. Castle Vichtenstein was once the most famous and most feared of river toll castles. Burg Neuhaus is the pure fairy-tale castle rising on the edge of the Giant's Wood above a treacherous rapids in the river, to sustain the atmosphere of silent forces of nature working darkly, ever ready to spring. At least twenty places along the reaches of the Danube were pointed out to me as the haunt of a legendary Danube Lorelei known as Lady Isa. Wherever she did have her "pitch," it is told in song and poetry that her alluring voice was potent, her victims legion. Legend refers to river sirens who lay in rocky caverns on the shores and even on a tiny island said to have anciently sheltered a Roman cave-dwelling tribe. Pagan rites persist along the Upper Danube reaches more than below Linz.

Every jut of rock accommodates a castle of ancient lineage. Rannariedl-on-the-Ranna was an early Medieval sanctuary, and during the Turkish wars was a refuge for persons of every condition of society.

This point of the Danube is a famous swimming center for those who like "sporty" river swimming, where one is constantly breasting devious rapids. The inns of the region serve a light fragrant local wine called Lustigwasser or merry water. This wine is also beaten up with white of egg and sugar into a kind of meringue to serve tired swimmers.

Of all Danube castles, the history of Burg Haichenbach is most marvelously varied and bloody. Its ghosts are accredited with screaming in the night and hurling rocks to frighten river boatmen. One woman ghost of unhappy memory I saw on a night of brewing storm, treading warily the ruined battlements. She was more than ordinarily luminous, for as she stumbled along the broken stones she gleamed green-gold from head to foot as if sheeted in phosphorus. Behind her there seemed to float on the night wind a phosphorescent ship rowed by a score of shimmering oarsmen. More a Danish longboat than one of Danube kind.

The story is told that a Medieval countess, to escape the savage cruelty of her lord, tried to flee downriver in a craft of some curious design. The husband caught the boat at the river edge, loaded it with rocks and sank it in midstream with all on board.

Once we had swung in a great winding curve around the Schlögen loop, a mystic silence, an unutterable peace, pervaded the atmosphere. The banks seemed almost deserted, as centuries ago when Roman drum-shaped forts were protecting the frontier. Suddenly a blast of brass-band music rent the silence. A water picnic boat was just setting out from Obermühl. Cheerfully occupied holiday crowds waved from canoes and swimming baths as we sped past in midstream. Herons encircled the massive towers (partly Roman masonry) of Ottensheim

Castle situated directly opposite the extensive buildings of the Monastery of Wilhering. Now as I approached Linz the valley narrowed, densely wooded slopes rose on either hand to become again perfectly solitary. At Linz, the busiest city in Western Austria, I would spend a few days before continuing the Danube trip to Vienna.

Chapter 10

LOWER AUSTRIA, ANCIENT LAND OF THE DANUBE ROBBER BARONS, CRADLE OF VIENNA

NIEDERÖSTERREICH, the regional name for this province intersected by the Danube, is sometimes described by habitual travelers to Austria as the "great holiday center at the gates of Vienna." A wide choice of holiday resorts provides opportunities for a variety of entertainments. The province may be said to consist of four quarters, each of distinctly personal character; dovetailed together, the whole forms the cradle of Vienna. The Alpinist may still ascend heavenward, for the magnificent crags and pinnacles of serried rock—the Alps that cross Vorarlberg, Tyrol, Salzburg and Carinthia—extend also across Upper and Lower Austria to finally fritter away, describing a series of gently undulating fern-crowned knolls and boskies in the latticed beech groves of the Wienerwald. South of Vienna Woods the river swirls in a mighty horseshoe bend. Here stretch the foothills of the Alps where crouch baronial villages, seeming remote, unapproachable as an eagle's eyrie. Some of the houses hewn from the living rock appear to be surveying the changing world diffidently—*in it* but not *of it*—from behind gateways carved with heraldic bearings of families who, down the centuries, have stormed their way across Danubian history.

The convivial traveler may regale himself in gay company on an epic wine-drinking spree at surprisingly small cost, considering the quality of the wines imbibed, by traversing the vine-clad hills bordering the river and making the acquaintance of a vineyard proprietor or a man who owns a *weinstube* with a sun-latticed garden under a grape arbor called *"weintraube garten."* *Stehweinhallen* (standing wine bars) out of doors serve all the great wines of this region. While the palate savors coolness and body of a light, sparkling Brunner-strassler, a less dry, amber-green Muskateller, the noble "proportions" (as you will be advised) of Gumpoldskirchner or the pale topaz-pink Wachauer, one's eyes are refreshed by the panorama: far reaches of vine-terraced slopes accent arrogantly Baroque monasteries on the heights, moss-rimed cloisters in the valley, ruined toll-castles, and crumbling buttressed towers rising from black firs or the burnished red beeches called Donau *"roteflagge."* These are symbolic of the hated red banner that was once flown from these same battlements as a signal to river barges: "Halt! We collect toll." Branches of this tree are carried by small boys, forever playing at robber barons, each boy bearing a painted shield emblazoned with the name of some desperado famous for plundering these riparian villages.

Stone symbols of power and wealth of the old nobility rise everywhere. They spread over the province, museums of art and temples to the grace of living. The river reaches and the surrounding estates are the setting for romantic castles or historic fortresses embedded in greenery, clinging to bronze stone towers that spear the skyline like exclamation points from Marchegg all along the winding riverway to Krems and Marbach on the border of Upper Austria.

Magnificent abbeys lending their names to identify some rare vintage wine, spacious manor houses, and pitch-roof farmhouses hung with clematis and climbing sweet pepper vines mirror their reflections in the waters of the swift, deep Danube. And in most cases all these places are open to view. Stop in such villages as Herzogenberg, surrounded by flower-pied meadows which in turn are girdled by the mysterious, witch-haunted forest of Dinkelsteinerwald, or Ybbs, a plateau raised above an ominous whirlpool and raging rapids. Then make excursions. Visit these surrounding villages by the various means offered. Rail, auto-bus, bicycle, motorcar, or on foot. However one chooses to get about, here is a chance to whet one's appetite for Vienna by getting the feel of Danube countryside. If possible, circle all around Vienna. Range the entire province which cradles this wondrous city.

Lace-making communities, like Tulln on the Danube, offer such curiosities as long, wavering, tortuously cobbled streets bordered by what appears at first to be high white walls roofed with dark-red tile sprouting a furze of wind-seeded meadow grasses. This is no wall but a relic of the Middle Ages. These are secretive dwelling houses. Gateways twenty feet high are of solid wood painted in massive scale, impaling five golden eagles on a sky-blue ground. Each gate is an armorial shield, emblematic of the province. Within these shuttered courtyards women work with their cushions and bobbins creating cobweb-fine lace. In thought and habits they are as far removed from the present time as are the women in harems of Bou Bajouda in Moroccan Marrakesh. No lace maker who guards her reputation *ever* removes her hair-concealing headdress, a Medieval wimple of linen and exquisite lace, when walking in the streets. Such immodesty would court the Devil's advances and in all probability a stiff beating by her husband.

Vienna is placed nearly in the center of the province, like the mask of Helios on his chariot of the Sun in the center of a sunburst. The myriad rays of this sun spread out from St. Stephen's Cathedral in Stephensplatz to become roadways that vein the province entire. It is proverbial that all roads lead to Rome. I find it interesting that so many of the wide highways over Austrian terrain, especially in Lower Austria, were built by Roman engineers two thousand years ago. For example, Linzer Bundesstrasse follows the erratic way of a Roman road, in places so close to the Danube that fishermen and washerwomen put road and river to daily use. Roman legions blazed the roads over the Strengberge to Amstetten, a town metallic-gray and grim, set like a Medieval knight accoutered in full armor, amid orchards of black trunked pear trees, the river meadows carpeted knee-deep with tangy wild mustard, a brigand weed strangling the red-bud stalks of barley.

I sat in Gasthof Kirsch at Struden, little dreaming I would be trapped by angry flood waters for five mortal days. The inn was once a riverside guardhouse built in 1400 to protect the entrance gate of a castle on the hill now in ruins. Walls of the room were of rough-dressed stone seven feet thick, built converging from the inner wall at a rake in the Medieval way. The windows were nearly as narrow as a crossbow aperture in the outer wall.

At Struden the Danube at all times churns up treacherous eddies and foaming rapids. Rain or no rain I saw a few hardy souls doggedly shooting the rapids in short canoes, the gunwales covered in rubber tarpaulin. This is a popular sport for campers along restless stretches of Danube water.

And still it rained. I improved my enforced inactivity by finishing drawings from quick sketches I had dashed off along the roads. Too, I ate prodigious meals, happily the larder at the inn being well stocked with food in plenty and of first quality.

As the days drew on, rain—rain—rain, I had time to browse about this intriguing old tavern. The furniture, impressive in scale, was all of carved spruce wood to harmonize with the buff washed walls rising unadorned, except for a crucifix or the ubiquitous stag antlers, to high, vaulted ceilings. In the attics a bewildering web of hand-adzed oak beams defied every law of construction, bold as some gigantic scaffolding in an abbey nave, intensely arresting in the evidence of power and ingenuity exercised by Medieval artisans who, however fanciful at the time of fashioning, built for the ages.

There were two objects at the inn I craved to own. The bungs and spiggots from the wine casks, old and rare, were not for sale. These were carved from chestnut wood in the form of river demons bearing a resemblance to Bacchus, the wavy locks bound in grape vines. I was able, however, to buy the tall, fat, yellow, black and white pottery "puzzle jug" which had been used to fool me like a gully. Liquids can be drunk from this jug without spilling only through the nozzle at the top of the handle, just where the drinker, if he does not know better, would ordinarily place his thumb.

When it cleared, I set out early for distant Raabs near the border of Burgenland. Vast forests, dark in tone as moss-agate, surround Zwett. Forests primeval seem to all but swallow the ancient stone-built town and venerable monastery. I noted that its walls, glowing under so many coats of color washes lightly applied down the years, prey to mold and mildew, have taken on the patchwork color of a carved Coromandel screen. In the Chapel of Our Lady of the Fields reposes an enchanting Madonna, patroness of all meadow creatures. Her veil is thickly encrusted with gold grasshoppers, each one bearing upon its back a bleeding heart of garnets.

The road wound like a switchback trail past dorfs set precariously on crags of rock or wooded knolls. These hillocks are a formation of turf-covered rock, perpetually decked throughout the changing seasons, as if for festival, in berry canes, fruit-laden brambles or swathes of wild flowers. Many of these communities consist of only a few beetlebrow-roof houses crowded together under the tall, thin spire of a white church or the vine-hung bastions of a derelict castle, old, silent, retreating into its Roman history.

Lower Austria has been called the province that "could not make up its mind" whether to ape the vaulting mountains enclosing lakes and river-watered valleys of adjacent Upper Austria, the more gently undulating reaches of Burgenland to the east, richly endowed with fruit and grain fertility, or the vineyard terraces of the Rhine and Danube valleys. So, unequivocally generous in nature, the province settled to embrace all three, to become a kind of preserve for scenic beauty glazed over with fruits of the earth in conspicuous abundance.

Where else in the world will one find such tortured magnificence in striated columns of rock- and fir-shadowed ravines, sliced from the mountains as by the sword of a Colossus to reveal black and prune-purple clay rock, as in the terrain around the Schneeberg and Semmering Pass? In the stark sunlight this is a region of resounding contrasts. Pale green foliage of hazel trees twisted into airy garlands mingle with the darker richness of emeralds and cobalt-dusted evergreens. Flame-pink and yellow daisies rill the edge of crevasses, the shadowed depths eloquent with the sound of torrents, of mysteriously wandering subterranean rivers which the eyes of man have never seen. Along the pass rise twisted columns of rust-red and silver rock, close-set as colonnades roofed only by a luminous sky, reminding me of some long-deserted pagan temple. Stark drama by day, surely it is on a shiny night of stars when the Milky Way emblazons the heavens that I feel Semmering Pass comes into its own. It is then that the crags and grottoes, pinnacles and ravines are illumined by a muted radiance more mysterious than the strong white rays of a full moon, revealing a world of faery as I visualize the mystic realms Lyonesse or Hy Brazil, the Never-Never-Lands of olden tales. There is unexpected loveliness here in the countless terraces of grapevines which appear to enfold the deeply gashed rock formations and to spread out beyond one's vision, a low, thick-set forest of endless silvered green, fragrant as a garden from the odors of grape released by the heavy fall of dew.

There are any number of small villages surrounding the eminently fashionable summer and winter resort of Semmering. Gloggnitz, for example, virile in character as the surrounding landscape. Pay a visit to one of the farmhouses as I did, and was immediately asked to stop for lunch. Spacious stone buildings under solid roofs of timber planks, weighted down by flat stones, are usually surrounded by a ring of hazelnut or linden trees, necessary as a windbreak against valley gales.

Gasthäuser and pensions abound, the rooms huge and airy, the beds as comfortable as goose-feather mattresses and monumental red sateen-covered eiderdowns can make them. The food is fresh, bountiful, healthy farm fare.

The luxurious hotels in Semmering, Südbahnhof and Grandhotel Panhans, were once, and to a great extent still are, world famous. In former days Semmering in winter was the playground for members of the Austrian Court circles. Hungarian nobles frequented the gambling casino to bet profligate sums of money. In summer the opulent Russian grand dukes took over, their amours and alcoholic shenanigans supplying heady scandal in the international drawing rooms and world-wide press. The hotels, cafés and restaurants are largely run by famous Viennese concerns.

The region known as Waldviertel closes in on the Danube. It is characterized by Eggenberg, a rich, Medieval city of stern architecture. Vast forests of "black pine" give the countryside a dark, rugged hue relieved by fields of gold and red swathes of oats and rye. I passed fields of flax where the sky-blue blossoms embraced red and white poppies among the green wheat, forming an undulating banner in tricolor.

Gföhl, of Celtic origin, a black and white timber and plaster town, cradles her mysteries and they are legion. For example, according to an old chronicle, "health of mind and body prevails." Through the centuries when plague in all its hideous guises intermittently "scythed the dead by the thousands across the land," the scourge never touched this walled village, although Krems and Senftenberg, the neighboring weaving and tapestry-stitching communities, were decimated almost to extinction. No reason has ever been found for this curious immunity of Gföhl other than the crystal purity of the water and the spotlessness for which the town is renowned.

Above the Bohemian frontier and in the broad Thaya Valley stand fortresses and castles in great numbers. Karlstein is Medieval with Baroque overtones. Gaunt Heidenreichstein is a gloomy if starkly impressive pile, with huge bastions and immensely circular keep tower. To my mind this is the most notable moated castle in Lower Austria. In the inner courtyard rises on lofty arcades a three-story dwelling house to which one might find a counterpart in the Renaissance town palace of a noble family in Vienna. In 1200 Count Otto von Heidenreichstein built the Waldviertel Tower to scan the beautiful Waldviertel Valley. The family is still in possession and graciously admit visitors to the castle. There are good hotels and restaurants to be found in the tree-shaded village of Heidenreichstein at the foot of the castle rock.

Rastenburg was built in the 12th century on a rugged, precipitous crag of sepia-purple clayey rock sprouting twisted trunks of black spruce, affording an eminence commanding the valley of the River Kamp for many leagues. Vastly romantic is the history of this castle. In 1460 it was occupied by Crohemma the Brazen, a Bohemian warrior-woman who is said to have hung the bloody skulls of her destroyed enemies from the stone cornice of her bedchamber, the better to gloat. Grimly evocative spear-point iron hooks in the walls are still in evidence. Crohemma also maintained a "stable" of brawny young peasant lads (kept prisoner when not needed) to lend variety to her libido.

It is said as well that between the ages of "sixteen and sixty" she bore thirty-two illegitimate children.

The valley sweeps suddenly to widen our perceptibly into an orchard-strewn plain stretching to pale green hills panoplied in the glory of sun-drenched vineyards. Beyond the hills I perceived the immense, silent beech and oak forests of Ernstbrunn where the red deer roam in their thousands. On winter nights when vines on the lower slopes are in danger of being frost-nipped, vintners light fires in braziers to be carried aloft and so temper the air with hot smoke. Then this vineyard land takes on an unearthly beauty lit, it would appear from afar, by elf-lights.

The population in this region has preserved to a startling degree its ancient traditions in dress, manner of life and, most of all, in archaic speech, a blend of Celt, Roman and Medieval patois as lively and deeply resonant as the roll of ocean waves.

Marriage festivities are of commanding splendor in banquet, dancing contests and richly embroidered dress for man, woman and beast. Horses, oxen and sometimes goats hitched to the *lustigwagon* or "laughing cart" which hauls the bridal party to and from the church, are bedecked with gilded cloth sewn with whatever fruits, flowers, acorns, sprays of wheat and barley the season dictates. It is here that Divina, the "Greek wine," is served. The vines are purported to be descendants of a vineyard planted by Phoenicians. Only one vineyard in all Austria grows the blue-black grape that makes this vintage deep purple, warm and passionately sweet. A fitting wine to seal the future for connubial bliss. I have drunk "wines of the region" in too many countries to mention here. The only parallel to this wine that I can recall is Mavrodaphne Achaia (The Tears of Daphne) from vines on the Greek mainland.

Restless flows the Danube through Lower Austria. Near Raabs-on-the-Thaya I came to a stretch of grassy river bottoms, a lost waste of bronze-green stubble and sour grass murmurous in the light river wind. This grass is unappetizing to cattle so that the region was empty of life. But I had come to see a curiosity, the greater-than-life-size Renaissance statue of St. John Nepomuk that presides over the river wastes, the heavily sculptured folds of his robe belling out as if in perpetual high wind, the ecclesiastical lace edging to his cotta as exquisitely carved as if fashioned from filigree silver. Slipped down over the figure to hug the knees was an "offering" in the shape of a "collar" of dried wheat, barley and meadow-sweets, like those which have since pagan times decorated the withers of oxen decked for harvest festival. The sensitive features of this "most beautiful of the martyr saints," as the poet Schiller described him, are set in introspective expression, hooded eyes gazing off and away toward the plains of Hungary. St. John Nepomuk is identified with beasts of burden, for unto the meanest of these creatures he is the protecting saint. I have tried to find out the reason why this magnificently alive and fluidly sculptured stone statue, golden, green, pink and gray from lichen and rust stains, should have been placed in so bleak a spot far from any church or chapel. No one vouchsafes more than a terse, "It has always been here."

The Castle of Raabs sits high above the river, bristling with spires, crenelations and pepperpot-roof towers, the outside walls washed in wide stripes of crimson, white, black and yellow, the myriad wooden shutters painted in heraldic pomp of "full odd beasties" and quarterings of noble families in grand array. The frescoes within the long, narrow rooms are vital in the extreme, the walls seeming to writhe with vividly painted grapevines, mulberry trees and excessively attenuated saints engaged in subduing by bolts of lightning that streak from fanatically gleaming, hollow eye sockets the legendary ogres of the Thaya Valley.

The road to Friedersbach, if not actually "paved with good intentions," is certainly lined with such, for on a mortally hot day I drove for five miles under the cool, arching shade of beech and linden, hazel and tulip trees.

I breasted a gentle hill to obtain my first view of Retz. An ancient Roman town now architecturally Renaissance and Baroque, it is set in a bowl of heavily foliaged trees, while tilled fields rise on all sides to stretch away in swathes of all the greens, golds, russets and amber of carefully husbanded fertility as far as the eye can see. "Rich Retz" for centuries has been the chief market-produce town for Lower

Austria. Its taverns and small inns are famous for roasted, broiled and boiled flesh of steer, calves, swine and fowls. Guinea hen cooked in sour cream and white wine is a renowned dish at Gasthaus Leber. Ham boiled in sweet wine and herbs is another specialty of Retz. The Krone Theatre, Music College and numerous warehouses for linen are built in the grand tradition of Salzburg Baroque. Because of its individuality in decoration, the house of prime interest is known as "The Life of Man." This is a "palace" of four stories, a cube-shaped structure with a high-peaked, blood-red tile roof. Embracing five tall windows across the façade, it is devoid of architectural embellishment that would in any way detract from the improbably magnificent *sgraffito* work (incised designs painted in chiaroscuro to ape the vitality of an etching). Every inch of the flat wall surface from sidewalk level to cornice under the eaves is etched in arresting vitality of technique. When first seen, the effect is that of an illuminated page torn from a gigantic book, illustrated possibly by Albrecht Dürer, set up against the sky. Across the top story a series of connecting panels tells the story of a rich man from birth to death. A kind of Rake's Progress. All the figures are life size. A wide banner painted under the panel imparts in exquisitely painted German Medieval Script the joys and sorrows of this man who at the last of tottering age is changed by the Devil into an antlered stag to be brought down by the slavering hounds of the king's huntsmen. There is a panel depicting in a chain of huge ovals alternating male and female figures experiencing titillation of the five senses.

The lower floor of the house is enriched by tall panels showing the triumphal progress through life of a woman of stupendous beauty who, from luxurious living in sumptuous raiment, becomes a hag of the byways in rags when her beauty fades. This remarkable feat in etched plaster and paint, using only the colors reseda green, sepia, plum-purple and charcoal-gray, was painted sometime around 1680 by Italian artists.

The Rathaus tower is again unique in style. A tall, square shaft, it is topped by a Baroque "pagoda" roof of bronze painted in swarms of gold butterflies. A gallery or colonnade set just under the "pagoda" encircles the summit of the tower. From this aerial pleasance I obtained a raking view of the patterned countryside, stretching away to distant cobalt-blue mountains.

At Wiener Neustadt lie entombed in great simplicity the bones of Emperor Maximilian I, who had carefully planned a burial of unparalleled splendor in the Hofkirche at Innsbruck, watched over by the existing throng of bronze statues portraying personages exalted in the Medieval history of Europe. The environs of the town extol the celebrated vintages of this valley. Along the roadside range an assortment of "caves." Steep flights of stone steps lead down to wine cellars through arcaded tunnels overgrown by berry canes and espaliered apricot trees. Glasses of red, green, blue, amber and purple Bohemian glass hang from pegs in the stone walls. The vintner in charge will approach you with a wine siphon. He will motion to you to choose a glass of whatever color you like. Into this he will direct a thin stream of sun-fragrant wine for you to sample, accenting his hospitality by shouting to the echoes *"Gesundheit! Gesundheit!"* On a table will be a "rack" hung with pretzels and circular rusks, for it is wise to eat something when tasting the various wines so that you will be able to negotiate the steep steps on your return journey into the vineyards.

The costume worn by vintners and tenders of the vine in this locality is arresting for its frankly Greek influence. Dark-purple linen breeches and paler violet linen shirts are protected by a voluminous amber-colored leather apron. A heavy silver chain is hung with keys. For cool days a sweeping circular purple wool cloak is worn in the manner of vine tenders on the mountain slopes of Corinth, and a wide-brimmed amber linen hat with usually a few grape leaves or a cluster of ripening grapes tucked into the green cord wound round the crown. The effect is that of a rakish Bacchus of the Wienerwald.

Gumpoldskirchner is the chief wine here. Unlike so many Austrian wines it travels well and has become possibly the greatest traveler of them all. Saloon keepers of the Yukon once called it "the only wine fit to drink." Casks of this vintage wine traveled round the Horn and the Gold Rush millionaires of San Francisco's Nob Hill served it at their fabulous banquets in preference to champagne.

I crossed the Ungarfeld, dominated at this point by the twin Gothic towers of Empress Maria Theresia's favorite building project, Theresian Military Academy. Beyond the wild and majestic "giants' playground, where trees grow at all angles from unimaginably tumbled rocks," lies the deceptive Rosalien Range. More mirage than reality, it loomed pale pink and violet, ever variable, tinged as a changeable taffeta will sheen and flicker in gold and green reflections. I passed, through Neuhöfen of the grim Gothic bastions, then on to Strenberg where hundreds of snow-white geese swam in wide ponds. Bred for the softness of their breast feathers, this delicate plumage is destined for the ubiquitous Austrian eiderdown, "the quilt that warms but may just as easily smother you," as an inn proprietor once told me on a sharply cold night. Many of the shop windows displayed luxurious eiderdowns seeming stuffed nigh to bursting at the seams, the satin covers as bright as the colors of a tulip bed.

The river reaches hereabouts are enriched by a dozen or more of the most famous riparian *schlösser* in the land, some of the castles stemming from Roman days when the Danube was "a Roman river and so my sword," boasted the Emperor Trajan.

Linz is a prideful city and with good reason. Its situation in a valley girdled with undulating forest-clad hills and meadow-topped bluffs rising sheer from the Danube, overlooked by the Alps, is salubrious. As a river port the site is comparable to Budapest a few hundred miles away, whose situation is very similar.

The city of Linz owes its origin to the Danube. This river was the boundary to the Roman Empire, and on the site of the present city the Roman general Silius built a fortress. He called the settlement Lentia or Lentium. So important was this town as a river port that merchants and artisans flocked here from all parts of Austria and Germany, and from as far away as the Italian Dolomites, to set up outside the gates of the fortress markets and ateliers for cutting, dressing and sculpturing stone, hoping to gain a share of the wealth that was being so swiftly amassed. That the extent of profitable trade was formidable has been amply substantiated down the centuries, for in Medieval times the boisterous and ever-expanding town, encroaching on both sides of the river, was known far and wide by an enviable sobriquet—"The Rich Town of the River Markets."

In the Later Middle Ages, around 1400, German emperors took shelter in Linz, built imposing town palaces, and in some cases remained to reside at this "imperial listening post for the length of the Danube," as it was once described by one of the Starhemberg princes, the hereditary overlords of Linz. Certainly Linz has been notoriously embroiled in political intrigue for centuries; also it has offered constant hospitality to deposed diplomats, nobles, and sovereigns alike. In spite of repeated fires and devastations, trade and industry always recovered so rapidly after each catastrophe that this talent for civic rehabilitation came to be known as the "Linz miracle." Today this oldest part of the city, the original Roman walled town, is something of a mysterious maze, its orieled and turreted houses and peaceful squares seeming altogether remote from the turmoil of the newer parts.

Now that the excellently manned Danube Pleasure Steamers again ply the river from Passau to Vienna, a trip of less than twelve hours, I believe that Linz will become one of the most sought-out cities in Europe. Linz is frequently chosen as a starting point for excursions: the Imperial Monastery of St. Florian, the Baroque "wonder of Wilhering," set in gardens comprising three miles of river frontage, tree nurseries and a score of farms; the world-renowned Lake District of Salzkammergut; the High Alpine region near the Pyhrn.

The stately and beautifully proportioned Landhaus is the most brilliant achievement of the Italian master-builders Cristoforo and Giovanni Canavale. In the courtyard the octagonal fountain is surmounted by a bronze statue of Jupiter.

The Trinity Column centering the widest market square in Austria was erected by the townspeople from public subscription in fulfillment of a vow for deliverance from an Asiatic plague which nearly obliterated the populace in 1709. Sculptured from pure-white Salzburg marble, the mélange of ascending angels bearing on a cloud the Holy Trinity was carved by collaborating sculptors, Italian Beducci and Austrian Stumpfegger.

In the Altstadt (Old Town) I traversed narrow, winding streets faced with the houses of rich merchants dating from the striated stone grimness of 1400 to the graceful High Austrian Baroque at its best. Ebullient imagination stands revealed in sculptured detail in rose, white or black marble, encircling windows and doorways or embellishing the engaging crescent-shape balconies set at the corners of houses, so characteristic of the definitely personal architecture of Linz. Color has not been spared. Exuberant color, too, so dear to the heart of the gay and humorous nature of dwellers in the Danube reaches of Wachau. A corner house is washed primrose, the marble trim in black. Heliotrope walls of one house are smartly pointed up with white marble cornucopias spilling out all the fruits of the earth, the grapes, pears and apples touched with green or bright gilt.

One Renaissance house, once the "palace" of a noble family, is now run as a *weinstube* de luxe by the monks of Kremsmünster. Pale grape-leaf-green walls are wreathed with gilt and silver grapevines. The inn sign hanging before the arched entrance is the traditional "bush" of linden twigs to identify a wine house. Standing beside the doorway is a life-size figure of a mitered abbot in gilded wood. He holds a flagon of wine aloft, posed as if pouring its contents into an ecclesiastical goblet. Within, the old vaulted rooms are engagingly, even wittily, frescoed in scenes pertaining to the culture of the grape in Roman times.

Wilheringerhaus in Altstadt 15 is the town house of the Kremsmünster Order. Here one sees the typical galleried courtyard with six flights of bronze-balustraded stairs leading to the upper reaches. From a cupola I had an encompassing view of the surrounding vineyards and orchards illuminated by the gleam of winding river reaches. These flower-hung courtyards, some of starkly simple Medieval origin, others in resounding elaboration of Baroque style, are a notable feature of Linz.

The wide Landstrasse is called "The Street of Churches." Within three blocks stand five churches, three of them of high prominence in the province. Floridly Baroque, its twin towers topped in bulbous roofs, the gold plates scaled like a dragon, its tiara façade pillared in pink marble, the Karmelitenkirche acts as a resplendent screen to protect from view a spacious Carmelite nunnery set in a garden behind its portals.

The Ursulinenkirche rejoices in a towering Rococo front resembling the fluted piece of Chinese embroidery used to cover the portal of a Confucian temple. The interior blazes and scintillates with gold and crystal adornment. The white and crystal Madonna wears the hooded Carmelite cloak sewn with huge pockets in which to collect alms for the poor.

At the far end of the street the Dom is a basilica, the Heart of Mary Church. This particular Virgin is the patroness of Linz. Here all is simplicity, or as nearly as restrained Baroque, built over a Gothic shell, can be. On holy days the sight of thousands of lighted candles, a veritable shimmering forest of flames, is a tremendously moving sight.

The Imperial Schloss, a triangular bastion elevated high above the river, was first built as a fortress by Frederick III to house his Imperial Governors. During a fit of rage at what he believed to be the treachery of one of his governors, he banished the devious incumbent and took up residence himself in the vast apartments that we see today. He built in 1489 the magnificently florid Frederick's Gate. This stunning, if ostentatious, portal withstood the fire which nearly destroyed the castle in 1800.

Empress Maria Theresia loved to come to Linz for the Spring Festival when the fruit trees burst into bloom to embroider the landscape in pink and white splendor, then to scatter the fragile, fading petals on Danube waters like crumpled carnival confetti. It was the Empress who decorated an enfilade of painted and damask-hung rooms, adhering to the sumptuous and profligate manner with which she enriched her favorite residences, allowing those she did *not* like to remain little more than state barracks.

St. Martin's Church, a simple chapel-like stone building of no pretensions, stands among bracken at the end of hill-climbing Römerstrasse, the ancient Roman Road skirting the Danube. Built on Roman foundations in the 8th century, it is proclaimed the oldest church in Austria. Architecturally unique—"a persuasive relic," Goethe called it

—the church illustrates the development of different styles in religious houses that have acted as hermitage, sanctuary and place of divine worship.

A long, tortuous road winds up from Urfahr across the river from Linz to a massif of wooded granite. Chalets and villas are scattered over the face of the rock. Hanging gardens adorn it. Presently one comes out onto the topmost crag to a kind of bewilderment. It seems scarcely possible that the church I had seen from across the river, unimpressive save for its aerial position, raising two slender turreted campaniles to the cerulian blue heavens as if in exaltation, could be one and the same as this mighty edifice, a very bulwark in tawny, pink and flame stucco and marble, rising sheer from the living rock. The actual immensity of the Pöstlingberg, when seen from afar, is dwarfed, an optical illusion if ever I beheld one. It is a Pilgrimage Church of the Seven Sorrows of Mary, built in the style of High Austrian Baroque by the family of Starhemberg in 1748 as a shrine for a miraculous image, as well as a repository for a large and splendid collection of religious art "for which there was no room" in the various family castles. It also ensepulchers in proper splendor the princely Starhembergs. The interior is immensely rich in gilt ornament. Six magnificent Murano glass chandeliers are fashioned from lusters whose variety in colors, smoldering in the light of myriad candles, shames the spectrum by disclosing tints it never knew. The mighty Baroque altar (1716) acts as a kind of reliquary for the miraculous image in carven wood.

There is a restaurant set on a flower-hung ledge under the buttresses of the church. Here one may lunch or dine in the quiet of an oak-tree-embowered garden and toast the view of Wachau and Alpine beauty in any one of an impressively various list of vintage wines.

I am extremely partial to the type of courtyard *biergarten* typical of the province. One will find these set amidst flowers and trees, hidden behind buildings in Landstrasse or Promenadestrasse, the two most frequented shopping thoroughfares in the city.

Largely due to the imagination of Viktor Pabisch there is one extremely agreeable hotel in Linz. This is Parc Hotel, a modern building facing a charming, small park in the residential part of the city.

Herr Pabisch has lived in England, and in America. He knows the hotel business from all angles. The rooms are small but extremely comfortable in furnishings and the dining room is presided over by a maître d'hôtel brought up in the great tradition of Suvretta House at St. Moritz. He and I discussed *haute cuisine*. Together we planned my meals, which could not have been better prepared anywhere in Europe. Linz has given to the culinary world a rarely delicious pastry, *linzertorte*, prepared with fresh apricots, raspberries or plums, the pastry crust arranged in lattice strips across the brandy-flavored fruit.

The morning I left Linz was a perfect day for river travel. The air was crystal clear, with a light, cooling breeze under a rain-washed sky. Once aboard the steamer *Schönbrunn* I sought the upper deck to watch the city on the bluffs recede into the distance. Like a painted theatre piece, the high-set Altstadt rose against the pine-dark slopes, a backdrop to silhouette the Baroque palaces and churches that crowd the streets running parallel to the river. Now more than ever, since I had a ground-level perspective, not a bird's-eye view, I realized that in the 17th century the city had been vastly enriched with a number of magnificent ecclesiastical structures in the highest Baroque style, owing to the efforts of religious orders which had come flocking to Linz to carry out the Counter Reformation.

The Baroque style breathes strength and vivid life into the old, gray and battlemented Roman and Medieval town. The gaiety of Baroque has triumphed. I felt its pulsing vitality. It was like the tuning up of an orchestra, ready to swing into the strains of Strauss' exuberant Rococo opera *Rosenkavalier*.

Chapter 11

VIRGIL CALLED THE WACHAU "WINE-FRAGRANT BACCHUS LAND"

THE historic name of Babenberg theoretically is carved on every tree trunk and across every stone in the Valley of the Wachau. The Babenbergs are the most powerful family to be identified with Austrian history after the departure of the Roman forces from the land. Chroniclers relate that two hundred and seventy Babenberg castles in what is now Upper and Lower Austria "fell to other liege" at the time the House of Babenberg became extinct in the 13th century, when Duke Frederick the Quarrelsome was "cut in twain" by the King of Hungary at the Battle of Leitha.

One of the ancient strongholds of the Babenbergs is the town of Grein. The theatre with its oval proscenium is the oldest in Austria. The castle is ruinous but extraordinarily decorative, pure theatre in itself. Jag-tooth pinnacles jutting skyward from a riotous tangle of trumpet vines, the strident red-orange blossoms blazing in the hot sunlight, it resembled a besieged fortress in flames.

This stretch of the Wachau dominated by Grein is called the "Greiner Schwall," a devouring whirlpool of horrendous memory. It is told that one of the early Babenberg dukes was feared by the townspeople as a monster of cruelty. For sport he would set his pack of savage hunting mastiffs on unfortunate villagers who crossed his path. When his retainers brought the mangled, bleeding, but still living victims before him, he would order them weighted with chains and thrown into the whirlpool. At night the shrieks of the drowned are said to disturb the rest of the good people of Grein.

From Grein the road and the railway closely follow the course of the river. (The Wachau Railway branches off at St. Valentin on the main Linz-Vienna line.) The Danube is plentifully strewn with small islands foliaged in willows and stunted hazel trees. Ordinarily these gravel deposits resemble shaggy green monsters crouching half submerged in the water. But close to the old fish market town of Struden, anciently famed for its smokehouses where fish was smoked to feed Roman and Medieval soldiers, looms the island of Wörth. A high crag of wooded rock showing the remains of a Roman drum-lighthouse. The silent and lonely ruin, Werfenstein, had its windows blocked up by great boulders in the 16th century as a sign of mourning. This gesture of woe extended to painting the riven masonry black with pitch. But within sight of the castle is the arbored river-terrace inn of Sarmingstein. Below the wall, fishermen sing while mending their nets, and huntsmen in the hanging forest across the river answer the echoes with a haunting, pagan "call of the hunt," a song called "Waldmann's Heil."

Pöchlarn is called "the town consumed by pride where ghosts of Attila and Kriemhild walk the stones at night," Kriemhild having journeyed with the Nibelungs down the Danube to marry the fabulous Hun. Celtic remains in roughly dressed star-shaped stone altars have been found among the rock crevasses. Archaeologists have traced the foundations of a villa built by the Emperor Claudius, who was known to have founded a military depot here. He kept a flotilla of canoelike boats for swift travel up and down the river. Old stone carvings show figures of boatmen in arrow-prow boats (the slabs possibly were pavings of an elaborate riverside quay) which appear to be progenitors of those used by fishermen in Sarmingstein today.

Aggstein comes boldly into view. It is set like a battle-ruined village of ancient stone buttresses, so high that it is not unusual on cloudy or foggy days for Danube steamer travelers to be cheated out of the sight of this hoary old castle that has a history for blood and thunder, rape and pillage second to no other castle in Austria. A more than ordinarily romantic ruin, preferably seen bulking against a cloudless robin's-egg blue sky, Aggstein was originally the seat of "the Kuenringer," the robber knights whose sport was to sack the baggage trains of early Crusaders. After it was besieged and almost totally destroyed in the 15th century the castle, rebuilt by "cruel Jörg," the Schrecken-wald "terror of the forest," acquired even more fearful notoriety. Jörg amassed great riches by plundering travelers on river and high-

CASTLE OF
AGGSTEIN.
DANUBE

way. He built toll castles along the Ybbs, the Enns and the Inn, to become in time the richest man in Austria. Perhaps his most pictur-esque fancy was to sleep in one of the towers at Aggstein in a macabre bed built like a Roman temple to Mars and composed entirely of human bones.

The boat slides past the quiet, gray, immensely ancient village of Willendorf. Not a ripple disturbs the lagoon backwaters here. The suspended activity of a sleeping village prevails. Somnolent even in waking hours, Willendorf's claim to celebrity is impressive. The squat, fantastically obese Venus of Willendorf, a limestone figure of prehistoric times bearing a striking resemblance to a figure by Brancusi, was discovered buried in river mud by a workman digging drains. The man, at first thinking it was a humorous toy, set it up on the quay to amuse the village children. The Venus is now housed in the Vienna Natural History Museum.

As one traverses the Danube, watching intently the castles and monasteries that appear, compel the eye, then fade away sternwise to become one with the river haze, it is the sun-gilded beauty of towers like that of Persenbeug rising above a welter of mauve-brown roofs that becomes the leitmotiv of the river scene. Although larger than most of the castles, architecturally its buff washed stone walls present the accepted plan of Baroque style superimposed on an earlier edifice. A steep, many-dormered roof covers the main building from which springs a tall, massive tower capped by an onion-shaped cupola, the verdigris-rimmed copper plates shimmering a particularly vivid emerald-green. Within a high buttressed retaining wall set about the center block are a score of smaller buildings, a chapel, and an armory. But it is the history of Persenbeug which sets it apart. When the Nibelungenlied was first set down on stiffened sheepskin by an obscure monk in an abbey "somewhere on the Danube," Persenbeug was conspicuously mentioned. A legend tells of Welf I of Altdorf, "a giant warrior who could wield a doublehanded sword in either hand with effect to shame the lightning," but who was killed in the Second Crusade. He sent back by squires his loot of infidel treasure in such amount that Persenbeug was called "the greatest treasure house in Austria."

Another page of its history gleams with romantic fire. Margravine Ita, reputed to have been a creature of remarkable beauty, was stolen from her hiding place in the crypt of Persenbeug by a Grand Vizier in the Islamic armies. The Vizier took her back and presented her "as a gift of Fatima," to a pasha. So instantly infatuated was the potentate that he fell ill. Ita nursed him to health, whereupon he married her. Her son became the Sultan of Aleppo. During the summers of his tragic boyhood the ailing Duke of Reichstadt, so poignantly presented to posterity in Rostand's play *L'Aiglon,* came to Persenbeug to spend his summers. Three paintings in oil of the son of Napoleon hang in the castle. All portraits show the boy as huge-eyed, pallid, his long gold hair nervously disheveled.

Near Oberarnsdorf, hidden within a girdle of trees, are unique Roman ruins. A deep, well-shaped pit contains crypts and alcoves once used for storing grain. There is a curiously interesting story concerning the "three Fates" villages of Arnsdorf, Ober-Mitter and Hof. It is said that during the time of Roman occupation of the Danube valley these hamlets were collectively called Cetium. It is known that there were three small temples in a ring, each one containing an altar for sacrifice. A black cock was sacrificed on one altar, a black ram on a second, and a black slave on the third. Mosaic pavings were found in 1927 bearing the designs of black cock, ram and Nubian slave, to substantiate this theory.

As the boat sailed past the sky-hung fretwork stones of ruined Dürnstein, I was treated to a particularly happy spectacle. The waterway narrows perceptibly under the soaring rock where the rickety shell of Dürnstein appears to cling perilously before plunging riverward. It was late in the afternoon. A westering sun burned the heights to a last blaze of fiery color. But suddenly I was conscious of what appeared at first glance to be banners of brilliant reds, purples, greens and blues, flicking back and forth on the perilous battlements and what is left of a once massive keep. Then I heard shouts of young voices. When we docked at Dürnstein it turned out to be a large party of children, under the guidance of schoolmasters, rehearsing for a pageant that is held annually within the ruined walls of Castle Dürnstein.

Here was life of knightly times portrayed in Medieval panoply, vivid as a fresco painted on the old lichened stones—stones that appear so insubstantial from the river level. Well do I know from previous visits, after toiling up the pathway hewn from living rock long before Richard Coeur de Lion was confined in a narrow cell waiting (waiting as it chanced for the sound of Blondel's voice singing madrigals), how everlasting strong the walls really are despite all the dissolution wreaked by the clawing elements through the centuries.

I have stayed at two inns, the Richard von Loewenherz and Blondel, or as they are called here, "At The Sign of King Richard the Lion-Hearted" and "At The Sign of the Singer Blondel," situated in the delightful town of Dürnstein. The town wanders erratically, a tangle of Medieval cobbled streets and alleys clustered around the base of the fabled Rock of Dürnstein. The local wine is famous, the food good farm provender with the accent on fowl, fish and fresh vegetables. The town boasts a beautiful library, a museum, ancient houses, and an armory. An elegantly decorated Baroque church bristles inside and out with sculptured saints, a few figures defying all the laws of gravity by flying upside down through space. Prelates in copes and miters are depicted omnipotent in heroic size.

In marked contrast to the rock-shard ruins of Aggstein and Dürnstein, imperishable sentinels to history, the pale ochre and celestial pink walls of Castle Schönbühel strike a more romantic note, redolent of serenity. The air of a house given to entertainment, the sound of sweeping strains of a Strauss waltz, preparation for a water carnival or *fête champêtre*, perhaps an imperial hunt in the encroaching forest. In fancy I seemed to hear the winding note of a hunting horn announcing to excited guests "Quarry away." Just below Stein the castle rises sheer from the river poised on a jut of moss-encrusted rock, forming a superstructure to the truncated battlements of a 13th-century fortress. Set foursquare to the Alpine winds, the tall, gracefully articulated tower is onion-capped in lead, the deeply grooved sheathing plates glowing with a patina of iridescent purple-blue. For suavity of design in High Austrian Baroque and for salubrious situation, to me the castle is the most beautiful in the country.

But for all its present air of elegant serenity there is deception here. Until the 16th century Schönbühel was a battlemented Medieval fortress, notorious as a highwayman's hideout as well as a den for river pirates who looted ships traveling along the Danube bearing rich cargoes for Vienna and Budapest. The castle is privately owned but during the summer months is open to visitors on week days. Long enfilades of high-ceilinged rooms present lovely pictures of luminous paneling painted white or in palest colors of spring flowers, the strong or delicately traced carvings picked out in gilt or silver leaf. For vital color, crimson damask curtains vie for prominence with the richest malachite green or apricot-pink of cut Genoese velvets and the tinsel-thread tapestries from the magical looms of Tournai. The walls are lined with paintings of court beauties and gallants famed in chronicles of Vienna society during the reign of Maria Theresia, of her son, and later during that of Emperor Franz Josef and Empress Elizabeth.

Nostalgia rides the frescoed corridors, for in one alcoved passage stands a spinet. On the yellowed ivory keys Marie Antoinette (in her childhood a close friend of a daughter of the house) learned to play a minuet. In later years the Queen devised new steps and patterns for the minuet to regale guests invited to her *cotillons* at Trianon.

It is certainly no exaggeration to regard the Austrian monasteries as a main cultural factor in the country during the Middle Ages and the beginning of modern times. Where art is so deeply embedded in the consciousness of the people it need not surprise one to find that a style of architecture once accepted was retained with great tenacity long after it had been abandoned elsewhere. Art, if it be really a state of heart, must be closely akin to the deep sense of piety that is as innate in the Austrian character as laughter or the lilt of song.

In Austria it is comparatively rare for a building to be so perfect that it gives no indication of its process of growth and no suggestion of its ultimate decay; nor does it appear unapproachable or remote outside the rhythm of everyday life. As most of the religious houses are centered in wide-spreading farms, there is an effortless give-and-take between monks and the farm community that administers to the needs of the abbey. I have seen women washing their linen at the sumptuously imagined Baroque fountain in some monastery courtyard and laying their heavy hand-woven linen sheets to bleach, spread over an ornate balustrade of the abbot's terrace.

The buildings of these monasteries were and are the most representative of Romanesque, Gothic and Baroque architecture in the country. Especially in the Baroque period these large monasteries flourished, and waxed vastly rich. In the middle of the 18th century the building period of the monasteries came to an end. Now attention is given by the monks to agricultural or scholastic pursuits in order to survive.

The Benedictine Abbey of Göttweig seen from the Danube evokes some fabled city in the clouds. Perhaps for panoramic effect and beauty of perspective, the position of Göttweig triumphs above all other monasteries save only Melk. The vast four-towered building, constructed from deep ivory stone (cut from the quarries of Steyr) veined like Parian marble in gun-metal and green, assumes many moods as the light changes from sunrise to fall of night.

Orchards, tilled fields, and vineyards surround the base of the abbey hill—a flowery dais in spring, carpeted in golden wheat in summer, a green sea of grapevines flecked with purple during the autumn vintage. Thinking back I believe the abbey comes into its own as an ice palace. I have seen it encrusted with snow and ice, set alight by prismatic fires from a winter sun.

Although Göttweig was founded by the "warrior bishop" Altmann of Passau in 1072 as a fortified Gothic church incorporating a monastic house and an armory, it was largely destroyed by fire in 1718. That supreme showman, architect Lucas von Hildebrandt, was entrusted with the task of rebuilding on a scale that would epitomize the zenith of Austrian High Baroque. He planned the magnificent building that crowns the vineyard-embraced hill and which we see only in part today. As with so many buildings planned by Hildebrandt, Fischer von Erlach and Matthias Steinl, to name only three of the grandiose architects of the day, for one reason or another (usually lack of funds) the great building schemes had to be either simplified or abandoned altogether.

At Göttweig, only one of the two staircases superbly representative of Hildebrandt's genius was ever carried out. The use of huge faïence urns, bone-white, gold and the illusive purple-blue of bloom-dusted grapes, lead the eye upward as the stairs ascend to a gallery enriched by a coved ceiling painted in sweeping strokes of pure color as brilliant today as when the brothers Altomonte painted Emperor Karl enthroned as the Sun God in the sky.

There are two splendid monasteries to be visited as excursions out of Linz—Wilhering and Kremsmünster. Wilhering, originally a "chain" of bleak stone buildings, was built during the Crusades on an isolated strip of river bank protected from river pirates by a "porcupine wall" of cyclopean stones set thickly with lethal iron spears. A few of these weapons are preserved in the museum. Only fragments of the Cistercian Abbey of 1146 remain. Two ambulatories are bordered by squat Romanesque columns showing traces of red, blue, purple and saffron-yellow paint in spiral design. Heraldic banners, escutcheons, and figures of armored knights attest to once elaborate frescoing. In 1733 it was rebuilt in Austrian Rococo style, boldly articulated but uncommonly delicate in detail. The architect of this most lovely Rococo building has not yet been identified with certainty.

Many artists of first repute collaborated in the rich interior decoration, among whom was Franz Joseph Holzinger, who attained fame while still in his teens. He loved the color blue to distraction; indeed, he was called "The Blue Wonder" by his colleagues. Johann Georg Uebelherr and his friend Johann Feichtmayr, called "The Genius of Augsburg," were responsible for the witty, scintillating stucco work. The exquisite color, muted yet of pastel clarity in ebullient brushwork, was "imagined" by Bartolomeo, the lazier of the two Altomonte brothers. The actual painting is said to have been done largely by the vital Martino.

These artist brothers, equally brilliant but poles apart in character, were born in the Tyrol with the name Hochberg. Together they journeyed to Italy, the Mecca of all painters, particularly those wishing to learn the supreme Italian art of fresco and stucco embellishment. After a long sojourn in Rome and Florence, the brothers decided to return to their native Austria. During the years the two Hochbergs had become more Italian than the Italians. The spirit of Italy and all it meant to them fairly coursed through their veins. So they decided to change their names from Hochberg—"high mountain" in German—to Altomonte—the identical meaning in Italian.

To me the unforgettably delicate beauty of the nave in the Church of Mary Mater at Wilhering is synonymous with music. The voices of boy sopranos spiraling crystal clear notes of all the *Ave Marias* that have floated heavenward to the painted cross-ribbed cornices seem never to have wholly died away.

The gardens at Wilhering are world famous for the unusual variety of flowers and even greater variety of trees brought from far countries. Tropical and subtropical palms and fragile "ostrich plume trees" from Zanzibar unaccountably seem to thrive, attaining impressive size and strength despite the none-too-temperate climate of Austria. Wilhering maintains a large school for advanced students. The monks work as well on fifteen large abbey farms which spread out for six miles along the river banks.

The road to Kremsmünster leads up hill and down dale past oddly silent waterfalls, the thread of pendant water so tenuous it appears not to have thawed from last winter's imprisoning ice. Spacious farmhouses are set back from the road on hillsides. The Krems, a deep blue, gentle river, meanders through meadows following the slopes of foothills.

The Benedictine Abbey of Kremsmünster is prideful of its ancient and noble lineage. In 777 Tassilo, Duke of Bavaria, called Golden Beard, was the fiery-tempered rival of Charlemagne the Great. He founded this oldest remaining abbey in Upper Austria. Early in the 17th century the old Romanesque Gothic buildings were beginning to heed the pointing finger of inexorable Time. The greater part of the historic abbey (which was partially devoted to a "palace" for Duke Tassilo) was torn down and the majestic Baroque structure, with its three soaring towers and immensely long wings surrounding a vast courtyard that we see today, was erected on a rise of ground surrounded by apple orchards.

Each time that I approach the village of Krems the long view of the abbey from the hill road impresses me anew. The mighty castellated walls, with their wide area of ochre-red tiling, are encrusted with moss and silver lichen. From the high belfry of the monastery towers with their helmetlike domes peal the sweetest toned bells in Austria, ringing out hourly praise to the Creator.

Michael Zürn the Younger, one of the most brilliant sculptors of the Austrian Baroque, carved the unique congregation of marble angels in an extraordinary variety of religious emotions from burning ecstasy to stern impassiveness. Over two hundred in number, these angels embellish the exterior and interior of the monastery and the church, enlivening the rather plain walls to impressive effect. The library, a suite of four deep semicircular rooms, some of them 230 feet long, represent to the hilt the type of High Baroque abbey library in which the preservation of the ancient parchment rolls and folios, some tied with hanks of "Frankish" human hair, and Cordovan leather-bound books of great worth, is the essential factor and not, as in the later Baroque period, the design of the room itself as a repository for imperial display. In a vitrine at one end of the library is displayed the graven copper and gold-alloy Tassilo Chalice dated 880, not only the greatest treasure of Kremsmünster Abbey but one of the chief national treasures of Austria.

The Imperial Apartments are a sumptuously appointed enfilade of twelve rooms. The walls of each chamber are hung with Italian damasks or Genoese cut velvet in deep, glowing jewel colors. The great feature of the Emperor's Room, entirely hung with tapestries depicting scenes of a royal hunt, is a white and gold tile stove which, far more than merely fulfilling its purpose of heating so huge a room, is a work of art.

Since earliest days the monks of Kremsmünster have been uncommonly interested in studying the planetary system. In 1748 an Observatory was erected near the principal portal of the abbey. The tower is 164 feet high. The problem of enlivening a tower structure with elements of palace architecture, notably the swags of carved sandstone fruit intermingled with signs of the Zodiac affixed pedimentally above the windows, has been brilliantly solved.

Take a leisurely walk around the water basins surrounded by closed-in arcades used for keeping and breeding fish. Three of them were built by Carlo Antonio Carlone in 1690 and a further two added in 1715 by the famous architect Jakob Prandtauer. Boldly sculptured stone statues of saints, holding in their arms huge wriggling fish with scales the size of those usually seen covering dragons, act as finials on the stone balustrades of the tanks. Rarely has so serene and graceful a piece of architecture enlivened with fountains been created for a purely secular purpose. I was told by the monk detailed to show me around that the fish here were once called to feed by the notes of a bell which hangs on a scrolled iron arm above the central fish tank.

I took lunch at a small inn built by the Abbey of Kremsmünster. It is a simple white building set on the edge of the Almsee, glittering like a patch of sequins flung at the foot of the Totes Gebirge.

Another of the most important sights in Upper Austria is the Monastery of Canons Regular of St. Florian near Linz. The roads and the rivers in this region seem to wind in company so there are three different routes out of Linz whereby one may reach the monastery. I believe the most rewarding highway from a scenic standpoint is known as the Klein-Reifling Strasse cutting into the Province of Styria near the "Iron Mountain" of Eisenerz.

It is the long approach, the hilltop view of soaring towers and the immense length of steep-roofed frontage at St. Florian that compels the eye. A world of carefully considered proportioning in stone and marble is revealed here, vast and majestic but never unwieldy. Below the green and purple shadowed heights of the Ennstal the towers of this splendid religious house of the venerable Augustine Prebendaries rise like fluted columns supporting sculptured marble urns against the shifting cloud shadows forever tracing patterns over the heavily foliaged mountains.

Breasting the steep hill, a surprise awaits the visitor. The celebrated Imperial Stairway is first seen through a tall wrought-iron gateway of springing vitality in design. The scrolls, flowers, fern fronds and vines appear as threads of black, lightly articulated as cobweb. Through this sharp, black tracery the winged stairways rise as a pillared colonnade on either side of the magnificent eagle fountain, the symbolical imperial monarch of the skies poised, saber-pinioned wings spread for flight.

In 1676 Carlo Carlone began to build. He laid out the original plan and is known to have designed the beautifully proportioned tiers of windows pedimented with a broken cornice centering alternating sea-shell and flaming-urn motifs. Carlone fell desperately ill at this point. Jakob Prandtauer continued the work. It was finally finished by Jakob and Michael Steinhauser in 1751. All were superior architects of their day. The marvel is that so closely did each succeeding architect follow the concepts of his predecessors that there is no feeling whatever of an abrupt change of ideas but rather a beautifully handled completeness of line and ornament.

The Archbishop's Gateway leading to the Eagle Fountain courtyard, one of the outstanding creations of Baroque Art in Austria, was designed by Prandtauer. The heroically sculptured figures and laurel-wreathed urn finials are the work of Giacomo Bianco. On either side of the gateway four Atlantides, denizens of Ocean, support upon a richly molded marble cornice figures of the four cardinal virtues. Nothing weak or softly "pretty" here, but rather drama personified. Helmeted, armored, or swathed in billowing classic draperies, the sense of vitality, of arrested movement of the female figures, is tremendous. This is a fiercely animated "conversation piece," so arresting that I suspect the collected "virtues" have enjoyed themselves mightily airing their opinions of the motley throng of individuals who have passed under their corniced stage for nearly three centuries.

The Collegiate Church or Monastery Church of the Assumption is a sweeping gesture in scale, unadorned spaces of gleaming bisque-pink marble so rarely seen in the ornate Baroque churches. Only the altar presents any significant ornamentation. Inside the church the great composer Anton Bruckner rests in a crypt beneath the organ named for him and from whose keys he drew for many years the music of simple melodies, impressive symphonies and religious themes, "sonorous music to confound celestial spheres."

Gallery after gallery of paintings unfold. The Danube School is brilliantly represented. A series of panels by Albrecht Altdorfer, whose name means "The Man From The Old Village"; portraits of emperors, popes, poets and artists in splendor of glowing colors reveal-

IMPERIAL STAIRCASE
ST. FLORIAN

ing the visages and diversely rich raiment of personages prominent in the history of Europe and in art down four centuries of time.

The exquisite Marble Festival Hall or Emperor's Room is located on the second floor of the southern wing of the monastery, reached by one spur of the Grand Staircase. Its ceiling is painted in the ultimate sweep of Italian bravura by Bartolomeo Altomonte, the less ambitious of the two painter brothers. Nevertheless, in this case he accomplished a prodigious feat of lyrical High Baroque fresco painting. The subject of the painting glorifies the blessings of peace and the victories of Austria and Hungary against the Turks. Altomonte employed a range of colors embracing all reds, pinks, orange-yellows and purple-blues, such as I have seen only when Nature in opulent mood enflames an autumn sunset. I had access to old "house books" pertaining to the building of the monastery. Part of the entries are a discourse by an abbot who decried the "waste of gold because of lethargy among artisans, their senses dulled by too frequent wine."

The double wings of the loggia staircase lead to the long corridor from which open many of the state rooms. For grandeur of design the staircase is unsurpassed. From the top of the stairs, reached through a pillared alcove, the celebrated Imperial Library, a large, octagonal apartment, repository for St. Florian's monumental collection of rare books, ancient and historic manuscripts, appears to have caught and imprisoned the sun itself. The day I wandered around the library was overcast, but the room was radiant from light cast by two immense chandeliers on the thousands of leather and parchment bindings tooled in silver and burnished gilt. As my eyes ranged the bookcases covering the walls from floor to ceiling, I sensed the reason for this improbable radiance. In the ceiling painting depicting the union of Virtue with Science, Bartolomeo Altomonte limited his palette to the use of yellows, deep ochre, the pulsing yellow of marigolds, of honey and amber, accenting sumptuous robes with pale primrose as a foil to patterned damask shimmering with threads of gold leaf.

The wine cellars at St. Florian are long, cool rooms in the west wing entered at garden level. Brightly frescoed and well lighted to dispel any somberness, these rooms elicit from visitors exclamations of pleasant surprise, largely due to the huge casks of vintage or "fresh" wines arranged in tiers along the walls. The collection of stone-china, carved wood, bull's hide, delicate porcelain and Bohemian glass mugs and steins is displayed in painted wall cabinets and on shelves.

As I drove away I turned to look again at the vociferously trumpeting angels perched above the gateway, an eternal hail and farewell to visitors, emblematic of the ecstasy with which religious art is portrayed in the Province of Upper Austria.

Farther along the road the Heidentor (Pagan's Gate) near Petronell looms in the landscape, a reminder of ancient times. The ruin of a Roman monument from the 3rd century, it is all that remains above ground of the great Roman town of Carnuntum situated at the crossing of the Danube waterway of the old amber, silver and gold trade route. The town was of such importance that it possessed two amphitheatres; Marcus Aurelius built one of them. Stones and statues from this arena have been excavated. While it was in the long process of erection the Emperor wrote his "Meditations" sitting in a loggia atop a tower he had built close to the theatre so that he might keep an eye on his project.

Septimius Severus was proclaimed Emperor of Rome at Carnuntum. Under the rule of Leopold III (The Holy) the "twin" monasteries of Heiligenkreuz and Klosterneuburg were founded. The memory of St. Leopold, the patron of Lower Austria, is still revered with almost fanatical ardor. Leopold called the monasteries "two pillars supporting my arch of piety over Vienna."

The Cistercian Abbey of Heiligenkreuz, long after its founding, was finally completed about 1135 by Otto von Freising, the famous historian son of Leopold III. It is one of the few abbeys in Austria which has preserved its Medieval aspect. The church is a three-aisled, pillared basilica in pure unaltered Romanesque style. I find its cool and airy clarity a symbol for the intellectual boldness of the time. The cloisters were built in 1220, long, wandering, colonnaded galleries, in all their parts indicative of the austere, unadorned elegance of line of early Gothic times.

The ancient Abbey of Klosterneuburg was founded in 1090–1136, also by Leopold III. At the beginning of the 17th century the abbey was beginning to show its age by monstrous cracks endangering its Romanesque walls, causing the main portal to sink down into a sand pit during the consecration of St. Kundra, killing scores of kneeling devotees. Abbot Perger (1707–1748) asked Imperial Engineer Donato Felice d'Allio to draw up a vast plan for the rebuilding of the abbey in the prevailing High Austrian Baroque taste. But complications marred the completion of the grandiose project. When Emperor Charles VI visited the abbey in 1731 he promptly stopped all work. In his characteristic curt way, he decreed: "I have decided to make the abbey an Austrian Escorial." Josef Kornhäusel, the great classic architect, brought the work to conclusion but completed only one of the four immense "parade ground" courtyards originally planned by d'Allio of the spacious ideas.

Fields of green, brown and gold stretch away in front of the domes of Klosterneuburg, away to feathery, pale green Wienerwald, to the blue spruce forested foothills of the Alps. The façade facing Vienna was intended for the Emperor's none too predictable approval as he sat in Vienna, leveling his spyglass, morning, noon and night, at the cupola, in which he had a chapel consecrated. This façade was intended to symbolize the secular, imperial might as opposed to the idea of divine power incorporated in the west façade. A refulgent note is struck by a large gold copy of the Imperial Crown placed on the cupola as if resting on a cushion. Everywhere in the abbey the carver's knife and chisel have been richly employed.

The finest expressions of carving are the tiers of choir stalls in the abbey church. One of the most significant contributions to High Baroque style in ecclesiastical embellishment, the easy, graceful flow of leaf and fern, grapevine and bracken frond called bishop's-crozier is from designs by Matthias Steinl, who attained unimaginable heights of delicacy in high-relief carving, doing justice both to the importance of the abbey as a repository of art, and the Imperial Court in a display of elegant luxury. The dark, waxed oak and chestnut-wood choir stalls are well set off by the glow of crimson velvet knee cushions, the pew curtains of gold galloon, and the embossed embroidery on altar cloths of white or spring-green satin.

The Leopold Chapel was once the Chapter House of the Romanesque abbey. In 1677 it was adapted in the Baroque manner by adding spirited carvings and a magnificently floriated wrought-iron screen. This protects the greatest treasure of the abbey, the enamel altar by Nicolas of Verdun, dated 1181. Astonishingly fragile in workmanship, as delicately colored as swathes of first spring flowers in an Alpine meadow, it is the largest and considered the most delicately executed work of its kind to be preserved from Medieval times.

Lilienfeld Abbey reminds me of a big, comfortable country manor house characteristic of the farmlands of Carinthia. Pale primrose-yellow washed walls, a rose-colored tile roof pierced by many wide dormer windows. The abbey church on the other hand presents an ancient face. Originally founded in 1202, the Medieval porch was left untouched when the west façade was rebuilt in 1703. Together the various styles of architecture afford an effective and original whole.

To me the most exciting moment of the Danube boat trip is when below Weitenegg the boat swings in a wide curve of the river through marshes thickly set with alder trees, the river fringe richly patterned with water lilies and exclamatory spears of sepia-furred cattails, to reveal Melk, the largest monastic edifice in the world. The monastery looms on its eminence above a small spear-shaped island spread like an aquatic prayer rug at its feet. Melk is a port of call for river steamers. I have found it an agreeable interlude to disembark there and stay at least overnight at any one of the three inns. The Goldener Ochse with its river terrace is a proven charmer in every sense of the word. Next day one can embark on the daily boat bound for either Vienna or Linz.

Melk symbolizes Austria at the peak of its world eminence. A rich museum of art, an imperial palace, a basilica and monastery, and an academy for boys all in one, it requires a considerable amount of unhurried time properly to absorb its manifold treasures. Conceived in the High Austrian Baroque style, rarely has any building that I have ever seen appeared so essentially a part of the surrounding landscape.

Set four-square to the river reaches, the abbey rises from a massive parapet of rusticated stone, throned in majesty. Prandtauer's glorious towers thus appear to command the entire Wachau. It has been said that every artist in whatever field creates one masterpiece—that is, one expression of his talent that tops all the rest. Here is the ultimate splendid achievement of Jakob Prandtauer. There is much of originality at Melk, as if the architect had let his imagination ride on a free rein, perhaps bringing into being ideas he had been saving against the "great day" that every artist dreams of.

The outer courtyard and east, or river, façade of the abbey is conceived as a powerful introduction and it is here that Prandtauer has created a worthy religious counterpart to the secular palace façade. Called The Prelate's Courtyard, the scale of the terrace is intensified by the supple rise of the elegant cupola, a palace-pavilion in miniature in itself. This cupola has been copied in Georgian architecture with varying degrees of success countless times in many lands.

History reveals that a Roman river fortress once rose on the Rock of Melk. It was the castle of Heinrich of the House of Babenberg before he became the founder of Melk in the 11th century. In 1900 a bronze shield was found submerged in Danube mud at a spot near where the river swings abruptly at the foot of the Basilica Rock, heading toward Vienna. On the shield was carved the arms of Babenberg, the name "Heinrich von B.," and the date 1067 as the founding of Melk. Building of the present edifice was undertaken in 1660 to be finished in 1726.

The interior gleams in its richly vital gold and silver leaf over red gesso, combining all the warmth of the sun and the cool brilliance of the moon, in contrast to palest rose, violet and icy green of Italian marbles. Unforgettable is the Organ Gallery. The forest of slender gold organ pipes are bound together with garlands of silver laurel leaves. The delightful carved concert of *putti*, twenty or more bouncing cherubs playing on every conceivable musical instrument, is the exceptionally free carving of Viennese organ-maker Gottfried Sonnholz.

The Prelate's Corridors and Side Galleries, as they are called, used

MELK
THE MAGNIFICENT.

by the abbots as audience chambers for "lesser persons," are definitely festive in decoration with their filigree lattices garlanded in flowering vines, cockleshells and seaweed swags. They are unsigned, though presumably these "innovations," as they are listed in a catalogue of improvements dated 1745 preserved in the library, are the work of the Imperial Theatre architects Antonio Beduzzi and Antonio Bibiena of Vienna.

The library is by far the grandest room in the abbey, even more splendid in its carved marble pillars and painted ceiling than any of the luxuriously appointed reception rooms in the Imperial Palace wing. Tiepolo painted the ceiling in clear radiant colors, his brushwork as free as the winds that blow the draperies about the limbs of his Muses representing arts and sciences. A notable feature of the library is the uncommon means of heating the immensely spacious apartment. Three circular trap doors are raised by great bronze rings to allow gusts of hot air to rise from furnaces burning in the bowels of the rock over which the library wing is built.

The librarian told me that as far as could be calculated the library was rated second in importance only to the Vatican Library. At Melk the collection of books, folios, and illuminated parchments on everything pertaining to Medieval chivalry is considered the largest and most comprehensive in existence.

In the Marmorsaal (room of Italian marbles) the ceiling is by Tiepolo. Here the juxtaposition of burning sapphire-blue and coral-red heightens in color value in contrast to the painted white architecture. It is the powerful foreshortening of architectural forms and human anatomy that breathes the festival gaiety, characteristic of so many of Tiepolo's painted rooms in Venetian *palazzi*. The luminous, melting blues and whites faintly touched in pink and gold "release" the boundaries of the walls until one's imagination leaps. In this room it is not difficult to evoke the great days when princely entertainments were held. This is a room in which music found its affinity in decoration. Here archbishops and cardinals, robed in crimson and ecclesiastical scarlet, paraded arm in arm with court gallants, or perhaps the reigning monarch himself, while Haydn or the shy young Mozart played upon clavichord and delicately painted pianoforte.

Each room within the Prelate's House contains a musical instrument, ranging from a great organ to a tiny painted clavichord. A world of music in itself, symbol, I thought, of that great love of music that is Austria's heritage.

Chapter 12

VIENNA OF A THOUSAND YEARS, THE
HEART OF *AUSTRIA FELIX*

V IENNA is to me a kind of lodestar. Vienna is an expression of life itself. Edward VII of England, a renowned *bon vivant*, loved this city on the Danube. "The Viennese," he once said to a friend, "know not of satiety but sing, dance and love in perpetuity." Old chronicles repeat that through ten centuries Vienna has persisted in the fabulous entertainment of the stranger within its gates by its natural and healthy way of life. Vienna has long proven the pleasures of the senses in expansive gaiety. An ivory-crimson, crystal and gold elegance pervades the city. Art and architecture join hands. Music sounds everywhere. When youthful Richard Strauss was once soundly birched by his schoolmaster for inking in the notes of a ballad on the newly varnished wooden top to his desk, he lamented, "Let me write my little music, for little music breeds *big* music. You'll see!"

Vienna emphasizes every attribute of a great European capital in its imperial architecture, its art galleries, broad avenues and esplanades, churches and glorious St. Stephen's Cathedral, its Opera House, its theatres, intellectual, sophisticated society, and its definite accent on schools of higher learning. The University of Vienna alone is world renowned.

For all its proud urbanity Vienna breathes a pastoral air, so close on its boundaries lie the exquisite glades of the Wienerwald. To the west in the region called Marchfeld spread the fields of early ripening golden grain. Within the short space of a pleasant morning's jaunt upriver the Danube winds through the storied Wachau, a landscape

239

of legendary castles that casts its spell to the very threshold of the city. The Alps themselves gently come to rest in a chain of vineyards, meadows latticed by icy mountain rivulets, and Vienna Woods (Wienerwald) that ends at the gates of Vienna.

From its earliest settlement Vienna holds such fascination for study in variety and colorful events that the whole parade of its growth from Celtic days unfolds one of the greatest stories ever told. Few cities of such antiquity have been so thoroughly chronicled, owing largely to Emperor Tiberius' enthusiasm for documentation of everything pertaining to his far-flung "imperial provinces." Later the Babenbergs, and still later the powerful Habsburgs and their satellites the Starhembergs, all kept Vienna and the nearer Danube reaches constantly in world focus.

Toward the end of Roman supremacy Tiberius strove to consolidate the rule of Rome along the Danube. To insure freedom from attack he built a chain of fortress castles, the chief stronghold situated at Carnuntum, which included Vienna and the nearly impenetrable wilderness of Vienna Forest. Traces of Roman tenure in buttressed walls, hugely circular cisterns and subterranean vats for the storing of wine are still to be seen in Vienna.

The Emperor elevated Carnuntum to the seat of the Governor of Pannonia. Here he erected the famed naval base and headquarters of the Roman flotilla. Because the garrison of Vindobona (the Roman name for Vienna) was largely composed of Syrian troops, the cult of Mythras was popular with the rank and file. Hence a temple was erected to this "hysterical warrior deity, a clownish roisterer and breeder of malcontents," wrote unsympathetic Marcus Aurelius in the shadow of a Temple to Jupiter Dolichenus, where doubtless the sacred rights were observed with proper dignity. So intense was Marcus Aurelius' love for Pannonia, that he spent twelve years there, "improving my mind and my days," and writing his celebrated "Meditations." He died in his "Villa of Solitude," in 180 A.D. To evoke this rich past, Roman relics abound in Vienna. In the Roman Museum in the Ringstrasse there is a "plastron" or chest shield of demi-armor (for ceremonial dress) fashioned of bull's-hide encrusted with silver filigree and mother of pearl cabochons carved from Danube mussel shells, bearing the Aurelian personal cypher, a branch of triumphal bay.

Away in the mists of time when one hundred trumpeters of the Praetorian Guard announced from the citadel of Vindobona the death of Marcus Aurelius, the muted notes sounded the death knell of the "illimitable" Roman Empire. Like runnels of quicksilver disappearing into the cracks of a tessellated floor (a famous pastime or game of chance for Roman patrician gamblers was to bet considerable sums on which direction a "throw" of quicksilver would take across an area marked out upon a terrace floor), disintegration spread over the Roman provinces. The great migration started in 375 A.D. across Europe. From the mountains, from the plains, vast hordes of peoples flowed like waves of a relentless sea. Across the whole continent of Europe, homeless, sullen, hungry, leaving devastation in their wake, these tribes moved toward a goal secretly chosen by their leaders. The goal was Austria. The Celto-Roman population, from the high-born to the peasantry, were submerged under the flow of Vandals, Slavs, Teutons, Franks, Samarians, Goths and Huns. The Huns were the most numerous, the most savage. Attila set up an "administrative" court on the River Theiss where, according to ancient documentation, chieftains of once powerful tribes numbering as many as forty races, all speaking different tongues, milled about in acres of knee-deep mud seeking some sort of promise for future security for themselves and their families. Here at one time the world appeared to be ruled solely by Attila the Hun. Into this maelstrom of bewildered, mourning humanity drifted stranger monks and priests, preaching in compelling voices a new religion. At this period Christianity was not new in Austria, although its acceptance was desultory and converts few, the sturdy peasants and warriors not relishing the role of religious martyr. The persecution of Christians which began in 115 A.D. under Trajan had grown in intensity to reach new and dreadful heights in 300 A.D. under Diocletian, "whose heart," according to an ancient lament, "was drowned in wine."

And so the centuries rolled on. Charlemagne built "resting places" or hunting castles in Vienna Forest, and in Vienna a palace (in which it is said he never slept a single night), rising from the Ottakring, the "Tief Graben" (canal) of today. As late as the 17th century portions of ancient Claudian walls were still standing near the old Freisingerhof, now the site of the Graben Café. Like the final rocket of an expensive pyrotechnic display, the last great burst of imperial Roman glory was the historic meeting at Carnuntum of four emperors. Haughty, profligate Diocletian, battle-scarred Galerius, tiny, mincing Maximilian and fantastically obese Licinius, who had to be borne in a litter "as hugely timbered as the ark" swung between the shoulders of four oxen. Like an omen, at the banquet held in a pavilion draped with the personal banners of the four emperors, each banner topped by a golden eagle, descending night obliterated the imperial eagles of Rome. With the relentless regularity of the tides, events of dynastic importance ebbed and flowed around the lodestar Vienna. The ruling Goths called the city Vidomina, everywhere erecting sinister rustic signposts devised in the shape of a cross, the crosspiece ornamented with human skulls. Barbarian Attila caused the walls of the houses to be painted red, black and yellow.

Shortly after, the struggles between the Franks and the savage Magyars reduced the fertile fields to a bloody morass. The city is first mentioned in documents of 881 as Vienna. This name, however, is seen traced in tarnished gold embroidery across silk banners used in processions to celebrate the Rights of Jurisdiction conferred on Salzburg in 816.

Under Charlemagne, the Empire of the Franks was established at Vienna with such pomp and circumstance as the peoples of the world had never before even imagined, let alone beheld. In 962 A.D., Otto the Great received from the hands of Pope Gregory the Imperial Crown of Rome. So came into being the "Holy Roman Empire," that historic intimacy of union between Church and Throne which, withstanding both foreign and internecine warfare, was to maintain its existence until 1806.

In 976 Count Luitpold Babenberg sheathed his sword for a scepter. A monkish chronicler recorded this momentous happening. "The sun burst forth full upon Austria until we gilded our hearts in the warmth of its rays." And so the House of Babenberg became forever rooted in the history of Vienna. Leopold of Babenberg, known to posterity as "The Holy"—often called by his impious, sports-loving brothers "the holiest man behind a beard"—built the Castle of Leopoldsberg looking away to the east. From the bastion-supported terraces Leopold and his saintly wife Agnes, daughter of the less than saintly Heinrich IV, Emperor of the Franks, could watch Vienna, rising along the Danube mud flats like a gold prospector's boom town. So enamored did both of them become with what they saw that Leopold bowed to the wishes of Agnes to found an abbey, Klosterneuburg, and a "stately palace, water girt," as a spot about where the Hofburg stands.

All this historical panorama of Vienna is uncommonly significant, considering that even today it persists as the very essence of the city. There is visible evidence of every epoch from the time when the Celtic river-traders built riparian villages, setting the flimsy huts, a clutch of tree-bark and woven reeds, high above the river currents upon log pilings. Beneath the elevated floorings crude traps were laid to catch fur-bearing river creatures—muskrat, beaver and *martilines* (water sable)—from which the characteristic voluminous winter cloak of the Celtic tribesmen was sewn.

From the first decipherable records there has always been in every village a "chief's house," a "governor's house," or, later, an "emperor's house" or chamber—the building in which the monarch gave audiences. So today the Imperial Palace of the Habsburgs, called the Hofburg (court of a reigning house), the last "emperor's house" in Vienna, is a great house indeed. On the two score acre spot occupied today by the white stone and marble Baroque Hofburg there once stood a 13th-century hunting castle, "a court of sweet music where minstrels sang of ancient days." Reinmar the Ancient, Poet Laureate to Duke Leopold V, sang in verse forms the moving legends of the great migration of nations articulated to him from the memories of the peoples. Ultimately these sagas found dramatic expression in the Song of the Nibelungs, the lyrical and poignant Song of Gudrun, and the long tale, embellished with startlingly pagan pageantry (Song of the

Nibelung), of how Etzel (Attila) and Kriemhild held their nuptials in Vienna.

Evening at sunset is a good time to become a part of the famous café life of Vienna. Then the renowned promenade, the wide Ringstrasse, comes brilliantly to life. Frequent visits to coffeehouses are as much an ingrained part of Viennese life as is the intentness with which a selection of a Vienna pastry is made. Coffee *mit schlag* (whipped cream) piled into a rippled cone half again as high as the cup, an assortment of pastries out of fable, and (or) a carafe of one of the numerous light wines from Wachau and Burgenland vineyards set the tone of refreshment for the favorite form of relaxation in Vienna. "For every ten houses in a street you will find a coffeehouse to supply them," the Viennese say. It was from Vienna that *coffee* set forth to conquer and delight the world in 1683.

Austria has always been predominately a wine country, although the competition of beer was recognized even in the Middle Ages. A friendly and generously disposed landowner often hung a *bierglocke* (beer bell) in the gable or the tower of his steward's house. At evening when work was finished for the day the bell was rung summoning all workmen to drink a stein of free beer to wash the dust of toil from their throats. Such a bell still tolls from the Stephansdom to remind the Viennese to refresh themselves with a glass of beer before starting homeward.

At the open air restaurant in the center of Stadtpark Gardens, tables are set on a flagstone court under lime and chestnut trees. There is a space for dancing as well. An orchestra plays from four o'clock in the afternoon until midnight. On a series of raised terraces surrounding the pale yellow Baroque building are the dining rooms, ballroom, and art galleries for displaying pictures or sculpture. Food is chosen from a varied menu to be served in latticed alcoves or under vine-trellised arbors. Fried chicken (based on a famous "country style" recipe from Wienerwald) and roast goose served with celery braised in white wine, the tender but firm stalks dusted with rye breadcrumbs sautéed in parsley butter, are two specialties of the house. Another is *faschingskrapfe*, a doughnut-type pastry filled with damson plum jam. The pastry has a charming history. In 1615 a pastry shop was opened under the name of its proprietress, Cecilie. Beneath her name on the sign that swings above the door a noble admirer had these words painted in gold: *The most luxuriously beautiful charmer in Vienna.* To show her appreciation (and perhaps with an ulterior motive?) Cecilie invented the rich, flaky pastry in the form of a wedding ring. It is said that originally the center of the "doughnut" was not, as presently, filled with jam, but hollow, dusted with almond-flavored castor sugar.

In any case the *krapfen* were an instantaneous success. Even today a young girl in love, when taken to one of the cafés by her swain, will order a *krapfe,* break it in two and present one half to the young man to signify that she accepts his proposal.

Torten—or tarts—of pastry filled with fruit are a Vienna specialty. So is *zwetschkenknödel,* a damson dumpling. The *knödel* filled with a juicy apricot or brandied cherries is popular. I am partial to cherry strudel or cream strudel filled with cheese curds and currants, a favorite of Viennese while leisurely enjoying a glass of wine, perhaps the aromatic Wachauer, Schlumberger Goldeck or sweet Muskateller, a wine that to me possesses an aftertaste reminiscent of the perfume of the dark-red Damask rose.

Whenever Vienna is mentioned I think immediately of the Prater, the Ringstrasse and Vienna Woods, three of the most famous recreation spots in the world for the population of a city and its visitors. The Prater was originally a vast game preserve reserved solely for noblemen to hunt its long forest rides. A famous story in Vienna has it that when the Emperor Franz Josef decided to open the hunting grounds to the general public, the noblemen were furious. Loud and long was the outcry that they would no longer be able to hunt with their equals. When a spokesman was sent to tell him of the noblemen's dismay, the Emperor answered coldly, "If I wished to be always with my equals I should be forced to take my walks in the Kapuzinergruft, among the deceased Habsburgs."

The Prater stretches in undulating open fields and brook-fed pools to the foot of the mountains. There are tracts of woodland, fern-grown gullies, magnificent old flowering chestnut trees by the thousands, and curious little conical mounds waving meadow flowers for all the world like the Easter bonnet of a giantess.

A wide thoroughfare, the Hauptallee, bisects the Prater. At one end rises the romantic Lusthaus where all betrothed couples must waltz to the strains of "The Blue Danube," as insurance for good luck in the future. At the other end lies the popular Trabrennplatz (trotting-race course), the Fun City, Sports Stadium and the big Ferris Wheel.

Vienna, urban, elegant capital that she undeniably is, identifies herself with the countryside by her inviolable love for the Wienerwald. This is bosky meadowland shaded here and there by immemorial trees. The feathery willow, the sturdy oak of dark burnished mitten-shaped leaves, the tall, shivering poplar, and the hugely girthed gnarled beech, revered in ancient pagan lore as trysting place of the Dryads, Nymphs and Satyrs.

The woodland encircles a greater part of the city and in summer its rustling leafage distills cool breezes from off the Danube to refresh all within the city purlieus, even to dwellers in the darkest of the narrow Gothic alleys, in the ancient section of Vienna built by the Babenbergs.

The Kahlenberg rises from a forest tract where rhebok and stag are hunted. Viennese consider this mountain the perfect retreat for a short holiday, the last outpost of Wienerwald before the fields are furrowed by a farmer's plow. Flower-pied fields and shadowy stands of deciduous trees mount Kahlenberg to form a natural park in which one can wander at will to pause a while and look away toward Vienna, to the green of Prater, or the white walls and verdegris-copper dome of the Hofburg pointed up by sunlight. Sharply defined is the tall, rapier-slim spire of St. Stephen's Cathedral. If the air is crystal clear the distant mountains can be glimpsed through the peristyle arches of Gloriette in the gardens of Schönbrunn.

On the crest of the Kahlenberg there is a marvelously situated restaurant poised as if for flight, as are so many mountain-borne buildings in Austria. Run by monks, it occupies one long wing of a monastery thrown out like an arm along the edge of a gorge. The Kahlen-bergkeller is an old wine house turned restaurant of the first class. Food is served either in a long room resembling the refectory of a monastery, which in a sense it is, or, if the weather is fine, on a long, arcaded terrace above the gorge. The food is famous here and the wine card will astound you by the number and variety of vintages listed. All the "little" and the "great" Austrian wines may be ordered by carafe or the bottle.

It is a memorable experience to sit on the terrace watching the lights come on in Vienna below in the Danube valley, while leisurely sipping some great vintage wine like deep golden, sparkling Brunner-strassler accompanied by its affinity, a delicacy called *kaserollen*, feather-light, individual cheese soufflés no larger than a gherkin-pickle. When ordering these cheese morsels, let it be a *double* order at least, for they are persuasive.

For a city so great of heart, its population unwaveringly devout Catholics, it is not surprising that Viennese will tell you, "The heart of Vienna lies in sanctity on the high altar of St. Stephen's."

When the old Romanesque church of St. Stephen was rebuilt in Gothic times the ancient West Front was preserved, being built into the new one, an act of piety unique at that time, a typically Viennese gesture. The Romanesque wall of "matched" red and purple-black ashlar, mottled and striated in bold strokes, has the effect of a Medieval tapestry hanging in massively molded folds and forming a partition behind which is revealed a fantastic world transcending reality, yet by its symbols revealing many links with the past. I stood at the entrance portal of the nave. Long, triangular rays cast by a blazing evening sun that slanted altarward through a forest of pillars spangled the incense-blue distances with flickering golden motes of dust until the atmosphere seemed alive with light vibrating from the strains of vesper music played on a hidden organ.

A wedding had taken place earlier. As I turned to leave the church I noticed an alcove chapel banked in white lilies and roses. I noticed, too, lying on the stones in front of a blue- and silver-robed Madonna, a pair of long white kid gloves, pristine gloves that had never felt the tug of searching fingers. Beside them lay a small, blue leather change purse, dropped unknowingly, I presumed, in the confusion of a departing bride and groom. I picked them up and laid purse and gloves at the feet of the gently smiling Madonna. As I did so I saw that this worldly offering to Mary Mother was not as odd as it might seem. For among votive offerings of jeweled pins, rings and so on, lay partially hidden in the folds of the Madonna's robe a pair of tortoise-shell side combs set with brilliants, tied together with a silver ribbon. I should love to know the story behind this furtive supplication. Somehow there was a tinge of finality, an end to escapade.

Outside in the twilight I regarded the South Tower of St. Stephen's. It is a rarity in ecclesiastical architecture. Begun in 1359, it took a century to complete. This widely praised symbol of Vienna is cele-brated as the most original of all the great cathedral towers of the Gothic period, surging upward, shimmering like a mighty jet of foun-tain water in unbroken ascent, tapering steadily from base to finial. The roof through which the steeple seems to pierce for freedom is ornamented with brightly glazed yellow and black tiles. The pattern of lozenges or dragon-scale tiles, featuring an immense double-headed Eagle of Austria in iridescent purple-green silver and black tiles seen also in old wood cuts of the 15th century, must have been then, as now, visible for many miles up and down the Danube.

Granted that Vienna is predominantly a city of wide promenades, spacious squares, parks, palaces and churches, there is still the Altstadt or Old Town, a quarter of deviously winding passages and alleys hardly eligible for even the courtesy title of streets. A complex tangle of cobbled *gassen* that repay wandering through to get a haunting picture of Vienna's ancient past. But there are some streets like vener-able Schönlaterngasse where the tall houses have witch-bonnet roofs and dormer windows set in tiers which appear to be sliding down the improbably steep pitch of black tiled roofs. Alt Universitätsplatz of Medieval memory, famed for periodic students' riots since 1200, smartened its house fronts in Renaissance and Baroque periods. The chief sight here is the lyrical Early Baroque façade of the Jesuiten-kirche, said to be haunted by the ghost of an old sexton who was strangled, on the morning of his one-hundredth birthday, by the bell rope he had maneuvered perfectly for eighty years. A charming church, the windows and door so placed in the front as to resemble a smiling face, is Zu den Neun Choren der Engel (The Nine Choirs of Angels). This church encroaches on a space where stands Am Hof. Here is ancient masonry where the Christmas Market, first established by the Babenberg dukes, is held at Christmastime.

Sonnenfelsgasse spurns to entertain houses erected later than the 14th century and has corresponding odors from bad drainage. Bäckerstrasse, on the other hand, is redolent of spices and the lovely, mouthwatering smell of freshly baked bread. Here are the bakeries and the old spice shops, spices from the wide world, so necessary to a nutmeg-flavored cream torte, or a cinnamon-sprinkled chocolate soufflé.

Walk down the Freyung to Schottenstift and see the permanent collection of the oldest paintings in Vienna, painted on iron, wood and ivory. Here, too, is the magnificently aloof Harrach Palace. Follow for a little way the Danube Canal where the musical Strauss family, all told fourteen in number, used to fish, loading their hooks in unison. Presently you come to the Ruprechtskirche, a church of venerable history where the interior walls and the floor blaze with all the colors of the rarest carpet out of Isfahan from the light that shines through the old painted glass windows.

Do not miss, in spite of war damage, Schwarzenbergplatz with its princely palace and houses of noble proportions lightly touched in sky-blue and gilt. And now to the Ringstrasse. Stand across from the Bristol Hotel. You are then in perfect position to see the over-all beauty of one of the most famous buildings in Vienna. The Staatsoper (State Opera House) often called the most beautiful opera house in the world. Designed by van der Null and Siccardsburg, the Opera House on the Ring was completed in 1860. Mozart's *Don Juan* was chosen for the gala opening. The splendid proportions of the building pleased the Viennese mightily. Here was the sweep and princely elegance, the grand air, a fitting addition to the architectural frame of their fair capital. The long loggia is embellished by statues of the

Nine Muses. The vestibule is a wonder of gold leaf burnished over sky-blue and ivory gesso. The soaring Grand Staircase is carpeted in crimson. Although greatly damaged by bombing, the Opera has been rebuilt and reopened, a harbinger of Vienna's future.

It was Maximilian I who originally founded the National Library. Later came the Great Hall classed as one of the largest rooms in the world devoted solely to housing books. The frescoes are painted with great power in the richest color by Daniel Gran. One million and a quarter bound books and nearly one hundred thousand papyri are so cleverly arranged that the bindings, brilliant cords and tassels of folios complement color in the painted ceilings.

By far my favorite church in Vienna is the Karlskirche. To me it is a masterpiece of architectural imagination, form, and proportion. During the year of the holocaust, when the most devastating plague that Vienna had ever endured claimed 70,000 souls, Emperor Charles VI made a vow to his patron saint, Charles Borromeo, protector against the plague, to build a church. Here we have a fusing of the two von Erlachs' brilliant talents. Johann Bernhard von Erlach, the father, prepared the designs. After his death in 1723 his son Josef Emanuel Fischer von Erlach directed the carrying out to the smallest detail of everything his father had planned. Set forward from the superbly articulated entrance porch are two triumphal columns. These columns act as sentinels, or a proscenium, to frame beauty in stone, to "present" the edifice to the visitor in a manner wholly different from any other known edifice. Reliefs modeled to perfection by Johan Straub and Jacob Schletterer, arranged spirally, depict the life of the martyr St. Charles. This church is one of the most compelling and independent *chef d'oeuvres*, not alone of Austrian, but of the entire European Baroque.

Vienna's Burg Theatre was built in 1888. The original theatre which it replaced had been rather sketchily improvised from a royal tennis court, nearly derelict from disuse, since the game of tennis brought from France had never caught on with the indolent or more equestrian-minded members of the Court Circle. The theatre at first was inadequate but intimate, and the story goes that actors had to shout their

KARLSKIRCHE
THE CORONATION CHURCH
VIENNA

lines to the echo in order to combat the incessant gossip among the fashionable box holders.

Most of the seats were handed down from one generation of courtiers to another, like the family jewels. The "Burg Theatre Style" of acting became synonymous throughout Europe for the grandeur of tragic drama. Students from afar, Prague, London and St. Petersburg, flocked to Vienna to enroll in classes conducted by the Burg Theatre luminaries. Empress Maria Theresia became an enthusiastic patron. She called it her Play House, in the sense not of play acting but of a place for relaxation.

One night during a performance of *Oberon and Titania* the Empress leaned from the royal box to announce the birth of a son to the Crown Prince Leopold of Tuscany, calling out to the audience in that broad Viennese accent the Habsburgs affected, "Children, my Poldi has a *boy!*"

In April 1945 the interior of the Burg Theatre was gutted by fire that started when the victorious Russian Army had installed a camp kitchen on the stage. Today the theatre has again opened its doors to present Classic German drama to the general public.

During the Baroque period the Vienna nobility formed a habit of running off to the country outside of the town walls to picnic, which included dancing and "release to love." Alfresco dalliance was the rage. The craze for pastoral pleasures spread, with the result that in addition to sumptuous town palaces, each family of any prominence had also to own a country mansion. Not a farm manor, but a villa of architectural eminence to glorify the nobleman's name and station.

Like all cities Vienna gradually spread out to encroach upon rural environs. Some houses have disappeared today; the surviving ones with their tree-embowered, flower-strewn grounds form oases of green in the town. Palais Schwarzenberg is identified by its gilded copper dome and pillared demilune wings.

The Lower Belvedere is a one-story pavilion. After it had been finished, Prince Eugen of Savoy found himself left with a wealth of grandiose ideas he had been unable to utilize. He immediately decided to build a new palace. This is the Upper Belvedere, and in it the architect Lucas von Hildebrand in 1721 created his masterpiece. This tremendously spacious pavilion was intended less for living than for receptions and festivals. Like some romantic dream, the palace with its shimmering reflections in lily ponds, goldfish pools, lagoons, fountains and acres of Venetian mirrors seems to float unreal and ethereal between the surface of water and sky. The panorama of Vienna viewed from the upper terrace of Belvedere, the silver and white city dominated by St. Stephen's steeple of stone lace, harmoniously sustains the dream sequence.

The interior of the Upper Belvedere Palace seems to me to be a gigantic cabinet wherein to display *objets d'art* of crystal, gold and crimson, the walls enlivened by intricate Cuvilliés scrolls in burnished gold and silver leaf. Rococo ornament is so rampant at Belvedere that it twangs. Room after room is hung with huge canvases of the hunt, not so much of the actual sport as of groups of huntsmen, all friends of the prince, sitting under trees or assisting ladies in shepherdess kirtles to wade in a brook. A military portrait of Prince Eugen mounted on a pure white Lipizzaner stallion, charging through clouds of black cannon smoke, is the high point of a scarlet and white breakfast room. The frame is bizarre but, complementing the lusty power of the picture, absolutely right for this room. It is composed of horns from mountain deer (rhebok) more delicate in line than stag antlers, rubbed with gold dust and lacquered, the points intertwining to form filigree, backed by Venetian mirrors smoky with age.

Walking along the Opernring to Burgring, the agreeable width of boulevards and open park spaces allows the sky to play its part in the urban scene unhindered. The dome of luminous blue, perhaps mottled with high-piled white clouds, forms a perfect arch to offset the Hofburg, that immense acreage of white walls garlanded with carved fruit and ornamented with over-life-size statues of classic deities and personages prominent in Austria's history. Some persons find it a cold, reserved frontage; actually it is not one building but a series of loosely connected frontages. But to me the gleaming stone exterior acts as a highly embellished screen concealing from the outer world a far more beautiful interior.

Above staircases winding into realms of gilt and crystal, sportive mythological creatures reveal color and detail that can be fully appreciated only in rooms of such thundering scale—a succession of gilded chambers, damask-hung apartments and a ballroom where from the frescoed ceilings hang fantastically conceived luster flowers, so arranged as to hold thousands of candles. It is when these candles are lighted that the dream world seems to spring to life, the elegant aristocracy once more amusing itself at cards or dancing to the sound of harp and violins. This Austrian Baroque, this fashion for sumptuous display which Austria gave to the world, here reaches heights seldom attained by architect, painter or sculptor. The style Baroque is here exemplified as the harmony of pleasing color and sweeping line, of luminous surfaces upon which sunlight or the light of candles plays as lightly as sensitive fingers upon the strings of a harpsichord. Surely this is the art and architecture for release of the spirit.

As an edifice to command attention the Hofburg is placed in its open quadrangle at exactly the right distance to hold one's attention for study of the whole architectural conception. One's eyes focus unwaveringly, hold in exquisite equilibrium the diverse elements of this Austrian Baroque prospect.

Vienna is particularly happy in its impressive number of museums, housing all sorts of treasures of arts and sciences. Indeed the art collections and archives seem inexhaustible. The Austrian's love and understanding of art have created permanent collections that defy cataloguing, hence must be seen.

Among the brightest stars are the Albertina Collection and the world renowned Czernin collection of paintings, sculpture, intaglios and jeweled *objets d'art*, which has now been dispersed among smaller museums, the Stadtmuseum and the Natural History Museum.

Among the palace-museums, Palais Questenberg gloriously fills the eye with its extensive Baroque frontage engaging eighteen windows across, arranged in diminuendo tiers so that the façade achieves a fascinating perspective in height, not alone a curiosity but an architectural *deceite*. I like the bold accent of its double entrance portals, surmounted by a frieze of Satyrs in hot pursuit of Bacchantes stripped for action.

The façade of Palais Fürstenberg is unusually graceful, displaying a pair of delicately sculptured heraldic grayhounds poised in arrested motion amid branches of oak above the central carriage portal. The most splendid of all these private palaces is Palais Kinsky, built in 1720 by Lucas von Hildebrand for Count Wierick Philip Daun. Perfectly proportioned for the narrow plot it occupies, the façade is sumptuous without being in any way overelaborate. A supreme repose seems to dwell about this building, like a notoriously beautiful woman who, when entering a room full of appraising eyes, lifts her chin a shade higher, lowers her eyelids, smiles slightly at the corners of her mouth, and quietly challenges anyone to find a flaw. The *bombé* or undulating line of roof balustrade is conceived in the highest beauty of Rococo taste, enriched at intervals by scroll escutcheons supporting flaming urns. The urns were modeled by Akzent, who also wielded his mallet and chisel with arresting drama in the four groups called *"Herkules-statuen"* (Hercules rending limb from limb four different wild beasts) that flank the two massive gateways to the Parade Ground Quadrangle of the Hofburg, where state ceremonies and military maneuvers were held.

All of these palaces may be visited, the interiors a bewildering array of corridors, galleries and apartments gleaming in white, silver-gilt, porcelain, crystal, variegated marbles and all colors of the spectrum in velvets, damasks, robustly imagined frescoes and painted ceilings. Perhaps most memorable when one has left the shimmering splendors of these palace-museums are the *ofen*, the characteristic Austrian porcelain tile-stoves. Some of these stoves are ornate in elegant Chinoiserie and Rococo taste.

If one is visiting the Palace of Schönbrunn for the first time, an entire day should be set aside. Meander through gardens, stable-close, conservatories, garden houses. From the terrace enjoy the sweeping panorama of the Gloriette, the peristyle set piece designed to frame arched vignettes of the countryside. Vienna lying silver, white, gold and green in its shallow bowl of contentment beside the bronze-rilled waters of the historic Danube.

The vast park of Schönbrunn, lying in the immediate outskirts of Vienna, was laid out in 1706 by Jean Trehet, a noted French garden architect and the favorite pupil of Le Nôtre, who designed the renowned gardens of Versailles. Trehet welded urban and suburban garden motifs to satisfy all tastes during a period when the most sophisticated French taste in all things pertaining to the aristocratic way of life was not only fashionable but nearly compulsory for members of the Austrian court circle.

Palace and gardens are open to visitors seven days a week. The frontage of the palace, viewed from the Gloriette, extends to an improbable length, a five-story structure embracing thirty-eight windows across, and as white as bleached bone. Schönbrunn appears immense, but Fischer von Erlach the Elder had envisaged a building of even vaster dimensions, far more grandiose in frontal ornamentation. It was to outclass Versailles not only in size but, designed to be situated on a hilltop, it would have greatly surpassed it in artistic domination of the landscape. The palace was begun in 1696 after von Erlach's plan, albeit greatly reduced in size. The interior decoration of brilliantly conceived though delicate tracery, ceilings, and robust caryatid figures supporting cornices and columns was not finished, however, until 1780.

The palace embraces an endless series of great rooms for audiences and receptions, small rooms, tiny closets or "retiring rooms," and ballrooms of such scale that the imagination staggers. Many of the rooms are extremely beautiful in Rococo style, still many others are dull, even dreary, the walls and fabrics for curtains and upholstery drab in color, the furniture heavy.

World renowned is the Salon aux Singes where hundreds of grinning monkeys clamber on trellises and swing from the branches of gold trees limned on a dark-red lacquer ground, so dark in fact as to appear a luminous black. This curiously shaped room is a blunted ellipse. A poignant aura hovers about the Salon aux Singes because of its dramatic association with the unhappy young Duc de Reichstadt.

In Rostand's drama *L'Aiglon* is a scene which is said to have in reality taken place in this room. The boy, wracked by the fires of rapid consumption, is driven to hysterical frenzy by the taunts of the unsympathetic Imperial Chancellor Prince Metternich, who to break the boy's spirit points to a mirror evoking a long shadowy procession of mad Habsburg ancestors. The prince seizes a lighted candelabrum and hurls it, shattering the writhing faces in the glass.

Even in an era when large houses for royalty, nobles and rich commoner alike were temples to "the spacious days of delight and delusion," this palace was considered gigantic. It flaunted Habsburg pre-eminence to the tune of one thousand four hundred and forty rooms (one hundred and thirty-nine of them kitchens) and sixty staircases. There were over fifty State Apartments of from ten to sixteen rooms, as well as "nurseries" for palace dogs, and a long room containing one hundred tables complete with gear for valeting where an army of ladies' maids and valets were in attendance around the clock.

The apartments of Empress Elizabeth are in direct contrast to those occupied by Empress Maria Theresia, which were full of Rococo gilt and crystal, ceremonial paintings and dark damasks. Elizabeth chose a series of not overly large rooms overlooking the great turnabout for coaches in front of the Imperial stables. She liked cascading muslin or dotted Swiss curtains and gay, spring-flower English chintzes. A court functionary chronicling events writes that when he was received by the Empress in the morning she would invariably be sitting in her window over morning coffee watching her Irish hunters and carriage horses put to the canter or the trot in the quadrangle below.

In the reception rooms there are many interesting examples of *Österreichisches Rokoko*, the nearest to an individual expression of Rococo furniture designed by Austrian craftsmen. I find that graceful boldness in the carving of fringed silk swags, acanthus leaves, wheatheads and shells lends flowing line to the curvilinear freedom of the frames of the furniture.

The room known as the Kleine Galerie (Little Gallery) acts as a delicately articulated antechamber, a kind of foyer to the Rococo splendors of the Grosse Galerie (Great Gallery). Designed by Nikolas Paccassi, these were the favorite rooms of Empress Maria Theresia for entertaining foreign ambassadors and personages of high rank. The parquet floors from Nancy in France are superb in basket weave, employing every shade of gold-colored wood. The ceiling evokes the four seasons, painted delicately in pastel colors in the small gallery and strongly colored in emphatic Italian bravura in the large one.

Lunch is served visitors to Schönbrunn in a restaurant occupying a large room overlooking the Fountain Garden on the first floor of the palace. The *Wienerschnitzel Nature*, veal steak sautéed in parsley butter partnered by tiny, soufflé-like almond and potato-flour pancakes, is a specialty.

A pleasant walk after luncheon is to the Royal Stables. By this gesture in stately Baroque architecture, pleasantly lightened with ebullient Rococo overtones, Lukas von Hildebrand shot his finest arrow. He repeatedly referred to his completed buildings as "an arrow from my quiver, Imagination." In style somewhat resembling his National Library and Spanish Riding School in Vienna, the stables seem to me less grand but infinitely more winning as evocative architecture. They are haunted by ghosts of long-dead Lipizzaner stallions whose resounding names—Robustier, Saladinmond, Goldener Kavalier, Empyrean, Lothario and Koenig von Donau—are lettered in gold on white marble plaques hung in the tack room of the stable. These milk-white horses, so it is reported by caretakers, are heard at night pawing the floor of the carved, gilded and black lacquer columned stalls, to be gentled by the soft voices of long-dead Brandenburg grooms. Once nine hundred horses were stabled here. When I walked through the stables in September 1955, there were only twelve horses retained for show purposes. A collection, rare today, of every conceivable kind of equipage is on view. Ponderous state coaches display a welter of gold carving, crystal windows and "mythology rampant" painted on doors and side panels. A set of four "opera chaises," a bijou closed-carriage without wheels, rather like a sedan chair, the domed top rising high to accommodate the three-foot "Versailles coiffures" and sprouting from a crystal rose panache of ostrich plumes to rival those adorning the wig of a court beauty inside. Harnesses of vermilion Cordovan leather, tricked out in silver, gold or jeweled garniture, glint like the spoils of battle looted by a conqueror from some Rajah of Ind. Saddles, gifts of nobles currying favor, have always been the "present paramount" for royal persons to exchange. Here the silver, gold, bronze and jewel-mounted saddles fill the eye. Even an iron filigree-lattice saddle slung over citron-yellow felt drips like rainfall with crystal and silver tinsel fringe. Perhaps the richest, certainly the most uncommon of all, is a saddle, gift of a Manchu emperor to Maria Theresia. The leather is of blue, green, purple and bronze, as iridescent as a kingfisher's wing. The pommel is a silver cup fashioned like an imperial Phoenix to hold largess for a scattering to the populace.

The Spanish Riding School in Vienna, actually a part of the Hofburg "environs," is an institution such as appears nowhere else in the world. Its whole inception is completely unique. The beautifully articulated *bombé* front, pierced by a boldly scaled entrance portal, supports sculptured groups of curveting Lipizzaner stallions. This is pure theatre at its best. Fischer von Erlach was the architect. It was as much a labor of love as a commission for gain, for he was an ardent horseman and enthusiastic supporter of the *Haute École de Dressage*, the complicated elegance of training, the high school method of teaching horses to perform in a ring for spectacle.

The interior of the building is a large oval arena surrounded by a high columned promenade, above which extends around the arena a wide gallery lighted by tall arched windows under a richly stuccoed covered ceilings. Everywhere is white upon white upon white, in plaster, painted wood and marble, startlingly accented by the red-brown earth of the riding ring which in turn reflects upward into the pendants of immense crystal chandeliers. The stark white of architectural detail is identical with the faultlessly groomed hides of the Lipizzaner stallions themselves. Startlingly attractive is the contrast of sepia and the black uniforms of the riders. In the great days when the sovereigns appeared at the high noon *matinée* performance attended by members of the court, the spectacle of the brilliantly colored dresses of the ladies and the fur-trimmed uniforms of swank cavalry officers must have been splendid indeed. There are any number of large paintings hanging in various retiring rooms to prove it. Paintings in oil and pastel, and steel engravings over seventy-odd years attest to the changing fashions of just this scene. In representations of great evening galas that were held at the Spanish Riding School the change in court fashions and in jewels is marked down for history.

CAPRIOLE.
SPANISH RIDING SCHOOL
VIENNA

One drawing in charcoal is a spirited representation by Aubry of the Greek statesman and philosopher Xenophon, who wrote the earliest book on riding preserved (about 44 B.C.). It shows him astride a spirited Cappadocian-Eumenes black stallion. It was Xenophon who laid down rules for training horses that are today employed to the letter in the curriculum of the Spanish Riding School.

Each morning at half-past eleven o'clock the Lipizzaner horses perform. I watched their "Croupade," when the horse leaps into the air, all four feet off the ground; the graceful "Levade"; the "Piaffe"; the "Courbette," when the stallion waltzes on his hind legs; and the exciting "Lacade" when he paws the air, shakes his head, mane flying, and leaps upward like a Pegasus taking wing. Leaving the building, I carefully read Xenophon's wonderfully revealing sentence, a motto on the margin of the drawing: *Something forced, not understood, is never beautiful, and would be, as Simon of Athens already says, as if we tried to force a dancer to spring about by using whips and thorns; in this way both the human being and the horse are hideous rather than beautiful.*

At Wels in Lower Austria where the Lipizzaner horses have been in training for their reappearance in Vienna, I was told that it was two hundred years ago when Lipizzaners were first taught their "ritual" of training. Spurs are never used. The principal aid is the modulated voice of the rider.

And now we come to the all-important subject of hotels and restaurants in Vienna. Immensely important because every Viennese is so justifiably proud of "Vienna cuisine." In Sacher's Hotel there is one of the truly great restaurants of the world. "Sacher's dining room," as the original owner and proprietor Frau Sacher chose to call it, will be found in the small square directly opposite the rear entrance of the Opera House. While the rooms at Sacher's Hotel are agreeable if a shade overpowering in summer, due to heavily ornate Franz Josef style trappings, it is the food that reigns supreme. *Sacher-Torte*, a delicately flavored chocolate pastry, has a charmed history. In 1832 Prince Metternich was served a *torte*, evolved especially for the epicurean chancellor by a young cookery pupil named Sacher. The Prince is said to have eaten a whole *torte* (intended to serve six persons) and asked that the same pastry should henceforth be supplied him daily at his residence. *Sacher-Torte*, which has since then blazed a trail across the world, is regarded as a symbol of sophisticated taste. This Viennese delicacy is served at the hotel at all times and sent by air to discriminating restaurants in London, Washington and New York.

The Lindenkeller in the Old Quarter of Rotenturmstrasse (Red Tower Street) lies in the shadow of the Old Fortress, in an angle of the Medieval walls of Vienna. In summer one dines in a garden which is walled on two sides by antique stone. There are also four large rooms in which to dine. Try the *Gefüllte Kalbsbrust* and *Kalbshaxe*

LIPIZZAN STALLION VIENNA.

(stuffed veal breast and knuckle, respectively). Rhine salmon, that delicious fish which was "nearly a war casualty," is slowly creeping, or swimming, back into the kitchens of restaurants famous for seafood —Urbani Keller at Am Hof 12, for example. Broiled with dill-flavored butter, accompanied by chilled beetroot and cucumber salad dressed with white wine, this is an epicurean dish. Here at Urbani Keller you will eat from heavy earthenware dishes, huge in circumference, the good old Biedermeier Vienna crockery. Remember that it was the

Roman satiric poet Caius Lucilius, a notable trencherman, who wrote: *One, bidding me to a banquet, killed me with silver hunger, serving famished dishes. And in wrath I spoke amid the silver sheen of famine: "Where is the plenty of my earthenware dishes?"*

When walking around the streets of Vienna searching out some particular restaurant, you will do well to remember that certain cities have their characteristic scents, but if we cultivated our noses we should be able to identify particular localities and even in time individual streets. Walking up and down the streets in the Domplatz area, or in the Altstadt along the Danube, you will realize this is preeminently a "cooking for the very love of eating" city. Drifting around corners of narrow *gassen,* the clean hunger-making smell of baking wheaten or rye bread is pointed up by the "warm brown taste" of baking meats wafted on the eddying breeze. Near the lively Bauernmarkt, where farmers and vintners eat more succulently at open air or glass-screened taverns, issues the musty tang of hops, the winy odor of grapes. The pastry and confectionery center is Singerstrasse, with its richly provocative smell of chocolate, the cloying sweet vanilla and all the spices that so memorably spike the famous Vienna *torten* and strudels. As I have done times out of mind, go your next walk for your nose's sake. Your experience may be on a par with a venture into the fourth dimension.

The Bristol Hotel situated in the Opernring directly across from the Kärntnerstrasse entrance to the Opera House has long been highly regarded by travelers, due to its central position. Kärntnerstrasse is the principal shopping street, where you will encounter the utmost in courtesy, and the highest quality in satisfyingly "different" wares. Discover for yourself the enjoyment of prowling the shops in Vienna for leather, silks, haberdashery, porcelains, and books beautifully illustrated in color on a variety of intriguing subjects.

Of all the hotels in the city I am partial to the Kranz-Ambassador, certainly agreeably central to shops and theatres, parks, museums and palaces, with its main entrance tucked away in quiet Raphael Donner Platz where the handsome bronze fountain of the Four Rivers by Baroque sculptor Donner occupies the center of the square. Rooms here are delightful, airy and charmingly appointed, and the food of Austrian renown. The smartest restaurant as a meeting place to gossip, famous for its food as well, is the Drei Husaren (The Three Hussars) in Annagasse.

Go out to lunch on the Kahlenberg or to Grinzing "above Vienna" as everyone describes it. But do not hurry. Be prepared to stay on until midnight or later, and then in the garden of perhaps Goldener Glocken (The Golden Bells) at Grinzing take your last glass of *heuriger*—"new wine," light, sweet, refreshing, but mortally heady if one is not wary. Drive back to Vienna by way of Cobenzl. Stop at any one of the open-late cafés or inns for a dish of *käseplatte*—cheese and eggs, a kind of flat pancake that is a wonderful "after-a-party bracer-upper." Gaze off to the horizon. Never will any city have looked more lovely, ethereal in the false dawn scarves of mist, than Vienna seen from the heights of Cobenzl or Kahlenberg. A beckoning place of quiet comfort, welcoming you for a good long sleep and more fun later on. It is small wonder that when Viennese get together at a country inn, or a restaurant near the ancient walls, they lift glasses to clink the old songs of *"Wien-Wien-Wien."*

Chapter 13

BURGENLAND BREATHES OF THE SOUTH, MAJESTIC STILLNESS OF ETERNAL NOON

L ONG, narrow, predominantly fertile, the Province of Burgenland extends eastward and southward along the Hungarian marches. A secretive, ancient border-country, its history romantic as that of the open, windswept Magyar steppes, it is smilingly referred to by herdsmen as "my brother the *puszta*." I have talked to many an Austrian who says this is his favorite province for a "get-away-from-it-all" summer holiday. "It is another world," they say, their eyes veiled with remembering. "In the summer we go to Mörbisch and Rust on Neusiedlersee to drink the great wines, as in winter we spend a holiday at St. Anton or Kitzbühel for the best in winter sports."

While the people of Burgenland toil early and late in the fruit orchards and vineyards, or fish with curiously archaic, hugely circular seines and long dragnets of braided horsehair in the Neusiedlersee, an air of timelessness, of unhurried, lazy contentment prevails everywhere that I have been in the province.

This territory is sharply divided into three portions completely different one from the other. The foothills of the Alps rise as the Leitha Mountains. The undulating fields of grain and farmlands produce in great variety and profusion fruits and vegetables for the markets of Vienna and towns situated in the unproductive Alpine reaches. The rich black soil gives abundantly of wheat and corn, barley and maize, in a wide belt of sun-drenched grain extending to the plains of bronze-red grass where once the ocean rolled.

The singular apartness of Burgenland stems from its nearness to Hungary. On every side I find evidence of how deeply ingrained is their nomadic origin in the traditions of the Burgenlanders. Here the blood of the Magyar clearly shows in physical characteristics in all but the mountainous part of the province. The men have broad faces, high, sharply defined cheekbones, narrow gray or black eyes tipped up at the outside corners, the profile either slightly flattened or the true Magyar look of a watchful eagle, the arched nose long and thin.

Women of Burgenland, for the most part tall, broad-hipped, famous for producing sturdy offspring in quantity, resemble more in features and coloring the fair-haired, brown or blue-eyed type of Austrian one comes to know so well while traveling through the nine provinces. Loosely braided plaits of honey-blond hair are wound about the heads of young girls, ending in giddy flyaway loops over the ears. A bright patterned gingham or silk bodice, cut with a wide flaring peplum, is buttoned high up under the chin with fanciful painted china, turquoise-matrix or rose-quartz buttons. Older women from the mountain districts wear a high-crowned beaver "top hat" ornamented variously with bands or loops of embroidered ribbon, and silk bodices edged in fringe or tassels. To fasten the bodice, brooches in the form of china plaques the size of a silver dollar, painted with birds and bouquets of flowers, are pinned closely in a straight line from waist to chin.

The women of Mörbisch derive their costume from ancient Magyar traditions. A kerchief of black silk covers the head, wound to frame the face severely like a Medieval wimple. Long fringed ends cross under the chin to float behind, rustling like the sound of a raven unfurling its wings. The skirt of ribbed black silk is ankle length cut generously full, totally unadorned and serving as background for a voluminous apron of white linen inset with appliqués of heavy white lace. To a somewhat somber costume this vitality of patterned white flowers and scrolls lends a touch of elegance. The design on the apron may be "the immortal vine," hung with huge clusters of grapes. Perhaps sunflowers with heavy heads, or strawberries being torn by rapacious starlings, symbolic of the constant menace to berry patches, cherry orchards and vineyards that causes the farmlands of Burgenland to be called "The Land of Scarecrows."

Under the grape arbors extending across the front of a farmhouse where I stopped, music from violin and *tamburizza* filled the air. Swarthy young men in baggy white breeches and dark-red jackets braided in green or blue, their thick black hair cut in a straight line above the eyebrows, partner the girls in a kind of breathless "sower's dance," an ancient measure where the girl is spun upon her toes hither and yon by her partner, a symbolic gesture as if he were scattering handfuls of wheat kernels into the furrows. This dance, I realized, would go on for a long time, probably until dancers and musicians alike were halted by exhaustion. The dance is exact, no lagging, no slighting the precise pattern. The wheat must be "sown," then "tended," which requires a good deal of panting, pawing and kissing, then "harvested" where the "sheaves," quite liable to be buxom, are "bound" (embraced) and hoisted to the backs of the young harvesters.

From my bench I surveyed a softly lighted tableau. The young married women were sitting decorously with the matriarchs. Over her black velvet bodice each woman wore her heirloom parure of Styrian jade. A choker or collarette, a brooch to pin a cross over the wearer's heart, and four wide bracelets. Set in silver of exquisite antique workmanship, the jade has a personal magic, an illusive quality, cloudy yet luminous, so sensitive to the changing play of light, in this case from candles, that one moment it glows black, changing to the burning green of Caucasian malachite as the light flickers.

At Gasthaus Goldene Krone, long after I had gone to bed in one of those built-in affairs with shutters against the night air, I could hear a sort of obbligato to the *tamburizza*, the high wild notes of a lonely, far-away gypsy violin. No violin strings on earth ever vibrate to passion as when the bow is drawn by the fingers of a Hungarian *zigeuner*.

The next morning I left Mörbisch, driving warily through flocks of gray geese tended by small boys armed with rattles on the end of a long goad, which they spun raucously. This was a prelude to the fortnightly market day solely for poultry. Roast goose stuffed with

267

mushrooms and served with sour cream and paprika hot potato salad is a grand dish of the Mörbisch district farmlands.

About a mile outside of town I came upon a gypsy camp. On a hillock of sharp green forage grass stood a tall pole, a pine tree at least twenty feet tall. Pendant from the scars of lopped-off branches, coagulated tears of amber resin convinced me that the camp had been but lately set up, because the gypsy children had not yet gathered these glittering resin "jewels" to make necklaces and talismans over which incantations for good fortune are whispered. I had before now encountered gypsy children hawking them along the roads. A group of improbably wild and dirty women, all bushy, tangled hair and raddled cheeks, were sprawled on blankets and vividly striped saddle bags around a smoking fire. A few horses with burr-stuck coats were tethered to some saplings. Strange, I thought, that no men were in evidence.

My interest here was the pine pole. At the base of the pole a low, widespread tent of ingeniously contrived patchwork was spread. From a few branches left intact at the top of the pole hung a heterogeneous collection of booty. A parrot in a bent and rusty cage yawked stridently. Strings of garlic, red peppers, sausages, surrounded a large chamber pot decorated in pink cabbage roses. A few sacks of unshelled walnuts, doubtless gathered along the banks of the River Raab where walnuts grow as large as lemons, clattered in the wind like castanets. Tanned skins of chamois, rhebok and red fox, a Magyar cloak of shaggy black goatskin, and pillow cases stuffed with goose down. Most seductive, not for personal use, I am sure, but rather to advertise that one could shop nowhere better than here, a peddler's tray of jewelry, ribbons, sleazy rayon shawls and flounced skirts, and a straw hat with a heron's plume. Grandest of all, and perhaps most incongruous, hanging by loops of ribbon, were a dozen or more pairs of women's French-heeled slippers of brightly colored leatherette, gaudy no end but somehow inexpressibly sly. Later on, during my travels through Burgenland and Lower Austria, I came upon other gypsy camps flaunting a tall pole variously hung with food, household utensils, trophies of the chase, in effect a perpetual open-air rummage sale.

I drove into a quiet, secret village with an engaging name—Minihof
—an abbreviation, I learned, of Mönchshof or Monk's Dwelling, for
in earlier times a pilgrimage hostelry was maintained here for the use
of pilgrims on their way to famous places of pilgrimage, such as
Frauenkirchen, Lockenhaus and Kloster Marienburg. For all the
cloistered calm of Minihof, I found myself considerably entertained
by an incident of the road.

Heralded by a sudden loud uproar, I witnessed a small boy of about
six years old being spanked along the road by an exasperated mother.
What particularly caught my eye was the youngster's rear elevation.
The coat-of-arms of Burgenland Province was emblazoned on the
back of his jacket. Against a yellow shield a fiery red eagle, tongue
protruding in defiance, wore a crown of gold Crusaders' crosses. The
wings outstretched, each pinion alert, this was a ponderous amount of
heraldry, it seemed to me, to plaster on the back of so small a boy,
no matter what his mischief. I learned from an older youth following
the culprit that this was Stani, a notorious runaway. He fared far
whenever wanderlust overtook him. This time Stani had decamped
in the middle of the night and had been found by a lorry driver from
Minihof wandering in the street of a nearby village across the border
of Lower Austria. In desperation his mother had recently taken a
festival banner bearing the arms of Burgenland, embroidered on it
Stani's name and village and his proclivities for wandering, then
stitched it to the only jacket the boy possessed. It appears that in his
last three adventurings this vivid advertisement of his extremely
juvenile delinquency had worked like a charm.

Around Pinkelfeld, a rust-yellow, cool olive-green and white village
where storks sleep standing on one leg guarding their nests built on
chimneys or the gable ends of steep black-wattle roofs, you will
encounter a charming, humorous people. "Burgenland is stork land,"
villagers will tell you, winking solemnly. "Look about you—thousands of storks, and," a smile widens, "thousands of fine babies." All
manner of curious superstitions prevail in the countryside roundabout.
In Oggau and Hornstein, if a girl is born in the spring, violets are put

into the oven to insure that during her first contact with the hot summer sun she will not get freckles.

On my way to Forchtenstein I passed along a road steeped in history and ancient legends. Across the Wulka Plain, relics of the early Stone Age attest to human progress. During the Bronze Age roadways for developing trade were blazed through impenetrable wilderness, and bridges were thrown across the gorges so numerous in the Leitha Mountain districts.

Bernsteinstrasse was a famous trading route of prehistoric times, centuries before the Christian era. Until the 12th century it was known as "The Precious Way," because of the rich caravans that passed along this broad, winding highway, carrying such treasures as olive-wood chests containing "tears of the sea"—the words of an old chronicle which thus described the honey-gold and dark red-violet amber from Byzantium and the Marmoran Sea that was used as both a form of princely currency and to set in gold as jewelry to deck some Madonna as a gift of expiation. The Counts of Mattersdorf and Forchtenstein gave such gifts of amber to the Madonna of Loretto in the Church of the Immaculate Conception. The entrance court has a soaring stone pillar supporting a statue of the Virgin dramatically silhouetted against the sky, supremely effective on a night when the heavens blaze with stars. When looking at a collection of church treasures in the magnificent Frauenkirchen Pilgrimage Church of the Assumption, I noticed that among the finest examples of the distinctive art of Burgenland were rarely lovely chalices, ewers and embroidered altar garnitures set with amber in all shades, from palest "sun shining through water," to deepest gold and red-violet.

I passed the heights of the Rosaliengebirge, a breeze on the lower slopes stirring the leaves to an undulant sea of color. As far as I could see, orchards stretched away. Orderly rows of cherry trees in full bloom, the paper-white petals etched against a webbing of crisp black branches, diminished in the distance. Apricot and peach trees tossed plumes of pale and deeper pink. Nature, I observed, had strewn color with a prodigious sweep. Swathes of flowering purple sage and wild blue lupins formed a background to the flowering fruit trees.

MAGYAR WELL SWEEPS
AND INEVITABLE CASTLE
BURGENLAND.

From far off in the plain I could see the Castle of Forchtenstein, its high piled walls and towers shining pale yellow and russet under the crisp black of inky-black tile roofs. This province of Burgenland owes its name—"The Land of Castles"—to its number of ancient castles. Many of them stem from 11th and 12th century fortresses, while others, like the great Esterházy Palace at Eisenstadt, is a resounding example of Austrian Baroque architecture.

As I drew nearer to the village of Forchtenstein, I noted that the castle today is in perfect repair. Every black tile on the roof is in place, the famous frescoed walls fresh in color. In the highest circular tower in the province hangs the deep-toned bell called Tota, to honor the sister of Bertram, Count of Mattersdorf. In 1200 this woman of Spanish origin was conceded to be peerless by all who beheld the splendor of her raven hair and alabaster skin. Troubadours from afar sang that her beauty had no equal throughout the world. A second brother of Tota's, called Simon, hung a bell in the tower to ring out each morning at sunrise and each evening at sunset the tidings of his sister's perpetual beauty. Today it still rings out. The legendary beauty of Tota is symbolized by the beauty of the flowering spring, the golden heat of poppy-strewn summer, autumn heavy with fruit, and the stillness of violet-silver winter.

Farms lie at the foot of the Rock of Forchtenstein. I wandered in the Friday market in the village. Stalls were piled high—the first early cherries, the small heads of fresh garden lettuce, perfect as a huge green rose, that are set for display in holes bored in a wooden wheel, in effect a "lazy Susan." Cauliflower, pyramids of strawberries, apricots, yellow and purple plums, reed baskets holding carrots, red and white onions, artichokes and bundles of extraordinarily long French beans. An assortment of cheeses varies from chalky-white goat's milk to a miniature mountain heap of lightly tossed curds as yellow as butter. Sprinkled with paprika or mixed with barley sugar and served with strawberries, curds are highly regarded. I felt as though I were surrounded by the immense still-life canvases of fruit and vegetables painted so magnificently by Flemish artists of the Renaissance.

I drove through lonely wastes. Grass, grass, grass, crackling, whispering, bending to the wind. Odd colors, too—livid green cut by swathes of purplish-blue grass dusted with a bloom like that seen on plums. As I drew nearer to the great marshes I noted that the color had turned strange and unpredictable. Reed cutters waded in the marshes, their brown canvas smocks bloused at the waist by wide bull's-hide belts studded with iron nailheads. A Medieval Pied Piper of Hamlin air is lent by pointed caps pulled low over the eyes as the men work cutting the reeds, lashing them into immense bundles, to float on the surface of this shallow waterland.

At sunset I beheld a transformation scene in this waste of reeds. The darkened lake reflected on its surface red and copper lights. An outer chain of copper-gleaming pools lay beneath low-lying indigo clouds. In a flash a blood-red sun split the horizon in a final burst of power, edging the clouds with gold and green vaporous light. For an instant this brazen spectacle held; then across the fiery rays thousands of white herons rose. Higher they flew, white plumage magically turned to crimson and gold, and as I watched, the sun sank, dying among the distant reeds, the high winging herons mere specks of violet against the darkening amber sky.

Through vineyards trailing every conceivable shade of green I passed a group of deeply sun-browned men. I recognized them as vine-dressers by their leather aprons and capes stained matrix green by the copper sulphate used to spray the vines. The wine district of Friedrichshof and Landsee spreads far and wide, the vineyards mingling with the farmlands around Edmundshof and the wheat fields encircling Eisenstadt. During the festivals in honor of Haydn in the historic Haydn Hall, a flat cake called Haydnbröt, favorite of the master, prepared of wheaten flour flavored with caraway seeds, angelica and sage, is sold from carts drawn by a team of mastiffs, as was the custom in Haydn's day.

Since Early Medieval times the banner of Esterházy has blazed against the sky of Burgenland province. The great Italian Renaissance palace of the Esterházy, at Eisenstadt, erected in the 17th century on the foundations of a Medieval fortress, is a dark barracks. Now its rooms are shadowed in dusty grandeur. A galaxy of hugely scaled terra-cotta portrait busts of long-dead Esterházys and Hungarian kings since earliest tribal days of Avars and Magyars add confusion to the pillared façade, the columns copied from those of the Parthenon in Athens. Social brilliance unrivaled in history, entertainments on a scale that will never be seen again, were the métier of the Esterházy breed. As late as 1929, balls and banquets of such staggering splendor were given here that every item of costume and jewels worn by the ladies, food served, and diversions of originality were recorded in the newspapers in the fashionable capitals of the world.

The Esterházy Palace presents its best face to the classic garden, evoking visions of Roman marbles and cypress allées in Tuscany. Terraces descend to fountains, to "tapestries" of parterre in the formalized mood of Le Nôtre, to grottoes latticed in sun and shadow, until the eyes become exhausted discovering new beauties of garden contrivance long before one's legs tire of walking. Esterházy Park extends to the largest private game preserve in Austria, a maze of leafy rides and grassy clearings stocked with all manner of game including the uncommonly vicious wild boars from Poland. This marvel, in its heyday, was the talk of world sportsmen. So rare a treat as broiled boar steak is still called *Eber Esterházy*. Invitations to the great shooting parties held by the Esterházy were framed as collectors' items, for they were painted in scenes of the hunt by famous artists on the ivory-yellow dressed skin of the small wild pig called peccary. Fifty years ago brown bears from the Carpathian Mountains in Rumania were hunted in this preserve. The breed of ruddy-brown bear that in times past used to wander in scattered groups, called "families," down into Austria from their cave fastnesses in the Carpathian Mountains is now nearly extinct. It was the cubs of this breed that hunters caught, selling them to mountebanks who trained them to perform tricks—the famous dancing bears celebrated down the centuries for slyness, mimicry of human antics, and the clumsy comicality of the traditional clown. The historic Nibelung of Eferding on the Danube, an historic race worshiping Nature and its creatures, made companions of bears, believing them to be forest deities.

Every year reports are circulated among hunting enthusiasts that bears from Yugoslavia have wandered into the forests of Carinthia. Bad Villach and Eisenkappel are centers for shoots. Mountaineer guides in this region call a Yugoslav bear *schwefelkopf*—because, they say, "Its head is full of brimstone."

I spent a night in Weiden. Ochre-yellow is the earth under the vines in this region. Ochre-yellow is washed over the plaster under the sloping dark-brown roofs of the houses and long sheds where stand the wine presses. The golden quiet of wine-drinking time, when tending the vines is done, enveloped the towns and the vineyards. I drank Rulander and Welschriesling. Another famous vintage is Blaufränkisch-Venus. It is told, even sung to the clinking of glasses in rhythm, that Venus, tired of her diet of lettuce and ambrosia with a beaker of Olympian dew, leaned out from her cloud bower, espied a wedding ceremony here and caught up from the bridal table a flask of golden Rusterwein which trailed ribbons of gold and a spray of red poppies.

At the foot of glowering Geschriebenstein an unfrequented road leads to a ravine. Buried deep in forest greenery lies the Castle of Lockenhaus, stronghold of the Knights Templar dating from 1200. A stone keep, the walls fourteen feet thick, rises above the Gothic Knights Hall, an arch-vaulted chamber of soaring proportions. Through a horrific act of treachery whereby three score knights were massacred while at prayer, the Templars lost the castle. Forever after, this has been called "the bloody hall of blasphemy." The altar stones are still streaked with dark-brown stains. Knights in tabards of the Templars still haunt the castle. Whenever this visitation occurs the bloodstains weep and a reek of carrion pervades the Gothic Hall.

A winding road near Strem traverses for miles upland and lowland country, undulant as ocean swell. Here the road is bordered by groves of acacia trees. Farther on, almond trees grow in soil of silvery pink. Umber and blue clay wastes appear where no herbage thrives. Then the eye catches the ochre-yellow earth where grapes mature.

I drove over a dusty white road near the Hungarian-speaking village of Oberwart. A sallow-faced herdsman, his sooty black hair hanging in tight braids from beneath the upturned brim of his *cziskos* hat, sat straight in the saddle, regarding me warily. The wind stirred the heavy folds of his white wool cloak, the hanging sleeves and wide, triangular collar embroidered in a design of eagles and running horses. The herd numbered thousands. As far as my eye could see, streams of cream-colored and black and white cattle were being driven to the drinking wells.

The churches hereabouts often stand on wooded hills or crags of rock surrounded by castellated walls, presenting a picture of a small fortress, even though rising from this defensive wall is a spire topped by a cross. This religious seclusion was necessary during the time of Turkish invasions, for these Janizaries and Mamelukes were ravishers and marauders who held nothing outside of Islam sacred. Charlemagne, defeating the Avars in 800 A.D., pursued them along these southernly roads. Centuries later, the retreating Turkish soldiers were drowned by the thousands in the heron marshes before they reached the blue clay roads, widened by the Romans, that lead to Kittsee.

In the region of Bernstein and Schlaining and Landsee, Burgenland lives up to its name in resounding manner. Everywhere castles rise. Most of these are ancient, Early Gothic, Medieval, or rebuilt later in Baroque style on early foundations. There are a few magnificent pure Austrian Baroque *châteaux* such as Kittsee.

The plain to the north of Neusiedler Lake has always been a region of vast estates situated in the midst of dairy farms of the feudal land-owners—Batthyány, Esterházy, Daun-Kinsky, Erdödy and the "cloth of gold" Questenbergs. This *"nom de richesse"* was gained because members of the family always appeared at a court function or whenever receiving at their own residences resplendent in sumptuously bejeweled cloth of gold.

Kittsee was designed in "high" Baroque that is unblushingly ornate, probably by Lucas von Hildebrand who, with Maulpertsch and Fischer von Erlach, is known to have designed many of these great country houses. The plan is a wide sprawling mansion of ivory-white stone. Set in heavily foliaged gardens, the acacia walks surrounding "Diana's Bath" are splendid. The entrance porch is an expression of architectural character unique for its massive male and female cary-atids, eight in number, supporting arches of a terrace where balus-trades of richly scrolled ironwork are signed by Künner, ironmaster of Vienna.

The interior of Kittsee has the usual arrangement for a house of this style. Enfilades of reception rooms, painted and gilded galleries alternating with the *"petit salon"* so much in vogue in the 17th cen-tury for withdrawal of guests to play cards, gossip or arrange assignations.

Nothing could be in greater contrast to Kittsee than Burg Bern-stein near Edlitz. Visitors may stay in this castle. There are eleven rooms with bathrooms, and meals are served. Bernstein was built at the end of the 12th century. Situated on a commanding rock, a garden fragrant with syringa and roses is hidden from sight behind high bastion walls until one enters under the portcullis. There is a banquet hall on the first floor, its panel-vaulted roof richly painted, the stucco work remarkable for fluidly sculptured scenes from Greek mythol-ogy. A torture chamber containing all the devices to wring truth from unhappy victims "put to the rack" has the usual fascination for guests of the castle or for casual visitors, particularly when they are shown the sword that was used in the last execution of a murderer described as "truncated with visible loss of blood" in 1842.

Catherine Frescobaldi, even before her demise, was known to be pale as a ghost, her beauty of skeletal slenderness. She was myste-riously poisoned here in the 15th century. Now, dressed in "white samite coiffed and hennined," she roams at will through Castle Bern-stein. It is told that an elderly woman guest, avid for a fourth at bridge, accosted a tall woman—a stranger to her—whom she thought rather oddly dressed. Sputtering at what she thought crass rudeness, the woman told this tale at dinner. "Shocking manners. She did not answer me. She walked—well—I could have sworn she walked right through the stone wall."

I visited Burg Schlaining and found it still wrapped in its romantic past. History swirls lazily through the vaulted passages, for life is unhurried here, a stillness of listening "all the world away" remote on a high wooded rock. The Tauchenbach roars in tumult at the foot, forming a natural moat where fish leap and woodcock, snipe and quail flutter in the reedy brake. Built in the 13th century by the Counts of Güssing, the frescoed library houses a great deal of inter-

SPIKE TEAM
CASTLE SCHLAINING
BURGENLAND

esting lore concerning its tempestuous history, accumulated by the family of Batthyány, owners of the castle since 1648. All this is now on view, along with magnificent armor and heraldic accouterment used in tourney and at court. The dungeon is known as the "False Tribunal"—false accusations, safe conducts repudiated, promises broken, until, as an old chronicle has it, "the sound issuing from those damp stones is the sibilant treachery of the Judas kiss."

Chapter 14

LIKE CERES IN THE ROMAN *MASQUE OF SEASONS* SWITZERLAND, WALLED BY FRONTIERS, PRESENTS FOUR FACES

DURING my stay in Vienna while waiting to journey during the autumn vintage through my favorite of all Austrian provinces, Burgenland, I met a Swiss friend from St. Gallen. He suggested that later I meet him in Liechtenstein where he was flying next day. "After all," he said, "you have never been in Liechtenstein. A surprisingly individual country. Better join me and afterwards come on to La Suisse as well."

Driving to Bregenz a few days later, I mused on Swiss history, on the unique position of Switzerland in Europe both geographically and politically. Ringed by a barrier of mountains, it remains somehow poles apart from the present wrangling world. Too, I thought that near Tivoli in the Alban Hills above the Roman Campagna I had once seen a mosaic pavement, possibly the atrium of an antique Roman villa. A woman was the principal figure in the elaborate design depicting a pagan rite of the four seasons, undoubtedly the popular Masque of Ceres. The Earth Mother sat enthroned upon a mound piled high with all fruits of the earth. In her hands were four masks. Flanking this mosaic stood two steles, tall plinths of moss-stained marble. Each shaft supported a sculptured torso of a lesser deity, attendant, I presumed, on the Earth Goddess. What placed these moss-encrusted figures apart from any I had ever before seen was the fact that where the faces would ordinarily be, four masks—Spring, Summer, Autumn, and Winter—formed a sort of casque. Each mask was crowned with a diadem indicative of the season. Meadow flowers proclaimed Spring; latticed wheat ears, Summer; apples and grapes were redundantly Autumn; and a wreath of icicled bare branches distinguished Winter.

While traveling in Switzerland shortly after seeing this fantasy in symbolic pagan sculpture I was forcibly reminded then, as I am again years later, at this writing, of the four archaic faces gazing north, south, east and west, yet composing a single consistent design in the round.

When one motors up and over the Swiss Alps traversing the sky-borne St. Gotthard Pass down into Italy, Lugano on the Italo-Swiss frontier is one's destination. But the traveler begins to be conscious of an Italian atmosphere when reaching Bellinzona thirty kilometers from the frontier. If one enters Switzerland from Feldkirch in Austria, for example, crossing the Rhine where it emerges from Lake Constance, the first sight of Appenzell (capital of the historic "Inner Rhoden" district of Canton Appenzell), Walzenhausen and Heer-brugg will still seem essentially Austrian. Atop the towers of the old town halls the cupola roof will still be shaped like an onion.

Once St. Gallen looms on the skyline, its silvery stone towers and medley of Medieval pinnacles proclaiming the abundance of ecclesiastical buildings within its ancient walls, the road winds through fruit orchards terraced on the surrounding hills. Then the accent everywhere becomes unmistakably Swiss. At Neuchâtel and Montreux in Canton Vaud fronting the French border, a locality famed for its mellowing Medieval fortresses such as Château d'Aigle, and exquisite 18th-century *châteaux* like the lovely ivory-pink Château d'Hauteville, the suave French air prevails. Even so is the delicate touch in preparing food. At the simplest appointed *restaurant paysan* the cuisine is predominantly French—subtly fragrant vegetables, tiny spring chicken sautéed in butter with a pinch of green herbs with, perhaps, in season, a *soufflé aux cerises* and *marrons glacés* to follow. However strong in some of the border cantons may be the influence, even on speech and costumes, of the foreign "lands across the frontier," the interior cantons nevertheless present the "face" that is *Switzerland* alone. A "portrait of true features with sufficient background to decorate," as Hans Holbein used to guarantee to produce for his clients. A portrait of the proud Swiss, so indomitably patriotic.

I started out for Switzerland via Liechtenstein from Bludenz on a sparkling July morning, so early that changing lights on the mountains struck the snow-clad peaks of Drei Schwestern (Three Sisters) with such brilliance as to create a kind of Aurora Borealis in fanlike rays of color. The road starts to climb sharply once one leaves the valley meadows. A steady climb to Schaanwald, the frontier town. Solitude reigned. The inhabitants were long since up and about their business. Wooden shutters painted in bright heraldic stripes, red, black, yellow and white, swung wide, each window sill a repository for the family bedding, the eiderdowns prodigious fat from goose-feather stuffing with a lavish hand.

The air was cold with tingling, invigorating freshness. At the village of Triesenberg I took coffee and rolls—a new experience in rolls, the dough having been folded over butter, a dab of creamy cheese and caraway seeds before baking to a proper crispness.

This is an Alpine village with a difference. The houses are tall and narrow rather than low, wide-windowed, and the roofs nearly flat. The shingles are long strips of mossy bark rent from the trunks of Alpine spruce. This sheathing of bark is weighted down, against tempestuous winds, by great flat stones. I reflected on how strong the beams of the roof must be to bear such dead weight.

There is a distinct change of scene in Liechtenstein difficult to express somehow, considering it is still mountains, terraced vineyards and valley farms. But now the leitmotiv is softer vistas, the lovely blue-misted Rhine Valley, the Grisons' mountain flanks colored pale chalky silver, diagonally striped by strata of violet and black rock with here and there a vein of gamboge-yellow and rose-red. These mighty flanks of rock might be the marbleized walls of the throne room of some prehistoric giant king from out of old German folklore.

I took "second coffee" on the terrace of a tiny inn, Villetta Kermess, near Sücca in the Saminatal. The balcony of the inn was ornamented by a rustic gazebo, a noticeably unstable contrivance hung like a swallow's nest over a torrent-splashed gorge where giant rust-red and sulphurous-green ferns grew, forever dewed with spray. I looked off and away to the three prongs of a spur of mountains. Malbun rises

STILT
SHEPHERD
Wild GRISONS
LA SUISSE

above a tunnel cut through living rock. Near its summit opens a view of the Bettlerjoch (6,925 ft.) where Liechtenstein, Austria and Switzerland join. Here is the starting point for the dangerous ascent of Naafkopf (8,440 ft.). There is a mountain shrine, Chapelle Ardente de Dux, set at the top of a tortuous path which, notwithstanding its apparent inaccessibility, is visited every day by the devout who must as well be strong of heart. The Madonna is of ivory, robed in the splendor of crimson, gold and royal blue. The altar screen is a bizarre collection of votive offerings.

The road to Vaduz, the capital of the principality, describes here a sudden hairpin loop. Through a sort of natural bridge of rock cut through a towering crag I had one of the breath-taking views of my life. Far, far away, in another world, I thought, luminous, illusive, in the last rays of setting sun, the three cloudland crags of Drei Schwestern appeared, for all their impregnability of rock, shimmering ephemeral as mist.

Liechtenstein is only sixty square miles in area. The entire population numbers roughly 14,000. There are very few towns one can regard as more than a village. Vaduz has a population of 3,000 persons. But you will hear the topic of population variously discussed in the taverns. "We *should* have a larger population. There is room for more. But," shoulders are shrugged, "everybody is too busy working. Industry is important to keep the world noticing we are here at all."

The economy of the principality is based on agriculture and, in recent years, textiles and delicate precision instruments. Valley lands and gently rising fertile slopes are devoted to cultivation of cereal (the chief grain crop is maize from which is made *türkenriebl*—reminding me of Scottish oatmeal at its thickest—the staple food of the country people), tobacco, flax and hemp. Vineyards abound and a large amount of fruit and vegetables is raised for exportation to Switzerland. There are no large estates, as in Austria or Germany, although white red-roofed country houses stand amidst vineyards or orchards of ancient lineage which still doggedly bear their annual yield. Small manor farms of from three to five hundred acres are usual.

The present ruler, Prince Franz Josef II, lives on an estate comprising six hundred acres in all. The greater part of this he farms with imagination, being intensely interested in all modern means of agricultural development. The erratic surface of the terrain throughout the principality, however, precludes extensive use of American farm machinery save midget-tractors and small, easily maneuverable plows and harrows. The majority of farmers still rely on primitive, albeit extremely picturesque, methods of husbanding the soil. As in Austrian and Swiss valleys, or the remote upland farms, teams of that antique beast of burden, the noble oxen, are still used for plowing and fetching in the hay and harvest.

Near Vaduz I saw in the dying evening light, silhouetted against the sky, three teams of rust-brown oxen plowing with wooden shares —surely the simplest and one of the most important implements ever fashioned by early man. As I stood watching, an eagle, soaring on its evening quest for food, stooped to attack a plowman's whiplash as it would a snake. Here upon this ridge of meadow, earth-brown men and oxen limned a pastoral frieze evoked out of Attic mists.

The history of Liechtenstein from 900 to 1719 roars with tales of monstrous tyranny, decimating plague, witch hunts to the death, treacherous and bloody doings on the grand scale to a point seldom encountered in the history books. Anciently it was under the banner of the ruthless Counts of Hohenems from "up the Rhine" in Austria, whose dossier of depredations as torturers and land-grabbers during the Middle Ages reads like an invitation to Hell. In 1648 the Hohenems had plunged the country into ruin by their extravagances. At last the people rose and in a body sought relief from their oppressors by appealing to Emperor Leopold of Austria. He turned the Hohenems out of the country and confiscated their estates, dividing the spoils among the beggared populous. But, unhappily, it was too late for any lasting peace. Attributing their misfortune to a few women who had been creatures of the Counts Hohenems, whole families turned against one another, hurling accusations of witchcraft. This outbreak of witch-hunting to the death ended in wholesale massacres. Before this maniacal wave of superstitious butchery had waned, a far more lethal misfortune struck. The Black Death breathed out of the Graubünden marshes. Here the camps of mercenary soldiers, recruited from God alone knows where, paid by the nobles to fight the Austrians, "diced with Death" by consorting with harlots, refugees from Adriatic ports rife with plague. It was the season when the Föhn blew, a kind of sirocco. Warm winds have ever been handmaidens for spreading plague. It is recorded that the Föhn blew ceaselessly for two months. In an effort to escape death, the people fled to the highest mountain fastnesses. Many died there. The survivors stayed, creating a hardy mountain race which prevails until this day.

A century passed before Liechtenstein's population numbered twelve thousand souls. In 1700 the long period of misery drew to a close. The principality, as we see it today, was purchased by Johann Adam, Prince of Liechtenstein, and placed under the aegis of the Imperial Black Eagle of Austria. With Switzerland, it was one of the few countries in Europe whose neutrality was respected throughout two world wars.

Schaan lies at the end of a valley. A village of utter quiet, as I drove in, save for the concerted honking by a flock of zany geese disporting themselves in a vast duck hole. Taxidermy flourishes here. The dusty windows of shops, where taxidermists stuff and mount in "life-like attitudes" outstanding specimens of game shot by sportsmen in the mountains, reveal some astonishing, even eerie, sights. Favorite with hunters as a reminder of their prowess is an eagle in a glass case, hanging in mid-air, wings outstretched, against a crudely painted canvas backing, commonly a representation of Drei Schwestern or the Grisons, the crags preferably bathed in cerise, magenta and orange sunset glow of horrific brilliance.

The approach to Vaduz is felicitous. At the farthest reaches of a long valley, the lower slopes wear a kind of coronal of fresh sap-green leaves and tendrils of grapevine, the vineyard terraces mounting to the darker onyx-green of pine and spruce at the timber line. Overlooking the town, three hundred feet above the market place rises the Castle of Vaduz, called by its earlier overlords the Adlersturm, the Tower of Eagles. The barbican raises a massive tower of rough-hewn stone, rendered more friendly than forbidding by the softening swags of moss and waving wind-sown field grasses. A huge circular bastion lends the fortress-touch. Above this are massed a collection of pale yellow plaster and half-timbered buildings under steep raisin-brown tile roofs. A mélange of gables defines the living quarters, which are enclosed by a castellated wall, sinuous as a dragon, tracing the irregular crest of the escarpment. From afar off, or from directly below in the town, the castle resembles the huddled villages bristling with balconies and turrets that I have seen on the illuminated pages of old German fairy tales.

The reigning prince, Franz Josef II, resides here with his family. From a terrace overlooking the town the personal banner of the Prince flies a perpetual welcome. The banner emblazons the Black Eagle of Austria, predominant among numerous quartering of noble relatives. The castle is open to visitors six afternoons a week. From the broad terrace one looks across the town, away up and down the Rhine Valley. The encircling range of mountains opens a vista, a proscenium to frame the Grisons. Here is great theatre, staged by Nature, one of the magical panoramas of the world. In one day I have seen it shimmer in rain, in drifting mist at morning, in shifting sun and shadow at midday. This is eagle country, remember. To see an eagle anywhere is always an event. Here he reigns emperor of the skies—usually deigning to glide close, then sweeping haughtily upward to encompass his airy pavilions among the Alpine wastes.

I suggest a leisurely period to inspect the armory and the picture gallery in the castle. In the former, a superbly proportioned and frescoed apartment in itself, the collection of articles of knightly accouterment of varying periods—some of it Hohenems and Habsburg armor strangely fashioned of mysterious workmanship—is marvelously damascened. Studded horsehide jupons, chain mail in knee-length shirts, and iron scale-plate forged for a giant were dug up from fields in the Schellenberg area that were once battleground or, as historians say, "a slaughter yard," during the Thirty Years' War. Troops of many nationalities and tribes used Liechtenstein as a corridor for advancing and retreating through the endless years, pillaging the country as they went. The picture gallery contains a collection of outstanding worth. The Flemish School is fortuitously represented. Rubens, and Van Dyck at his most grandiose, his equestrian portraits of princes priceless documents of the times. The set of Gobelin tapestries brought by Wenzel von Liechtenstein from the Court of Versailles glows in all greens and a surprising range of yellows and gold. Indeed, it lights the whole gallery as if the threads were incandescent.

ANCIENT CASTLE
VADUZ.
LIECHTENSTEIN

While I was studying the vigorous design in the altar cloths and vestments embroidered by Medieval nuns that adorn the Royal Chapel, I was conscious that a pervading golden light seemed to grow more brilliant. I walked out across a paved corridor, through the red and gold audience chamber hung with banners of tourney, the edges "dagged, tongued and boar-toothed" in heraldic parlance, into a courtyard that I had not known existed. Here, burning bright in a saffron glow of the dying sunset, stood the principal treasure in armor from the Middle Ages of the entire collection. Had I not sought the source of the radiant golden light I would have missed this suit of German armor, complete to the last hasp and stud, hammered out for a tall man with broad shoulders and long, slender thighs, poised on a base of corniced oak—arrested motion in every fluid line. The date of "forging" is 1465. In detail and entirety this is quite the most beautifully articulated suit of full battle armor—designed, by its richness, for a great nobleman—that I can remember having seen. Except for the peplum of a rouge-velvet cote-hardie shown between the thigh pieces, there is no color—only burnished steel. Supple as velvet is the flexibility provided by overlapping flanges which "pin" the steel. Smooth the rhythm of "concertina" shoulder pieces designed to facilitate ordinary movement in raising the arms, as subtly curved as the calix of a Madonna lily. The gauntlets in themselves are a work of art, each bone on the back of the hand and fingers being identified by indented scroll chasing. The helm sets firmly upon the gorget, the cheek pieces curving away from a single eye-slit to a low point in the back. But to me it is the foot pieces that triumph. The instep is delicately ribbed and as flexible as the prehensile paw of an armadillo, the shoe-ends, which measure twenty-two inches, forming a hollow steel point sharp as a stiletto.

What makes individual suits or fragments of armor in this collection exceptional is the curious nature of its discovery. When digging out the stump of a lightning-blasted tree, farmers found the skeleton of a man in sumptuous mail. Around his neck hung a leather bag of jewels and gold florins. Another grave gave up armor of Eastern forging, perhaps Saracen or from the Turkish army of Suleiman. One discarded casque of German make was found in a bog. Hanging from it were black horses' tails, fully preserved.

Philatelists consider the leading attraction in Vaduz to be the Post Office Museum. In an impressive array of glass cases are displayed specimens of all stamps issued by the Principality. Vaduz does continuous business selling her stamps to collectors all over the world.

In Vaduz I was shown the prize piece of the precision-instrument industry. A real beauty—the Curta pocket calculating machine, smallest in the world, no larger than a stem-winder watch.

The hotel situation in Vaduz, considering its size, is surprisingly good. A hotelier takes great pride in comparing his hotel with "the best that Austria or Switzerland can offer." The Prince also keeps a watchful eye out to see that a standard of excellence is at all times maintained. Hotel Vaduzerhof perhaps leads the list. The cuisine is exceptional. The chicken, diced ham and egg omelet is a specialty. Hotel Schlössle is spacious; many of the rooms and the dining terrace afford a sweeping view of the Rhine Valley. Hotel Adler has a famous wine cellar; its fruit punch, made with a local Vaduzer wine, is cool and refreshing on a summer day. Then there are delightfully situated pensions. Usually these are centered in gardens or, like the historic "manor house" Röte Haus—actually a small red castle—rise in the midst of a vineyard. Pension Santis and Pension Sonnenhof are greatly admired. At Waldhotel, a sportsmen's lodge, I found roast venison prepared with proper reverence for its succulence, garnished with all traditional condiments.

After a long morning of exploring the mountain paths around Lavenna, I set out after lunch from the Brenzer Hütte to tramp the rise, a path leading to the timber line on the flanks of Falknis. Perhaps one thousand feet up I came out on a ledge screened on two sides by a stand of gray-blue rock spruce. Here spread a curiously appealing little meadow no bigger than a clipper ship mainsail where the grass was vivid green, cool as moss, inviting me to lie down and take a nap. I happened to notice that the edge of the meadow sheered off to a precipice with a considerable drop into what novelists call "infinity" or "limbo." I walked over to look down, when with the suddenness of lightning a fawn dashed headlong out of a thicket behind me. Like a brown furry bullet the creature sped past me to the rock edge, plunging over in flight as I heard the beating of great wings. I stood rooted where I was. No more than a yard above my head an Alpine eagle flashed meteorlike past me, swooping with a never-to-be-forgotten dive for the deer. I caught at the trunk of a small tree and hung out over the drop. Perhaps a hundred feet down the rock flank the deer had come to rest, lodged, powerless to move, against an outcrop of rock. Then it all happened in a flick. The eagle, legs rigid, talons spread ready to clutch his prey, great wings arched, the pinions like steel sabers hissing in the upcurrent of air, stooped for the kill. A slash of the strong talons, a shriek from the trapped fawn, the fierce beak did the rest. I sat down at the foot of the tree, feeling a bit weak in the knees after such high dramatics. I heard the beating of those tremendous wings as the eagle flew through the ravine below the level of my eye back to his lonely eyrie.

For dinner I ate a distinctly gamy venison ragout, thereby keeping alive the wild mountain motif of the afternoon's experience. From the aerial terrace of the Waldhotel I saw Vaduz below sharply etched under the pale sheen of a half moon. The beams were strong enough to pick out the reaches of the Rhine pursuing its undulant course downvalley. I was reminded of the "wavery" Toledo blades beaten out by Spanish armorers to ape running water, yet strong and biting as a bolt of lightning. I had seen them in the Apprentices' Museum in Toledo and but lately had seen identical blades among the collection of armor in the mountain crest Castle of Vaduz.

Next morning I set out shortly after dawn for Switzerland. With visits to numerous villages in between, I planned to wend my way from St. Gallen to Zürich, on to Basel, to Neuchâtel, to Bern and Lucerne, Fribourg, Interlaken to Lausanne and Geneva, cross the Pennine Alps to Andermatt to Disentis in the Rhone Valley where the upper and lower rivers meet. The glorious monastery on the banks of the raging Rhone, as it roars at the foot of the Grisons, is set amid fields that in summer wave with golden wheat pied with daisies, poppies and cornflowers. Upward to St. Moritz. From the incredible heights of Pass Bernina I would take the recently completed Bernina Electric Railway down to the ancient and lovely Italianate town of Poschiavo on the frontier, where the soil of Switzerland and Italy mingle.

I stopped briefly at Wallenstadt on the Wallensee. The delightfully temperate waters cause this quiet old town, with its half-timbered houses, to draw water picnic parties from surrounding towns, even from Bern. Regattas for small sailing craft sail from Stadt the length of the lake to Weesen. There are little settlements of villas all along the shore. It is a standing joke in Bern that fashionable mothers park their small children in charge of a nurse in these villas and forget about them, going off for holidays to Paris, the Lido of Venice and so on.

In Appenzell, the tall gable-roof, timbered houses have great character. This is a town that lives for its Corpus Christi celebration. Notoriously thrifty folk of Appenzell put on the most sumptuous show imaginable, famous all over Switzerland. The procession has been known to reach eight miles in length with magnificent display of costumes of the canton, the ancient "Inner Rhoden" attire, and floats depicting the Stations of the Cross.

The art of embroidering velvet, moiré silk and satin ribbons stems from Roman times when early ancestresses of the present embroiderers enriched the peplums and ceremonials togas of Roman generals and governors who paid heavily for appointment in this salubrious region. I was taken to a big, square house where a great deal of the cutting and sewing for these *trachten* (costumes) is assembled. The house itself was an oddly ramshackle building to find in Switzerland, a land of almost pretentious neatness. Midway down a narrow street a high, wide frontage rose. Once inside the arched gateway the atmosphere underwent a magical change. At oak tables in large airy rooms, the walls gleaming white, the ceiling latticed by black oak crossbeams, sat about fifty embroidery workers, middle-aged women and young girls. Like the Fates, their hands and arms moved monotonously as they affixed glittering sequins on white satin, gold tissues and velvets of ruby red, celestial blue or midnight blue that deepens to violet, destined to be cut into mantles for madonnas used in the Corpus Christi procession.

In the College of St. Anton I saw supremely beautiful choir stalls carved in motifs of angels bearing all the fruits of the earth redundantly emphasized by the carver's chisel.

The castle is reached by a slight incline, where immemorial oaks form a gateway to wooded heights and valleys of the Santis group of peaks. Wandering paths lead up and down through larch groves and ferny bracken to Weissbad, a small spa, quiet, remote, the hotels like spacious chalets, greatly favored by the old Bern aristocracy.

Just outside of Appenzell I passed a country wedding party wending its picturesque way out of the gates of ancient Schloss Wartensee. The bride wore the blue and white, silver-embroidered costume of Appenzell, with a lovely, trailing black lace shawl. Her headdress of fluted white lace rose in two flanges on either side of her face like the wings of a marsh heron about to take flight.

There are a number of old castles topping wooded hills along this road to St. Gallen. A good many are more Austrian than Swiss in character. The crumbling Castle of St. Anna near Trogen, however, is pure legendary Swiss. A stone tower, tall and slender as a campanile, dated 1100, has been a landmark hereabouts for centuries because of twin pine trees which grow straight as a ship's mast from the battlement. The trees, perfectly shaped as the traditional Christmas tree and approximately twenty-five feet tall, have flourished greenly but never, down the years, grown an inch.

In St. Gallen, parks and flower gardens of surprising magnitude lie on every side. Culture rides the air and has done so since 612 when a weary band of Irish monks from the Irish Monastery of Bangor, under the "staff and tutorage" of St. Gall (or Gallus), had accompanied St. Colomban to Lake Constance to spread Christianity. Consumed by the flame of piety and a deep desire for meditation, St. Gall withdrew from the group around St. Colomban who, he considered, was becoming too worldly. He built himself a cell in the loneliest tract of the virgin forest of Arbon, through which the River Steinach rushes in torrent. About the year 720, Abbot Othmar formed on this spot a Benedictine monastery and abbey. Persisting and growing as a center of learning, it was the school for sons of the Carlovingian kings. Each succeeding ruler on his coronation enriched the abbey with treasure. Sons of nobles from as far as Bavaria and Germany were sent here, so widespread was the fame of the Abbey. An upsweep to great power took place in the 15th century and the Prince Abbots became absolute rulers over wide estates from Toggenburg into the Thurgau. It was during this renaissance that the building of the Cathedral, the palatial Abbey buildings and Abbey library was under-taken—not, however, to reach completion until the middle of the 18th century. In 1803, under Napoleon's "Act of Meditation," the present Canton of St. Gall was created, the ecclesiastical domains being incorporated into it.

It is important to keep this long eventful history in mind when visiting the unique ecclesiastical and civic treasures in St. Gallen. The variety is immense, the library exceptional. Here one can see the exquisitely illuminated representation of "St. Colomban and St. Gall on Lake Constance" from Codex 602 of the Abbey library, and a miniature from the *Psalterium Aureum* (Golden Psalter) completed in 910 when the Abbey was at the height of its fame. The psalter is a revelation in flaming color and panoply, luminous as peacock's plum-age. Ten knights in early fish-scale armor, astride purple, emerald-green, marigold-orange and black horses caparisoned in jewels, ride joyously to a Crusade. The leader bears aloft a banner fashioned like a dragon, crimson, gold and green, the distended jaws belching flames upon the air.

It is a felicitous thing to walk around the streets of St. Gallen before going into the church and library to savor their carefully preserved antiquity. From the center of the *marktplatz*, where the old and new markets lie, the rows of houses encircling the heart of the town in wide curves indicate the plan of its former walls and moats.

The odor of ripe cheese pervades Speisergasse (built in 1600), for there are food shops and small restaurants where the famous fondue is served with its accompanying glass of *kirschwasser*.

In Parkplatz try lunching at Hotel-Restaurant Schwanen, under the clematis arbor facing the Cathedral, or inside where the red and white checked tablecloths match the curtains, and cold meat salad is the summer specialty. Also a pleasantly various *mélange de fruite* laced with kirsch. Order St. Gallen sponge cake with this fruit. It is firm and golden, fragrant with slivered lemon rind.

Wood carving in Medieval times reached a high degree of craftsmanship all over Switzerland. Characteristic of the patrician houses of St. Gallen are the oriel windows jutting out over the sidewalks from the second story. The House of the Golden Apple in Hinterlaubenstrasse reveals particularly exquisite carved ornament.

The Cathedral, facing a tree-lined square, is a prodigious expression in Swiss Baroque. Twin towers, curiously Eastern in feeling (1755-69), rise 225 feet at the east end of the long nave. A magnificently articulated series of ascending pavilions compels the eye to travel slowly upward, tracing the scrolls and volutes diminishing in scale as the apex is reached. Peter Thum, who designed the church, is said to have growled his way through the years saying, "I am cramped for money but not for space. So I will use scale instead of money to achieve my vision." This he did admirably. Powerful scale rules the edifice. Unbridled richness and imagination are displayed in the carving of oak choir stalls rising in three tiers, almost like panels of carved lace, which are the work of Anton Feuchtmayer.

In the Abbey library a carnival of all that is festive in Rococo decoration is achieved. The 100,000 books, bound in myriad colored leathers, line the cases but do not subdue the bravura of the painted ceilings. Perhaps the happiest of all are the delicately poised *putti*, twenty carved and painted cherubs representing the Arts and Sciences. More engaging creatures it would be difficult to find anywhere, nor the wit expressed in their accessories. Each cherub stands atop a boldly floriated Corinthian column dividing the bookshelves into sections. *Art*, for example, is gamin. He has wrapped a kerchief around his curls, stuck a paint brush upright at the back, like an Indian brave. His fat cheeks are smeared with cobalt paint, his palette drips all colors of the spectrum. In contrast, *Law* is a serious infant, nearly bent double by the size of square spectacles on an infinitesimal nose, an owl perched on his shoulder and a legal tome in both hands.

I was taken to a tall building in the oldest quarter of St. Gallen to see members of the Wood Carvers' Guild working on figures for a private chapel. Out of the bright sunlight I came into a Medieval workshop, steeped in shadow and dusk like a Gothic cathedral. The craftsmen had delicate sickly faces, such as one sees in ancient pictures. The men, working to the rhythm of soft mallet taps, were infinitely patient. I could see that they took no account of the passing of time. One carver was hewing a block of cypress wood into a semblance of the Madonna. Another was carving the locks of a tiny cherub to be affixed to the Virgin's canopy. I had a feeling that this man, whose mind was far away in the empyrean, was carving this treasure for his own private joy.

Hotel Walhalla is considered to offer the best accommodations in St. Gallen. I prefer the older Storchen or Pension St. Gallen near the Abbey School.

I left St. Gallen by way of Wildpark Peter and Paul. Specializing in all the existing Alpine animals, ibex, chamois, stag, red deer, it provides room for them to roam fraternally as in the wild. There is a natural enclosure of rocks, ravines, hilltops, and—to humor the chamois —narrow rock paths two inches wide, on the face of a cliff. Deer and ibex dash out from fir trees and bracken to stare at the traveler on his way to Zürich.

Chapter 15

AZURE LAKES AND SILVER MOUNTAINS LIE UNDER THE RED AND WHITE BANNER OF SCHWYZ

ANCIENTLY Switzerland was known as Schwyz. The old name prevails among the cantons. I still see it painted at the top of the wooden shields that figure so prominently in the landscape as I cross the border from one canton to another. These shields are extremely decorative, as are the solid wooden shutters on the castles, painted in the heraldic devices of the families who built them, and who in many cases still reside there.

For example, the shield of St. Gallen bears the Roman fascia, a golden ax upon a field of green. Rorschach displays two silver fish caught in a black fishnet on a yellow ground. Rorschach is the largest port on the Swiss side of the Lake of Constance. Fishermen here do not live in cottages but in tall old plaster and half-timber houses, leaning against the buttresses of 16th-century Mariaburg Monastery.

Romanshorn lies in a delightful situation among orchards on the shores of the lake. The tortuous lines of the old gnarled trees—pear, cherry, apple and quince—seem to be part of the boldly forged design of ironwork balconies on the houses, some of them built on, and from the stones of, early Roman fortifications.

The fishing at Untersee where the Rhine emerges from Lake Constance is an industry of ancient lineage. For centuries the *felchen* and blue trout have been packed in ice and sent in rush-leaf hampers to all parts of the surrounding country. Abbots and Prince Bishops in Switzerland, Austria and Germany, who kept a richly laden table, and even the Supreme Pontiff in the Vatican, prized highly presents of these large succulent *felchen*. It soon became known as "St. Peter's Fish." The fishermen along the lake adopted St. Peter's ring as their badge.

Through Herisau and Frauenfeld the Roman roads are still in use. I passed along a valley on one side of which runs a modern motor road, with on the other side an old Roman road.

I turned off the Roman way at Wil bound for Winterthur. I saw a number of fine Medieval castles in this area. Some, like Schloss Kyburg and Schloss Hegi, contain small museums preserving historical relics of the district. Hegi was once occupied by the rich and powerful Halwyl family, who were called for generations "the Pope's children" because so many became cardinals and Prince Bishops of wealthy sees. The castle has been turned into a museum entire; the sumptuously furnished apartments, frescoes and notable Bern and Zürich iron grillwork elicit the admiration of visitors, who purchase tracings of the designs.

The 11th century Castle of Mösburg is likewise open to view. Here two horrendous ghosts flourish. The young heir to the estate sometime in the 14th century was accused of cowardice by his father, a brutal warrior baron. To test the boy's courage, his father forced him to climb from the moat up the sheer stone walls to the top of the tallest tower and there to unfurl the banner of his House for all to see. Nearing the top, the boy slipped. In grasping a vine for support he became entangled in the tough tendrils and was strangled. It is said that in his remorse the baron lost his reason, ran amok and hanged himself from the same spot where his son had met his death. Down the years it is told that men passing on the road below the castle see the bodies of a youth in red doublet and hose and a great hulk of a man in half-armor swinging back and forth in the wind. Inside the castle, persons say that often at night there is the sound of armored heels hitting against the stonework of the tower wall. Also the sound of a man choking creeps in at the windows. In any case, to this day country people passing the castle at night cross themselves, murmur a prayer for protection, and hurry their footsteps along the dark road.

Schloss Liebenfels resembles more an ornate Baroque church with its tall, thin, scrolled tower. Schloss Wasserburg-Hagenwil is immensely old, scaly and grim, rising above a moat as big as a mill pond, a repository for a curiosity in the form of embroidered panels huge in size which narrate the story of "Judith in the Tent of Holofernes," the hands, faces and any exposed anatomy of the characters heavily padded in the manner of Elizabethan stump work to give a "lifelike" effect. More an oddity than a thing of beauty, yet completely in keeping with the Gothic-tales atmosphere of this old barracks.

Schloss Salenstein rises like a skyscraper on the skyline. Four immensely high towers set back to back surround a courtyard as narrow and dark as an airshaft in a tenement. The roof is cut in step-gables on which, as I walked around the tower, storks were building nests. Salenstein, a doughty old warrior hulk, gazes contemptuously down-valley to where Castle Eugensberg drowses away the years, content that the height of Swiss Baroque style is exemplified in the serene beauty of its long, low, primrose-yellow façade. The Aubusson rugs in this castle were presented to the family by Marie Antoinette.

At Schloss Arenenberg near Ermatingen, Queen Hortense, mother of Napoleon III, called "The Weeping Willow" for her constant hysterics, vapors and, as she lamented, "The misery of melancholy in which I exist," lived in a bedchamber hung with yellow satin with the shutters constantly closed against her migraines, and drank anise water.

Nearing Zürich I lunched at Pfäffikon at a chalet that bristled with innumerable balconies, swags of carved wooden lace on the wide eaves from which hung iron gypsy kettles. The black bowls dripped with purple and pink petunias. A mountain intruded in the face of the sun so that Chalet Eisl was in shadow. I sat under the hanging petunias and watched a fleet of small sailboats—the sails paper-white in sunlight—racing against the breeze. The Swiss are ever water enthusiasts, enjoying all craft from sail-borne canoes on small lakes to speedboats on lakes Léman and Lucerne. One finds the same throng of sports advocates for skiing and all forms of winter sport.

At the small village near here called Arth, Charlemagne erected kennels. Here he bred the mastiff considered by many dog fanciers to be the nobleman of the canine race. Charlemagne had been presented with a pair of Molossians (dogs of Epirus), bitch and stud, by a merchant of Tyre. The Emperor, when he promulgated his "Forest Laws," referred to "big, dun-colored hounds." Some authorities say that the Molossians bred at Arth by Charlemagne were progenitors of the mastiffs used so widely for sports in Europe during the Middle Ages. Charlemagne is said to have kept four mastiffs in attendance on himself. They were used alike for hunting and for war, being taught to hurl themselves with terrifying effect at the throats of the enemy and their horses. Later the mastiff breed was used for bull and bear-baiting in Elizabethan England as "Dunne Houndes." Again mentioned in Salzburg chronicles of the Prince Bishops as *gelbe Jagdhünde*" or yellow hunting hounds. Certainly the breed is seen in a great many of the tapestries and paintings of the chase and in castles and museums throughout Switzerland.

Zürich by its position on Lake Zürich, its art galleries, its splendid Gross Münster or Cathedral libraries and University, is perfectly fitted to entertain visitors on the grand scale. The ancient Helvetian settlement attracted Charlemagne, who founded the Cathedral. In 1218 Zürich became a free imperial city. At the signing of the Rolls for Swiss Independence the forest cantons of Schwyz, Uri, and Unterwalden were joined and Zürich became the stronghold of Protestantism.

In the Platz Promenade stands the Swiss National Museum. While Rembrandt and Rubens are represented here and little-known examples of the earlier Dutch and Italian Schools, the collection of paintings leans heavily toward 18th- and 19th-century paintings by Swiss painters who spread oceans of paint over acres of canvases, painting the huge documentary type of historical picture.

The chief thoroughfare is Bahnhofstrasse, extending from the railway station to the lake. The Alpen Quai is wide, tree shaded, a lovely strolling ground on which one may wander all the way to Mythen Quai. The oldest quarter of the town is a maze of narrow cobbled streets little more than alleys. Medieval houses with steeply pitched roofs shut out the sun, so that dwellers or shopkeepers on the ground floors live in perpetual half-light.

The ancient Wasserkirch on the bank of the Limmat is said to occupy the site of the martyrdom by sword and fire in the 3rd century of Felix, Regula and Exuperantius, the patron saints of Zürich. In the museum, curiously archaic images mysterious in origin depict these martyrs in wood, stone and moss agate from the Bernese Alps.

I think the most stunning view of Pilatus, the hyacinth blue mountain, is from the terrace of the University. In the middle distance Pilatus seems to float in some realm of the unknown. The jagged peaks of the Bernese Alps gleam rose and violet behind Pilatus as a foil to the icy whiteness of St. Gotthard Range and black-purple Appenzell on the left. Always at sunrise and sunset 14th-century Rapperswil Castle, situated on a wooded bluff above the lake, the most dominating spectacle in the city, changes color in rising or dying rays of the sun, shimmering as the crystal fragments in a shaken kaleidoscope. This effect is due to the isinglass and veins of quartz in the stone used in building the castle.

I was taken through a newly opened gallery at the National Museum by a knowledgeable and thoroughly entertaining gentleman who had had a hand in arranging the exhibition of old sleighs gathered from various cantons. Sleighs designed for private and ceremonial use have played a greater part in the Swiss scene than one would believe until viewing this collection.

Possibly the most powerfully conceived sleigh for sheer beauty of line and carving is one said to have belonged to the French ambassador, Du Lac. The rhythm of line in this sleigh reaches a high degree of perfection in the same scale and mood as the carved wood prows, garniture, and canopies for private barges produced in Venice by such master carvers of the 17th century as Rinucci and Pirianni. The frontal ornament of this sleigh is the head and front quarters of a sea horse, mane rippling in a sea breeze. The front legs are arched, hoofs warding off a breaking wave as swirls of foam-crested water flow backwards to support a huge, fluted sea shell which, tufted in sea-blue velvet, forms the seat. One errant wave rolls on to support a saddle at the back of the shell—a seat for the gallant to straddle, feet braced on the runners carved as conch shells, when taking his lady for a drive. Having carefully arranged the reins to pass through a kind of bit in the merhorse's mouth, formed from fronds of seaweed, the driver will place the butt of his whip in the clasped hands of a grinning sea

THE HONEYMOONERS
SUVRETTA HOUSE
ST MORITZ
18ᵗ CENTURY "SCHLITTEDL"

urchin carved sitting on a conch shell. Every detail in this conception tells that it is a symphony of the sea. Even the color of the lacquered wood suggests the sea on a misty day. Neither silver, blue, gold, or green, all these colors are stippled or dusted on until the surface gleams dully as will the texture of a sea shell.

Restaurants in Zürich are numerous. Dolderburg in a garden, and Eden du Lac attract visitors as much for charming location as for the excellent food served. Hotel Baur au Lac has an enviable reputation for comfort and the best in food. A hostelry in the grand and gracious style of *la belle époque*, its tables are set under the trees in a garden facing the lake for fine weather, if inclement in a glassed pavilion. Savoy Baur en Ville, as its name implies, is in the heart of the city. The old Schweizerhof is renowned for venison pasty and other game pies. The Spring Festival, when members of the city guilds carry decorative symbols of their trades and burn the Boogg, an effigy of winter, is enjoyable. Later to music and dancing Boogg's charred carcass is thrown into the lake.

Zug is the Medieval capital of the smallest canton in Switzerland, set beside its own tiny lake, the Zugsee. The early Medieval fortifications and castle built by Leopold von Habsburg are so hung with maidenhair fern and trumpet vines that the masonry resembles the stage scenery for an operetta by Franz Lehar. The Rathaus and Zytturm are built as part of the fortress walls. Altstadt and Dorf are the oldest quarters of the town. At Dorf the Market Vendors, as a guild, give a costume ball in Marktplatz in June. The costumes must be caricatures of local celebrities. Revelers join hands and dance around the caricature of "Mother Schwyz," which is a huge crone of fantastic ribaldry.

It is curious how two villages almost within a "hoot and a holler" of one another will have so different a viewpoint. This is particularly true of Fislibach and Baden on the road to Basel. Fislibach is the typical placid Swiss village of flower-garlanded chalets, where scarcely a lamp is lit after dark. Baden, on the other hand, is gay and high-toned. It has been a health resort from early times and, since the 19th century, a fashionable one. Lying amid lovely leafage on a ring of undulating grassy knolls in the valley of the Limmat, the town still retains distinct traces of Celtic origin. In Roman times Baden was popular with Roman patricians who came here and built small "pleasance" villas, to idle while taking the curative waters and rusticate among the wooded hills.

The Early Medieval bridges over the Limmat River, the builders using Roman masonry, are interetsing for carved entablatures of grimacing human faces and inscriptions of Hunnic origin declaiming historic victories. At evening from the tower of the Gothic Rathaus in Baden I saw the Jungfrau diademed in frosty splendor. Surrounding her rose the jagged pillars of Santis Range.

Hotel Verenahof & Ochsen is an old establishment, quiet and beautifully run. Hotel Bären exemplifies the traditional Swiss chalet of the story books.

Basel, situated on both sides of the Rhine close to the frontiers of France and Germany prides itself on being the most progressive and cosmopolitan as well as the largest city in Switzerland after Zürich. Under the name Basilia (often seen stamped on pottery presently made in the suburb of Birsfelden) a Roman fortress and cavalry depot established by Emperor Valentinian I, the city of Basel first makes its appearance in history. In 917 it suffered destruction of the "no stone left one upon another" kind by the Huns. For a century the ruins lay moribund. Basel was rebuilt by the Burgundians in 1033, to be incorporated into the Kingdom of Burgundy. The painter Holbein the Younger, when a stripling, drew portraits of passers-by in charcoal on the walls of houses near the Wettstein Bridge where he was born.

Shopping in Basel is an event. The shops are as excellent as they are varied. Jewelry shops predominate. Watches are everywhere: tiny jewel-encrusted watches set in bracelets and rings; watches the size of a thumbnail, showing the date or the time of day anywhere in the world. I saw a rose and blue enamel bijou, a bracelet that registered the pulse beats.

Silks of gossamer weave are dyed from palest to deepest shade of every known color by the Swiss vegetable dyes, a secret process in which they have long excelled. Lace- and hand-embroidered as well as machine-embroidered muslins known to the world as "dotted Swiss" and "Swiss eyelet embroidery" trail in fascinating disregard for yardage in the shop windows. Window display in the Swiss cities of whatever article dignified as "Made in Switzerland" has reached a high art.

Shopping thoroughfares lead out from Marktplatz and Gerber-Gasse which leads to Barfüsser-Platz. A piece of pure theatre is the façade of the 14th-century Rathaus. Painted long ago a violent crimson, it is undimmed by age or the chancy elements. The entire face of the building is adorned with cleverly painted shields of the original thirteen cantons—devices such as green leopards, yellow river craft, purple knights in armor, and a black bear of Appenzell—a tour-de-force of civic decoration in the heraldic spirit.

In January Basel holds its traditional Festival of the Griffon. A procession by the Guilds of Basel gathers at the Rhine Bridge. The "*Wilden Mann*," a fearsome figure representing "Wild Man of the Woods," comes downstream in a small red boat, where he is met by men in costume typifying the Griffon and the Lion. The three figures then lead the procession through fireworks, brass bands, dancing figures in extravagant *fasching* or carnival costumes to a banquet given to all inhabitants by the City Corporation.

Drei Könige is the leading hotel, but Eulerhof and Schweizerhof are more renowned for good food. Restaurants, like the romantically frescoed Alt-Gryff, serve the Basel specialty of roast baby lamb garnished with a variety of spiced vegetables.

I left Basel blanketed as with a London fog. The villages I passed through such as Reinach, Grellingen and Laufen were silent as if asleep behind gray veils. Scarcely a person was to be seen on the streets save in Laufen where small boys and girls were delivering milk by red painted cart with a big, shaggy dog of no recognizable breed in the shafts, his gaily embroidered harness hung with bells.

By the time I arrived in the market place of Delémont, mist had lightened somewhat. The silvery air revealed enough of the picturesque house fronts to convince me that Delémont is as French as its name. The Rococo Palace of the Prince Bishops of Basel, the balustraded roof decorated with statues of prelates in flowing robes, was so wreathed in mist that the effect was fantasy—a ballet of sky-dancing cardinals.

In time for a late lunch, I arrived in Porrentruy. The ancient town is close to the French frontier. The sun had now dispelled all mist. The town is architecturally important for students of the Baroque.

Notable are the Hotel des Halles, and the Bishops' Palace, an imposing group of buildings in High Baroque of French persuasion, reflecting *profondo* sculptured detail in the indigo-blue waters of the River
Allaine. The St. Geneviève Hospital entrance court is distinguished
by wrought-iron palings and massive gates. The beautifully fluid
design depicts flowering trees, wind-blown grasses and birds in flight.

In the Middle Ages this was a walled town and withstood a siege
of long duration declared by Count Guy de Gruyère. Traces of the
wall can be seen in the old quarter of Porrentruy. There is the
Refousse, a tall tower of great girth, and the elegantly proportioned
Porte de France, bristling with battle trophies originally intended to
elaborate the cornices of Versailles, sculptured by local craftsmen
who refused to deliver the trophies until paid, money in hand. The
payment never took place so the sculpture was presented to the town
to be used on top of the gateway.

La Chaux-de-Fonds lies deep in a mountain-walled valley of the
Doubs. It is the very heart of the Swiss watchmaking industry. It is
said the citizens have "precision minds" also. In the neighboring
villages it is said of them: "They have not intestines like other people,
but watchwork insides."

St. Ursanne is a great fortress in miniature. A tiny fortified town,
grim and gray rising sheer from the River Doubs. The Port du Pont
leads one across a 13th-century bridge, the pylons curiously carved
in acrobatic gargoyles. The roads in Canton Neuchâtel wind through
a countryside of vineyards, the leafy vines appearing to be draped
like great swags of glinting silvery-green silk on the terraced hillsides.
Sometimes a thrifty vintner hoists tall poles under the vines so that
long fronds heavy with fruit arch across the roadway. This causes a
voyager to pass through tunnels of fragrant vines, a kind of enchanted
allée dedicated to Bacchus and the fruitful vine. Immense vineyards
extend down the slopes to Lac Biel in Canton Neuchâtel. Wine-
distributing centers like St. Imier, Lignières, and Corneau are wholly
French in character, and the speech heard is that of France. St. Blaise
and Colombier on the intensely blue waters of Lac Neuchâtel are
summer resorts long favored by the Bernese who come to drink the

famous wines and spread crusty bread with cheese of Neuchâtel. Red-brown Twanner and pale, golden Schaffser are the wines of the Jura hill vineyards, cool and dry on the tongue, infinitely refreshing and fragrant in memory.

Neuchâtel is a wonderfully situated center from which to make trips up and down Lac Neuchâtel to places like the engaging old fortified town of Estavayer. High on a crag of rock, lonely and serene, stands Château Estavayer, an Early Medieval Burgundian castle, romantic now in its ivy-hung desuetude. I climbed the stone steps leading to the ruined battlements. From here I had the sort of profligate view that Switzerland so royally presents to her visitors. Below the town itself, backed by vineyards, the whole picture reflecting in placid lake waters, were the adjacent lakes of Biel and Morat, where the shores are terraced in vineyards.

Chaumont lies (3,880 ft.) a little to the north of the town. The summit, which can be reached by funicular, reveals Mont Blanc and the rose-tinged Dents du Midi, Weisshorn, Blümlisalp famed for deep red-purple Alpine roses, and towering above all, flashing blue fire, the crystal peaks of the Bernese Oberland from the Jungfrau to the Mönch and Wetterhorn, behind the famous ski resort of Mürren. This panorama encompasses an impressive swathe across the center of Switzerland.

There is an air of stately elegance in Neuchâtel. Broad avenues shaded by heavily foliaged lime and linden trees are planted to flower beds. Begonias, salvia, verbena and gardenpinks are set out—"embroidered" in the formalized French taste of the Luxembourg Gardens in Paris. French is the language spoken. The overtones are Parisian, but the point of view for the most part is the *ancien régime* austerity I always sense in two of the most elegant cities in France—Nancy and Aix-en-Provence. Yellow limestone houses, indicative of this canton, wear black mansard roofs sprouting chimneys like a tricorn hat decked with cockades. There are shops in Rue de l'Hotel de Ville where tortoise-shell, silver-filigree and enamel snuffboxes may be purchased as well as several mixtures of snuff with which to fill them. *Zephyr* is a delicate snuff perfumed with a touch of amber, affected by elderly belles and beaux. *Fanfaronade! ! ! ! !* is for the lusty steamboat captain, a pinch of this producing sneezes, as Disraeli liked his, to "blow the toupée off a rival at twenty paces."

The Picture Gallery of the Historical Museum contains a fresco rarely vigorous and decorative in treatment. Paul Robert, more famous for his classical subjects, painted the wide staircase wall with scenes of Neuchâtelois working at pursuits as vintners, cheese-makers, watchmakers, designers, and welders of iron for the handsome hanging signs seen swinging from shop fronts and taverns throughout the city. No hostelry in Switzerland entire has the personal magic, or so it seems to me, of Hôtel des Six Communes—certainly none has so engaging a sign. The wrought-iron and painted wood sign is hung high, because of its extreme size. Silhouettes of famous beaux and military men who have stopped there are on it, and shields of six towns—Boveresse, Couvet, Môtiers, Buttes, St. Sulpice and Fleurier—form a panel across the bottom of the sign. A wide ribbon of bronze boldly proclaims to all who run and can read: *Ici On Loge à Pied à Cheval.* (Good accommodations for Man and Beast.) The cuisine here is renowned. Gourmets come from Basel, Bern, Geneva and as far as Zürich to eat roast goose served with artichoke bottoms and brandied applesauce. Just before the goose is brought to table a glaze of the brandied applesauce is spread over its breast, then the bird is slipped under a hot flame. I noticed that the richness of the hot, dripping sauce glowed like polished bronze.

Dézaley, from the sunny slopes of Lake Geneva, is the wine to drink with the goose. The taste of brandied applesauce and the wine seem to complement each other greatly. To follow the goose, instead of a sweet I suggest salty biscuit and Tête de Moine or Vacherin, creamy soft-textured cheese made during the summer months by cowherds in the Jura District. The cheeses, stored in round boxes cleverly fashioned from tree bark bound with braided cord in brilliant colors, are hung in clusters from exterior walls and let ripen until winter.

In the old quarter of Neuchâtel the houses are of somber Medieval aspect, bleak, tall, narrow, the windows on the streets mere slits barred with murderously jagged iron sword blades. This was the walled precinct of the ancient Counts of Neuchâlet, feared for their cruelty, who rode abroad armed with ox-whips which they used impartially to clear their paths. The 15th-century Market Hall in the old quarter above the Place Purry rears from the cobbled street in great dignity, set high on massive steps. The arched Gothic windows retain the original glass—violet, icy-green, and topaz—a great rarity for the early time the Hall was built.

Hotels in Neuchâtel are commodious, furnished in the French provincial style. Hotel du Lac and Hotel des Alpes have fine interior restaurants as well as alfresco, the tables considerately placed in gardens enabling the diner to enjoy at the same time a supreme fondue and a view of the emerald, blue and silver setting of vineyard, lake and mountains.

Entering Yverdon, lying at the southwestern end of Lake Neuchâtel, after dark, one is treated to festive welcome—a town aglow with lights. The lake steamers are festooned with electric lights of carnival colors, bands play in the Promenade bandstand. Small white steamers offer a moonlight sail on the lake with buffet food, dancing, and all the wine one can drink. This gaiety constitutes a purely French diversion. Yverdon is built on the site of a Roman settlement, Eburodunum —documented in the library of Fribourg as "a retreat for relaxation commended by Roman governors and idle patriarchs." I find it was a gathering place as well for expensive and accomplished prostitutes who were "retained" by the military nabobs and patricians in small villas on the shores of the lake. Strapping women of less beauty were employed as bath attendants in the sulphur spring baths. These hugely thighed and muscled creatures appear as acrobats in some of the pavement mosaics lately discovered under layers of mud on the lake shore.

All the villages along the road to Fribourg are dedicated to the culture of the grape. Little boys and girls sell wine in *petits flaçons* of either glass or earthenware at the roadside. I noted in these youngsters flaxen hair and intensely blue eyes contrasting sharply with dark complexions, black hair and brown eyes, according to whether French or Swiss parentage predominated.

I believe that Fribourg, capital of the canton, has no rival in all Switzerland as a place to stop for a holiday. Lying nearly encircled by the River Sarine, Fribourg is attractively situated, agreeable as to climate and romantic in its Medieval character. All university towns the world over have a distinct air of culture. Students from many lands come here to study during the special courses of modern languages at the summer school.

As contrast to long, broad boulevards and shady promenades along the river, the Old Town is a mighty fortress, now somewhat mellowed with years of disuse but none the less mighty in import, stunning in boldly conceived masonry—particularly the ramparts and battlements of the Fortress Castle of Duke Berchtold IV of Zähringen, who fortified the town in 1190.

The University comprises a group of handsome mansard-roofed buildings suggestive of Versailles. There are countless small pensions and open-air restaurants in the old quarter and along the Promenade Rivière. The food in Fribourg is, in the main, excellent and certainly by standards set in Bern, Lucerne and Geneva surprisingly cheap. Hotel de Fribourg and Hotel la Suisse are large and usually crowded to the eaves. Close to Fribourg there is an excursion to Grotte de la Madeleine, a 17th-century *chapelle ardente* hewn from blue clayey rock. In a niche tinted in silver a gentle-faced Madonna resides. Only white or blue flowers are placed in the silver vases at the Virgin's feet. The day that I went to pay my devoirs to the Virgin was overcast, the rock chapel wreathed in mist. I noticed there had been a ceremony the day before. The shrine was a pavilion of flowers. Delphiniums six feet high, white peonies, carnations, and white sultanas, heads heavy with their own cloying scent, were placed in hanging baskets to form a spraying nimbus around the Madonna's silver-diademed head.

I drove out of Fribourg across pages of history. History and legends hang all about the Route de Berne where it climbs through "warlock, witch and werwolf glens" to the Pont de Gotteron. A suspension bridge 250 feet high is thrown across a ravine, a torrent crashes with a roar—to cause earth tremors somewhere in the misted depths below.

Bridges of great age rule the scene. Pont de Berne is constructed of timber bound with iron chains. I crossed it to the obbligato of creaking, grinding and the sobs, almost human, of straining timber beams. But I remembered that an accident has never been known on this bridge.

Farther along the road I passed a group of young women wearing the costume of this canton. A summer festival, I was told, to Saint Ildegond. All carried large baskets of flowers save one tall girl, who carried under either arm a circular Gruyère cheese large as a cart wheel. The costume consists of a full ankle-length skirt of a purple material tracing a black and red cross-bar stripe. An overskirt of crimson is kirtled up in panniers. The blouse is white, with a wide square yoke edged in crocheted lace. A black bodice is laced across a wide plastron of the same crimson. The hat reminds one of those made famous by Marie Antoinette when impersonating a shepherdess at her farm Le Hameau in the park of Petit Trianon. Of wide-brimmed natural straw (a particularly bright yellow), the crown is wreathed with red cabbage roses embedded in loops of crimson and black ribbon. Singing as they went, the girls were met farther along the road by a number of youths who stood grouped around a big hay wain. A team of the heavily muscled cream-colored farm horses from the district of Brig was harnessed to this festival chariot. Everyone was garlanded with meadow flowers. Each horse sported a topknot of poppies and daisies.

The political capital of Switzerland entire is Bern, lining both banks of the broad River Aar. The ancient fortified town, the walls constructed in 1160, describes nearly a full loop of the Aar, which at one time formed the frontier between Burgundy and Alemania. It is written in old chronicles that so treacherous were the Burgundians that the Alemans would not trust them for "the length of a night of darkness." All along the frontier tall poles were set up, spaced one hundred feet apart. Huge iron-lattice baskets filled with flaming pitch were hoist on the poles at sundown, to burn brightly through the night to ward off surprise attack. In the Gothic Cantonal Hall are preserved four of these basket lanterns. The pitch-flame lanterns were called "The Eyes of the Bear," for the bear has always been the symbol of Bern. Across the Nydeck Bridge the famous Bear Pit draws crowds daily. Succeeding generations of shambling brown bears, their ungainly frames surmounted with a small head, the tiny red-rimmed eyes intent only to seek out more sweets, have been kept, sometimes thirty at a time, in the pit, over a period of four hundred years.

At one end of Marktgasse stands the most potent magnet to draw admiring crowds in all Bern. Here we are back in the German tradition of ingenious mechanical toys, a prime fascinator the 16th-century Zeitglöckenturm. In chiming the hours the clock tower sets into motion a marvel of display. Puppets galore: knights bow to ladies; troubadours play upon guitars; Saracens decapitate simpering roués, dogs attack wolves, historical figures accompanied by trumpets prance, and elves pull the yellow braids of fat, pink-cheeked *fräuleins*.

The Swiss Alpine Museum contains relics of pre-history found embedded in rock and glaciers; musical instruments and jewelry, for example, the like of which passes conception. The German Gothic Canton Hall in Rathausplatz has a stunning outside staircase mounting at a perilous rake, designed in great beauty of carvings that feature mounted knights and warriors in full battle array.

It is one of the distinctions of Bern that the narrow cobbled streets are lined by arcades in the Italian Renaissance tradition. Near an old house, the Kornhauskeller, where one windowless wall of a raftered hall is taken up with a wine vat in scale nothing less than gargantuan, stands a fountain in the great Italian Renaissance tradition of those *"monsterosos"* in the gardens of Villa d'Este at Tivoli. An ogre, gaping jaws edged in fangs, wild matted locks, eyes blazing, a very henchman of Fafner, is portrayed in the act of devouring a child who seems complacent enough in all conscience. Whatever else effect this hobgoblin representation may have on its beholders, it has certainly been a boon to mothers with disobedient offspring. The threat—"I'll give you to the ogre in Kornhauskeller if you do not quiet"—has for long quieted countless obstreperous little Bernese.

I suggest the Bellevue Palace Hotel for its airy, spacious rooms. I have stayed here in summer, a summer when an unaccustomed heat wave spread over the canton. I have also liked Hotel Bristol with its elegant white and gold restaurant. The local specialty is *miskratzerli*, tender young roasted cockerel stuffed with purée of garden peas and served with pan-browned potatoes. In Aar Quarter restaurants you order *bernerplatte*. A soup tureen contains a stew of pork chops, sausages, ham, sauerkraut and French beans. Thick slices of *gesund-bröt*, a Stygian whole-kernel rye bread with which to sop up the pungent gravy, accompany this dish.

I set out for Interlaken by way of Thun soon after sunrise on a cracking bright July morning. Galleons of white clouds piled up over the far-distant mountains, but so clear and fresh was the air that I could see in the distant vineyards teams of oxen already being driven to their loading stations. The world was all *morning*, early morning. A rose-gold light struck radiations from the mountain peaks. A purely grand time of day to set out for Wilderswil in the willow wood, the heart of Bernese Oberland, called the "footstool" for the glittering Jungfrau.

Chapter 16

SUMMER SUN, WINTER SNOWS, LURE
VISITORS TO ENGADINE, PORTAL
TO STORIED TICINO

THE road to Thun on the Aar, longest river in Switzerland, is a sort of continuous triumphal highway of small villages. An undulant flowery chain, the houses all of chalet type surrounded by gardens, the balconies festooned with the ubiquitous hanging baskets of a trailing pink flowery vine called in this region Engadinaisa. Incidentally, this is a vine with a history. At the moment the vine was in full flower the Romans dipped it in a brew of gypsum which preserved its vitality and color. In the wintertime when the greatly favored January festival (which is still called in the prevalent Romansch dialect *Schtitteda Engadinaisa*) ruled for one week, garlands of the vine decked sleighs, dancing pavilions, were even twined as fillets for the head, the blossom resembling a somewhat larger fragrant arbutus flower.

The town of Thun, built on an island where the Aar leaves the lake, straddles water. Thun owes its never-failing popularity as a summer resort to many attractions including all water sports and, from any point in the town, an uncommonly exciting view of the piling-up of the entire galaxy of Bernese Oberland peaks. Sunset over the still waters of the lake, coupled with Borealis lights on the mountains, paints the whole visible world in crimson and saffron-yellow.

Most ancient is Kuh Bridge crossing the Inner Aar. Giant pine trees thrust skyward like spires of forest greenwood castles to flank the extremities of the bridge. On festival days painted banners and streamers of brilliant silks are hung on the branches of the pines. Old houses with beetle-browed roofs of purple tiles front Bälliz, the lime-tree-shaded main shopping street. Castles, ancient and hoary with lichen and wind-seeded meadow flowers, line the shores of the Thunersee. Dominating the old quarter of the town which covers the island, Kyburg Castle rises from a high, buttressed ramp, a confusion of turreted towers. In the vaulted chambers at Kyburg the Historisches Museum is housed.

Small, charmingly situated hotels line the lake shore at Oberhofen and Spiez. Faulenseehof and Hotel Hilterfingen-Thunersee on the south shore are extremely pleasant. Restaurants are open to the lake breezes.

Situated between two lakes renowned for deep, gentian-blue water —the Thunersee and Brienzersee—Interlaken beautifully lives up to its name. It has been described by the English artist Turner as "the center loop of a bowknot of azure satin ribbon."

The German language predominates in town and countryside; likewise the viewpoint of Interlakeners is wholly German. The costumes of the women bear close resemblance to the dark, slumberous colors, the silk and beaded fringes, and the black headgear with flat or conical crown that I associate with the somber traditional attire worn by women of villages huddled in the clearings of the Black Forest in Germany.

The water of Lake Thun is an indescribable shade of deepest sapphire-blue with undercurrents of emerald-green and shadows of darkest purple—veritably like the Mediterranean's "purple from Tyre."

Interlaken is a town of sharp contrasts. The extravagantly modern Strandbad is equipped with every sort of contrivance to attract timid bathers to aqua-paddle out on the lake. There are long stretches of water dredged deep for fearless swimmers to dive and race in and exhibit their dashing prowess. Unterseen is a beautifully mellow old quarter of 16th-century houses. In the bakeshop and *weinstube* area the air, aromatic from seepage of the herb-flavored wine of the district, mingles with an enticing odor from baking ovens. An illusive vanilla and almond odor issues from bakeshops where the famous

Interlaken sponge cake is made. Much firmer in texture than is usual, as chewy as caramels, the golden delicacy is baked only an inch thick. When cool, it is cut into long strips about two inches wide. Each strip is tied in the form of a large pretzel; then a whisk of almond-flavored icing is brushed across. Its popularity with all ages is limitless. Boxes of sponge "pretzels" are sold at landing stages on the lake, ski lifts, railway stations, and Alpine huts where mountain climbers gather.

Hotels to suit every taste and purse abound. Many have reputations for long-established excellence. The Beau-Rivage, a name which apparently fascinates hoteliers in Switzerland, Victoria-Jungfrau, and Royal-St. George with its high-bosomed Victorian air are far less expensive than formerly. The Carlton maintains a notable cuisine with specialties named for famous composers, such as *Torte Franz Lehar*. Swiss Baroque is the style of architecture. The houses, washed pale pink, primrose-yellow, hyacinth-blue and the faint green one sees in the shadows of a glacier, present an air of quiet elegance.

Wilderswil is a resort withdrawn into the solitude of mountain forests. For two centuries it has been a summer retreat for royal personages and celebrities in the international social world, as well as the world of arts and science.

Driving toward Lucerne, the country becomes an enigma. Stands of tall trees rear, densely foliaged. In no time the forests give way to grassy slopes where stand ancient villages like Alpnach, Hühnerwadel and Hergiswald. Here stripling youths tend tawny-yellow cattle in roadside meadows, the boys bare-legged and wearing red or blue puff-sleeve jackets over the briefest of leather breeches. I noticed a number of fair-haired youngsters resembling the frescoes painted across house fronts depicting the courageous son of William Tell. The dun-yellow cows wear immense bells of pewter-bronze alloy hanging from cut-out-work leather collars. During the winter months, when the cows are shut in a house-byre, these collars are used to belt the heavy frieze coats worn by the males of the household.

Lucerne has been called the most renowned summer resort in Switzerland. This may well be true. But in winter too it is gay. "Fritschi," a winter *fasching*, or carnival, delights revelers dancing in the snow-banked streets and wearing costumes of such unbridled fantasy, displaying bewildering flights of the imagination in Oriental design and color, that one is persuaded Harun al Raschid had brought his court of caliphs, viziers and houris to disport themselves amid the snows of usually circumspect Lucerne.

The Twin Brother mountains, Pilatus and Rigi, sweep heavenward at either side of the city at the western end of the Vierwaldstättersee. The oldest part of the town is of Roman origin. Ancient ramparts erected in 1208 rise from the north bank of the Reuss. The river flowing from the lake is crossed by a pair of old wooden bridges. The timber beams and upright stanchions are extravagantly carved with figures of historical characters, animals, and dancing folk in traditional costumes. Every panel or carved beam depicts a story from Lucerne's unquiet history. These bridges are in themselves a carnival of Swiss folklore, the carved and painted narratives to be read slowly, relished as one would read illuminated chronicles of another time.

Löwenstrasse, a long esplanade, leads to the Lion of Lucerne, a monument of power and point in sculpture. Thorwaldsen carved the couchant lion in 1821 from solid rock, hewn from the gaunt flanks of Pilatus. The lion commemorates nearly one thousand officers and foot soldiers of the Swiss regiment of Palace Guards, killed by a mob of revolutionists surging on the Palace of the Tuileries of Louis XVI and Marie Antoinette on the 2nd and 3rd of September, 1792.

Never have I seen a more "animated" structure for decoration of timber than the Spreuerbrücke, the lower of the two wooden bridges across the Reuss. Roofed in bronze-brown timber, the roof beams were first soaked in "tanners' soap" until pliable, then woven as one weaves willow withes when fashioning a basket. The closed walls of the bridge are entirely covered by 17th-century decorations extraordinarily vital in line and brushwork, the Medieval allegory a macabre "Dance of Death."

Shops for embroideries, silks and the famous Lucerne chocolate, either bonbons, liquid, or in pastries, are sold in *patisseries* of passing elegance. Many of these, like Le Cygne which faces the lake promenade, are small shops charmingly decorated. Le Cygne—or as it is better known in German, Der Schwan—is fitted out like an 18th-century salon, in honor of Madame du Deffand, the witty epigrammatist. From Lucerne she wrote to her great crony Voltaire: *Come to Lucerne. If the sun is warm I am rowed about on the lake. If not I hold forth at Der Schwan in a pink salon extemporizing over pots of chocolate. I instruct the slow Swiss in the art of swift repartee. I call it my Boudoir de Cygne.*

The old Swiss restaurants along the river attract many visitors. Lamb cutlets prepared with sour cream and paprika are a specialty, and cool, fragrant salads of every description, spiked with the fresh herbs that all Lucernois raise in their window boxes.

Lucerne is an infinitely leisurely city. Promenades stretch away; gardens and secluded flower-decked squares, lined with cafés for chocolate and coffee, induce a kind of languor that makes it hard to rouse one's self, hard to make decisions, to engage in the various excursions on the lake. It has been called Lucerne Fever, a summer lassitude. In June the Night Carnival on the lake, with exquisite floats drifting amid music and showering fountains of fireworks, is a rarely lovely nocturne.

Nearby Flüelen, in the Reuss Valley, is a resort of quiet hotels set in old, bee-browsing rose gardens. The bathing is considered the best on a lake noted for both vigorous swimming and for more gentle bathing. Where Flüelen is set in an embrace of solitude, the Bürgenstock abuts on a great promontory claiming attention as with a blare of brass. Bürgenstock-Palace Hotel seen from below seems to ride the clouds. For atmosphere of the *ancien régime*, pure Empress Eugénie, stop at the Schweizerhof in Lucerne, its red and yellow façade lighted up by the rising sun as welcoming as the smiling face of a beloved old retainer when one has returned home after a long time journeying. Hotels Europa and Montana set high above the lake amid boskage and flowery terraces invite one to take at least a meal— a fairly late dinner is best. I had dinner one moonlight night on the terrace of the Montana. Over coffee and liqueur brandy I contemplated the sweep of lake shore. Clusters of winking lights like fireflies illumined the shadowy reaches of oak, beech and linden trees above the shore. Surely Lake Lucerne bears a cultivated, as well as a romantic, air. Always there is an impression of ease, a sense of beckoning, an unspoken invitation to come hither, identifying this lovely stretch of water and its peopled shores as forever Lake Lucerne and no other.

Along the Axenstrasse (one of the most famous mountain roads in Switzerland) I made my entrance into ancient Schwyz in a downpour of cloudburst stature. Brilliantly painted frescoes pertaining to victorious ascents as well as to stark tragedies of Alpinists essaying the Grosse Mythen (6,191 ft.), and other nearby peaks, stare from the walls. Streaming rods of rain did not dull or obliterate the ramping color of Medieval Rathaus or the houses in the old arcaded Axenplatz.

After Schwyz the road winds circuitously through the verdant Valley of Alp-Trachslau below the Etzel Pass. Small farms are watered by a network of fiercely rushing streams. Fertility raises her wheat-crowned head; the odor of ripening apples rides the air.

As one approaches the Monastery-Basilica of Einsiedeln from either Zürich or Lucerne (the monastery lies midway between) an intense, almost overwhelming quiet encircles the valley of the River Alp. I know it well. As I drove through the hushed countryside, only bird-song stirred the stillness until a carillon of bells pealed out, startling the birds. The sound of the Angelus reverberated downvalley.

Encircling the monastery lies a fruitful farm where a religious order, Brothers of Our Lady of the Hermits, has devoted nearly one thousand years to the husbanding of wheat, millet, corn, all sorts of vegetables and the raising of fowls. There is a large dairy for butter and cheeses. I heard the whir of saws in the sawmill mingle with the thump of modelers' fingers on clay in a long shed, the *tuilerie* where dark sepia-red tiles are made for constant repairs to the acres of roofs of the many buildings, in general huge in scale, which comprise the monastery.

The millennium of the Order of Our Lady of the Hermits was celebrated in 1948. In the mists of antiquity—797 A.D.—a wandering monk named Meinrad, younger son of Count Otto of the Swabian House of Hohenzollern-Sigmaringen, was the first to penetrate the alleged ogre-haunted interior of the Black Forest. A rudely constructed shelter of boughs and bark constituted a shrine for the devout monk. Meinrad chose as the site for his hermitage a cave beside a rushing stream of clear water in the mountains where today stands the Abbey of Einsiedeln. With the assistance of a pious woman, the Abbess Heilwig of Altendorf, an offertory chapel was built close to the cave. Soon his gentle manners, coupled with his profound learning and generosity toward the afflicted, caused a large following of divers sorts of persons to seek out the hidden shrine of Hermit Meinrad. One night two malcontents sought sanctuary in the cave, attracted by rumor that treasure was hidden there. As Meinrad lay sleeping the thugs attacked him, bludgeoning him to death. This crime did not go unpunished, for legend says that two ravens who shared the hermit's solitude followed the assassins through the forest to Zürich, flying in circles above the heads of the distracted men, croaking incessantly. This clamor attracted the attention of the authorities. The men confessed the crime. They were forthwith bound by townspeople and burned at the stake. From that day two ravens have been emblazoned in the coat-of-arms of the monastery.

A fountain in the village of Einsiedeln is crowned by two black-bronze ravens. In 948 the skull, which still bears the mark of the gnarled club that caused St. Meinrad's death, was taken to the chapel of Einsiedeln where it now reposes in a kind of tabernacle at the feet of Our Lady of the Hermits.

The first actual abbey was an ambulatory erected in 925 by Benno, Bishop of Metz. St. Eberhard, of the princely family of Baden-Baden, built the first stone monastery. This was as much fortress as abbey, for the times were treacherous. Historically the abbey is deeply impressive. The first recognized miracle occurred in 948 soon after its dedication. St. Conrad, Bishop of Constance, was invited to consecrate it. The bishop, who had arrived in the midst of a tumultuous storm, was preparing for sleep when the wind howled to a crescendo. As a terrifying clap of thunder abated, a resonant voice, seeming to issue from the heavens above the high altar, proclaimed, *"Frater, cessa, Deo consecrata est."* (Stay, Brother, this chapel has been consecrated by God himself.)

Four times the monastery-basilica has been destroyed by fire. First in 1029—the last time in 1577. Our Lady escaped destruction each time, although her vestments were consumed and her wooden image charred. That is why she is black today. Miraculously preserved from the flames, Our Lady of the Hermits is revered *in excelsis,* in the sumptuous robes which habit the slender blackened figure, appropriate to the beatitudes. Her features are delicate, her expression one of utter simplicity, gentle as a maiden tending her flock of goats in the Engadine. But her robes, vestments for every momentous occasion in the religious calendar, are regal, as splendidly conceived and fashioned as a chalice of Byzantine enamel mosaic. I was unable to discover who designed these vestments, for the nuns fashion them in secret. The taste displayed is faultless. Forty-five robes comprise the celestial wardrobe. One is deep Burgundy-red velvet embroidered in a flowing design of *repoussée* lilies. The most striking and valuable crown of all, with parure and emerald cross, the "Courland Jewels," accompanies this regalia.

The story concerning this collection of jewels, bequeathed to the monastery on her deathbed by the 18th-century Princess Matilda of Courland, varies in import. It is said that this was a gesture of expiation for a life of flagrant sin. A dome-shaped crown of olive leaves is encrusted with emeralds and pigeon-blood rubies of almost incalculable value. Always in the arms of the Madonna rests the Christ Child habited identically. I am partial to the "Christmas Mantle," a spreading robe of vermilion silk, all-over embroidered in a tracery of gold and silver frost crystals, banded at the sleeves and hem with gold galloon heavily sewn in rubies and diamonds. The breath-taking effect is heightened by the Madonna, standing silhouetted against a nimbus of opalescent glass clouds. A recent *pèlerinage* from Nancy and the Department of Lorraine, numbering thirty thousand persons, filed past the High Altar. Next to St. Peter's in Rome, Einsiedeln is probably the most important basilica in the Catholic world. It is the proverbial wealth in treasure at Einsiedeln that has amazed the world at large.

As Einsiedeln stands today it presents a tremendously long façade nearly bridging the valley. The stone, quarried in the Vorarlberg, has a greenish-beige cast on dull days. But in full sunlight it assumes a warm ivory-yellow tinged with rose in the shadows. The present edifice is Swiss Baroque, strongly laced with Italian. Consecrated in 1735, it was designed by a young lay brother of the order named Moosbrugger. Two hugely proportioned entrance gates of rusticated stone flank a curtain-wall following the curve of a balustraded ramp, allowing for a rhythmical sweep of thirty steps to the entire rise. The interior environment at Einsiedeln is ornate, in the best traditions of Swiss Baroque, for there is a lightness of touch, a generous spacing of curvilinear design, whether in gilt or white stucco, gracefully superimposed upon walls of pale colors. The nave of the church is wide, paved in marble, the tessellation small at center graduating to large squares of black, golden yellow and Italian pink. The Hall of Princes is a long gallery planned and indeed frequently used for the entertainment of royal personages, often patrons of the abbey, at banquets. Portraits of Franz Josef and Empress Elizabeth add flashing color to the white and gold room.

To me the library is an exhilarating room on all counts, beautifully proportioned, designed as a long gallery with two naves. Green and white predominate, with a lovely accent of orange-vermilion labels on thousands of white parchment volumes. Many are rare manuscripts nearly one thousand years old. The *chef d'oeuvre* is *Regionator Einsiedelnsis*, a topographical description of Rome in the 8th century.

There, in its bowl of green valley, stands the Monastery-Basilica of Einsiedeln, like a huge country house, surrounded by farmlands. It is a great house with the door always flung wide in welcome to its treasures, both spiritual and temporal. No matter what one's belief, a pilgrimage to Einsiedeln is good for the soul.

One's senses are so dominated by the basilica that the town of Einsiedeln itself passes scarcely noticed. There are old, frowning houses nearly swamped under jutting roofs. Shops selling holy relics are, of course, legion. Hotel Pfauen, designed like a massively proportioned Swiss farmhouse of brown timber and white plaster, defines itself by having a peacock embroidered on its linen and painted on its china. Rooms are airy, comfortable; food is excellent.

Altdorf is the capital of the ancient Burgundian "warrior" canton of Uri, set deep at the bottom of a kind of well of towering mountains famed as the mating grounds for chamois. The old town of Altdorf shows timbered houses black with age, yet colorful, frosted with ripe green moss and gilt lichen. This *dorf* attained its immortality as the birthplace of William Tell (actually at neighboring Bürglen to the east). The house is now a chapel-shrine decorated in lurid scenes from Tell's obstreperous journey through life. A theatre is maintained in Altdorf to present each summer Schiller's drama *William Tell*. A bronze statue of Tell by Richard Kissling all but erupts, in curly wind-blown locks and beard, slashed doublet, wide-brimmed, be-plumed hat and Alpine bow, at the foot of a 13th-century watch tower. The tower is said to be the original site of the tree to which Tell's son was tied to undergo the ordeal by arrow shot. Women of this region are famed for buxom charms but, alas, for goiters as well. Many young women cleverly conceal this unseemly growth by wearing bead- and sequin-embroidered collarettes.

It was not far from Altdorf on the ravine road to Andermatt that I heard the doleful notes of an alpenhorn, blown by an expert as I could tell by the codelike spacing of notes. I suddenly came upon a picture that to me more nearly presented "Schwyz" as I always evoke the land than all I had heretofore seen on this trip. I stopped the car, alighted, to sit astride a boulder beside the road and watch. Above me rose a series of serried rocks like cyclopean steps mounting to an escarpment. On the topmost crag stood a tall bronzed youth sharply silhouetted against a pellucid turquoise sky; clad in white, heavily ribbed long-hose, black leather knee breeches, a white blouse with the Medieval capped sleeve of the mountaineers, and a black velvet cap festively embroidered in blue, red and green Alpine flowers. Here stood "Young Schwyz" at the traditional task of calling—perhaps a summons to civic duty, possibly the announcement of a posting of marriage banns—to an unseen hunter dwelling alone in some rocky ledge mountain *hütte*. An alpenhorn is a long wooden instrument, anciently carved, measuring sixteen feet in length and shaped somewhat like a slender classical Horn of Plenty. Capable of sending its sonorous notes over long distances, the blower rests the large open end on the ground and toots on the smaller end. The message boomed on. An eagle wheeled, darting close in anger, then rose to disappear from sight over the mountain crest. Still immovable, the trumpeter carefully spaced his notes. Far off I faintly heard three sharp barks

THE LISTENERS
ALPINE HORN—
The GRISONS

of rifle fire. The boy on the rock ceased his calling and licked his numbed lips. His alpenhorn message had been received.

It was just then that this picture of another-worldness was considerably heightened. A girl and boy, brother and sister no doubt, who had been tending a flock of black and white goats off to one side, suddenly raced pell-mell down the craggy path. The small boy came toward me, touched his Alpen flower-wreathed straw hat and shyly presented me with a rather bedraggled posy of cerise Alpen roses. Knowing that the boy was immoderately curious as to what I was sketching, I made a quick drawing of him hugging a black goat kid. His sky-blue eyes widened. He let out a high-pitched shriek of surprise. *"Ein Schatzmeister Sie! Danke, mein Herr, danke!"* He was profusely thankful to have met a "treasure-master." And he lit out to show his "treasure" to his sister.

Having arrived at Andermatt, I shall take time out to describe the diverse attractions of all the world-famed Swiss winter sports resorts regardless of geography. For the most part, excepting Gstaad and Bignasco, the villages of this region lie forged, by reason of terrain advantageous to skiing and bobsledding, like links in a circular chain.

Andermatt is a famed resort in the Urseren Tal at the foot of the St. Gotthard and Furka passes. The famed descent from Gütsch, if negotiated with success, lives ever after in the skier's mind. Hotel Bellevue is distinguished in comfort and cuisine. At Hotel Krone life will be gayer and less formal.

Kandersteg, in the Oberland, like all these winter resorts, starts its season in mid-December. The Christmas holiday is carnival time. Inherently gay in nature, the Kandersteggers welcome visitors all year around. In the high Gemmi and Wildstrubel region skiing continues into May.

Klosters has an ancient reputation for the carving of traditional alpenhorns long before foreign sensation seekers on skis crowned its Parsenn Run with Olympic laurels. Oddly enough, the alpenhorn carver who takes youths at the age of fifteen years as apprentices usually is a retired chimney sweep. No one has the answer why. There are five main runs here. From Gotschnagrat to Klosters there is an unobstructed descent of 3,300 feet. Grand Vereina Hotel is elegant in its accommodations and sets a notable table. Sporthotel Silvretta, one of the oldest hotels in the Grisons, caters to summer and winter visitors with equal aplomb.

Coming back to the Oberland, the situation of Mürren is unique, teetering on a wide shelf over the Lauterbrunnen Valley. Good snow conditions, owing to its height, are proverbial. The Mürren Ski School is the oldest in Switzerland. Kandahar Ski Club, sacrosanct in skidom, annually holds its famous Arlberg Kandahar Run in March. The Inferno Race from the Schilthorn down to Lauterbrunnen is a classic.

There are many persons who prefer Pontresina to all other Swiss winter resorts in the Upper Engadine. With St. Moritz and Davos it enjoys a fashionable clientele, starred with great names in international society. Shopping in the village smacks of rue de la Paix or Boulevard St. Honoré in Paris. Hermès, Cartier, Perugia, all have branches of Paris shops here. The climate is noted for long hours of sunshine, and starry nights when the Milky Way puts on a superlative show.

In winter, Kronenhof-Bellavista and Schlosshotel present constant entertainment in musicals and balls. Everyone who attends dresses to the teeth and enacts elaborate charades, an old-established custom in Swiss winter resorts. Proprietors of pastry shops where one takes eleven-o'clock morning coffee boast that to have a choice of less than one hundred different varieties of pastry would be niggardly. Bernina, Engadinerhof and Park Hotel come vitally alive in winter, to drowse, but carry on listlessly, in summer.

Zermatt reposes beautifully serene, content in her knowledge of supremacy as one of the largest and most favored skiing areas in the Alps. I admire Zermatt but feel it is always too crowded, with too much milling about in the narrow streets. To procure a room at Seiler's Mt. Cervin, the Monte Rosa, Waldesruhe or Zermatterhof, one must book rooms practically at birth. The popularity of Zermatt is unassailable.

For relaxation I like best Lia's Bar. And I may add I am in company with legions of visitors. It is by sheer personality alone that Lia lures you to her establishment. But then it is her smile, her conversation and her martinis that hold you there. Zermatt's ski lift is a voyage into the unknown reaches of a world away in ice, clouds and snow that you will long remember. The chief skiing grounds are centered around Blauherd (8,475 ft.) and the Gornergrat (10,280 ft.), from both of which one may enjoy long, pulse-quickening descents. A beautifully conceived and presented summer festival held in August features a procession from hundreds of tiny hamlets in the mountains, which converges at the Schwarzsee to honor Our Lady of the Snows. A "chapel shrine" composed of pine, larch and spruce boughs interlaced in basket-weave effect is set up in which to place the Madonna. Her robes are forest-green so thickly powdered with crystals that she is verily "of the snows."

To me, Davos represents nostalgia for Edwardian days, the fragrance of roses, portraits of *femmes du monde* by Boldini, the froufrou of lace ruffles under satin trains when, in the summer evenings, ladies under silk sunshades walked for tea to the little chalets set like slightly overscaled sedan chairs among the trees.

At Stolzenfels or Café Scaletta the strawberry tarts, topped with cream whipped up with kirsch, cannot be equaled anywhere. The climate is dry all year and phenomenally sunny. In winter the great event is the Parsenn Derby. The run is from the summit of the Weissfluh to Küblis, a total length of seven miles and a drop of 6,000 feet. The skating rink covers seven and one-half acres. If one wishes, light meals are served while leisurely skating. Skating waiters are in demand, and once I found that there was a skating Glee Club with a predominance of Italian tenors. Palace, Belvedere and Berghotel Schatzalp are old established hotels, warm and luxurious, excellent as to cuisine in winter. But in summer I prefer breezy, green- and white-curtained Schweizerhof.

Without question St. Moritz is the most famous winter sports resort in the world. The magnificent opportunities it offers for every known form of winter sport have elevated its reputation to the mountain peaks. By the same token it is the playground, winter and summer, for royalty (present and ex) as well as notables of the stage and screen. One American film star famed for her pectoral magnificence once told me, "If you haven't broken your leg or fractured your reputation at St. Moritz, you might as well jump off the Piz Nair Alp." Private skating rinks are maintained by most of the hotels—Palace, Suvretta House, Kulm and du Lac, to name only a few. Cresta Run for "skeletons" (bobsleds) is world renowned for the stiffest sport of its kind. The famed Bobsleigh Derby is usually held at the end of February.

Summer is quiet in St. Moritz. The smart shops are mostly closed. The climate in summer is chancy. "Summer rain weeps for winter sun," is an adage of the villagers. Still St. Moritz has always had a staunch clientele of summer visitors.

I was attracted by a huge poster in the square at Bernina Pass: RAILWAY OVER THE ALPS. NO COG-WHEELS. ELECTRICITY ALL THE WAY. This I decided to investigate. Most people who know Europe well are familiar with the famous St. Gotthard, the Simplon and Mont Cénis tunnels. But few seem to have heard of any other tunnel leading into Italy. Yet one exists. An amazing exhibition of engineering skill, a meter-gauge railway. It crosses the Alps at the height of 7,500 feet, at no point using the annoying cog-wheel method of traction with its bumpity-bump, whir-clank, drop-and-catch-again distraction. The line first runs over the flower-spattered mountains to Pontresina. A 13,000-foot wall of ice and rock confronts the eye: the four stupendous peaks of Bellavista; Piz Bernina's grimacing face of striated snow and ice; Crest d'Aguzza; and the peerless purple-quartz and copper-sulphate deposits of massive Piz Morteratsch itself. Far below lies the terminus of an enormous glacier, a frozen mound of debris, remnants of tornado storms that broke the earth in pieces millions of years ago. The train enters the tunnel to emerge finally onto the ledge where stands remote Bernina Hospice, sole surveyor of the savage wilderness of bronze, black, gun-metal and slate-blue mountains. A world apart painted in monotone.

Alp Grün, a mountain hamlet, seemed inhabited solely by dun cows, each one burdened with a huge metal bell which in a curiously sepulchral way peals as loudly as those of most churches. There is a gaunt mountain inn that it would seem is held suspended by divine intervention against destruction over the Alp Grün ravine, a formidable abyss if I ever saw one. From the terrace spreads one of the fabulous views of the world, providing a vast sweep of the Alps in every variation of color and rock formation. The Italian Alps rise far, far away, almost the ghosts of mountains, ethereal blue and violet against a sky that Giotto might have painted as background to his fresco of St. Francis of Assisi—"the impossible blue of Giotto," said Byron.

In the lower middle distance lies Poschiavo, a Swiss market town entirely Italian in thought and habit even to its speech, set beside a lake only a few shades darker blue than the distant sky. Graceful campaniles from out some Tuscan dream rise from ancient Romanesque churches, and the fretted arches of a derelict Roman aqueduct glow redly in the haze. Poschiavo is the last town in Switzerland before the lovely frontier town of Madonna di Tirano, where a midnight-blue Virgin with golden halo is painted on the outside wall of the customhouse.

From Poschiavo the train runs beside the lake. On every side are vineyards, the vines shimmering in the sun, saturated with copper-sulphate spray, the grape clusters hung in cheesecloth bags against the ravaging birds. Another one of the great pictures Switzerland offers is the one presented as one traces a curve in the road from the San Bernadino Pass through Olivone and confronts the Benedictine Monastery of Disentis at the western end of the Rhone Valley, where the confluence of the Upper and Lower Rhone meet at the foot of encircling mountains Piz Medel (10,510 ft.) and Piz Muraun (9,512 ft.). Not so large in frontage or height of Baroque towers as Einsiedeln, this religious house is one of the noblest buildings imaginable. As I drove across a winding road in front of the great sweep of pale-yellow masonry, a river breeze riffled the stooks of richly golden wheat that had been piled one upon another like pavilions. Backed by the darkly green forests that rise to the timber line of Piz Acletta, the monastery glowed in the sun as a carillon of bells, calling to evening Mass, reverberated across the wheatfields and the rushing Rhone. The clamor of bells mounted the pine-clad slopes, to clang on the mighty anvil of snowy rock that is the summit of Piz Medel, gleaming in its empyrean behind Disentis Monastery.

Bellinzona, capital of the canton Ticino, is "most old" as Medieval chronicles tell. It was most old when the Romans built a great fortress on the craggy heights above the town and set up a cavalry depot in the plain. The remains of the Roman town, later the Medieval stronghold of the Dukes of Milan and the powerful Pallavicini, is still ringed round with three sets of walls, each one dominated by the 14th-century castles San Michele, Montebello and Corbario. Scaly, flame-ravaged, thickly hung with blood-red blossoms of trumpet vines, these hoary piles of towered masonry more quickly evoke the turbulent past of Schwyz fighting for her freedom than anything else in the land.

There is a Byzantine church, Alo St. Michele, in the old Medieval quarter, wherein the crudely painted Byzantine frescoes molder on plaster walls. Still visible are the stark visages of martyred saints, noble warriors, prelates. Archangels wielding flaming swords slay the miscreants, as all huddle together in a mass of human misery. A terrifying sight of Christ's wrath as administered to mortals by His hierarchy of angels.

In the Church of St. Peter and St. Stephen a Crucifixion above the High Altar is said to be an unsigned work of Tintoretto.

To return to our resorts, summer or winter, it is all one to the villagers in Gstaad. They are so used to entertaining with renowned hospitality the year round that they bend their backs and work proudly night and day to keep it this way. In winter the long ski runs attract the more serious ski-minded. "Lower slope" Wasserngrat and Lauenen compete with sportier "higher slope" runs on the Wildhorn and Diablerets, both being among the stiffest in the region. Gstaad sets high on a fertile upland plateau surrounded by orchards and vineyards. The spacious farmhouses and village *dorfhäuser* all represent varied conceptions of the local architecture. Wide overhanging roofs, extending sometimes twenty-five feet, are supported by ingeniously devised openwork wooden consoles or corbel brackets. To my mind this is the finest regional architecture in Switzerland.

The Mühlenhaus at Lauenen is a *dorfhaus* of striking character. Commanding the slopes above Gstaad, Mühlenhaus, a private chalet, is by way of being an architectural pilgrimage, so magnificent in vitality is the wealth of carved and interspliced cedar, chestnut wood and pine timber of this structure. Gstaad Palace, true to type, is the usual big, sprawling summer hotel, a mélange of gables and balconies. I suggest stopping in summer at one of the better class *gasthäuser* such as Oldenhorn or Posthotel Rössli where bronze pine cones big as pumpkins and aromatic with resin, thrown on the open fire on a cool night, burn with purple, green and blue flames. As each cone is cast on the flames one customarily chants the name and crime of an enemy, end-

GLEANERS
GSTAAD
JR.

ing "Consigned to Purgatory." In winter, Alpina and Bellevue offer evening entertainment, aping more sophisticated Zermatt, Davos, and Mürren.

Quite different is Lugano, lying on a bay in the long, pear-shaped Lake of Lugano and predominately Italian. Arcaded streets, shading shops of every description, stretch for over a mile in the old part of town that is set back from the lake Promenade. Monte Bré and Monte

San Salvatore are the Due Reggi (twin kings) of Ticino canton. The Cathedral of San Lorenzo is redundant in Lombard Venetian style, as are most of the old *palazzi* of the wealthy Ticino wine growers who prefer to live in town. Piazza Rezzonico presents richly frescoed buildings and from here one looks away to the heights of Monte San Salvatore. At night a restaurant, Stella del Monte, is a beacon; its façade, luminous with blue and violet floodlighting, is reached by funicular. The Bristol and Park-Hotel au Lac are excellent hostelries. At Hotel Flora one might be living in a cool shuttered Italian *palazzo* of the Renaissance.

Locarno is again all Italy. It just manages to be within the borders of Switzerland. Lying in a sheltered position at the northern tip of Lago Maggiore, it is sometimes called the "Nice of Switzerland." It is a greatly favored summer resort. An air of tranquillity pervades the palm-shaded squares. The houses are faintly *pastiche*, delicate in design, washed pink, blue, yellow and mauve, each behind a tracery of iron balconies. There is a glorious Renaissance mansion, Casa Borrani, facing the lake. Myriads of white and *only* white flowers embower the house. Palm and magnolia trees cast dark shadows to create an intensely romantic mood. Piazza Grande is extremely elegant. Ladies correctly gowned and hatted and addicted to floating veils still drive in open carriages at eleven o'clock in the morning, shop for an hour, lunch, siesta, then drive again at seven o'clock in the evening.

Back near Lac Léman, Gruyère is proud, and with reason. When one ascends the tortuous roads to Gruyère in the canton of Fribourg, none but the legendary Swiss atmosphere prevails upon the grand and sweeping panorama of mountains piled, seemingly, one upon another like the playing blocks of some giant's child who had started to build a new world to pierce the sky and then suddenly abandoned it. The castle of the Counts of Gruyère who once owned the valley rises from rock bastion, a pinnacled cathedral, to dominate the surrounding valley for twenty miles.

When one reaches the base of the rock masked by a dense growth of larch and walnut trees there appears to be no way of reaching this castle. Actually, hidden from prying eyes, there is a secret tunnel road hewn from the living rock by prisoners of the Gruyère counts. This fantastic piece of engineering, in which human hands took the place of machines, is still in use. When the wild snow-laden winds of winter howl out of Jaun Pass the castle is not isolated from the village, because the sheltered roadway is free from snow.

From the terrace of the castle which is the roof of a dungeon keep dated A.D. 1000, one is regaled with the sight of the "Ceinture de Dents," a girdle of teeth. Here rise the jagged, spear-point-sharp peaks of Dent de Corjon, Dent de Lys, Dent de Jaman, pine-clad Dent de Broc, and Dent d'Oex, supporting on a ledge near the summit the dungeons of Château d'Oex where once recalcitrant female relatives of the Gruyère counts were sent to be incarcerated in duress vile. As an outer girdle range the Rochers, Verraux, de Naye, Cray and Moléson. Thrusting above all, ice-crowned Grammont reflects his stark white face in the icy green waters of distant Lac Léman.

The castle is a museum of antiquities encompassing a thousand years in time. Great banqueting halls are frescoed with vivid color and vigor of draftsmanship in scenes from battles and the chase pertinent to the lives of the powerful Counts of Gruyère. The three inner courtyards are surrounded by the ancient style of openwork timber loggias, with crazily balanced outside stairways connecting a rabbit warren of small chambers. From the walled garden the pungent odor of herbs, lavender and the dark moss rose wafts up into the Armor Gallery where I brushed against painted silk banners faded to the indescribable color of myrrh, the tattered folds gently stirring in a latent breeze.

There are a number of uncommonly interesting sights to be seen in the village of Gruyère. Perhaps most indicative of the canton are the vast winding subterranean caves where the cheeses are stacked on wooden racks to age properly. Alcoves are illuminated by flickering lights which are reflected in the amber eyes of scores of wild cats kept underground to rid the caves of the armies of huge, vicious rats which are drawn here by the magnetic aroma of ripening cheeses. So untamed are these cats that the men who tend the cheeses, turning them constantly in the racks to produce an even blend of flavor, carry long rawhide whips with lethal iron-weighted knobs to protect themselves. The day I visited the caves, possibly a dozen fat cats stalked along a high wide shelf which runs around each cave about fifteen feet from the ground. Balefully these overfed felines regarded me from their perch above stacked Gruyère cheeses. My guide hit the butt of his whip on the stone wall, the cats growled like hounds but did not budge. In the villagers' kitchens (everyone runs a "*fabrication de Gruyère*" as a means of additional income) or inside the long production shed where the finished product is prepared for export, age-old iron pots, eight to ten feet in circumference, wooden ladles, stirring paddles of wood, and pine-splinter "poignards" to test the cheese are used.

In any discussion of traditional Swiss food one invariably hears of *fondue,* how satisfying when prepared in one's own household or favorite inn, how often indifferent when served elsewhere. I agree that this dish of cheese melted in white wine, dashed with kirsch and dusted with nutmeg, can be superb. But I am more partial to the Vaudois *raquelet* when served on a cold night before a fire of spruce logs in some mountain farmhouse. I had this experience in the house of a vintner of the Vaud—a wide fronted brown and white house set on the lip of a meadow above the vineyard near La Tour de Trême within sight of the lights of Montreux. The room consisted of the typical white plaster walls, corner cupboards and furniture of golden spruce and balsam wood, hand carved by the original owner of the house. The hooded fireplace was set in an angle opposite the doorway. It was a cool night but the fire had been built up to the hot-ember stage necessary to prepare *raquelet.* Through the open doorway cold stars spangled the indigo sky. The family of father and mother in black or dark-brown garments, and three tall, broad-shouldered, fair-haired, bronzed young sons, each wearing the hand-embroidered short jacket with the Medieval page-boy puff sleeve, arranged their stools in a circle in front of the now redly smoldering fire. Then the ritual of removing the cheese box from under its hand-woven linen hood was performed by Monsieur Reylé. He murmured a blessing over the lid, then removed a noble Gruyère cheese, fresh from the ripening. These heirloom boxes, I may add, are a work of art. Thin strips of white pine are fashioned into a kind of ceremonial casket, the bands of thin wood interlaced in "fingers" secured by hand-molded pewter studs. The top is shaped like the low-crown, broad-brim black velour hats worn by the women of Canton Vaud. The handle of carved wood apes the twist of black silk which decorates the crown of the hat.

Now the mood of expectancy heightens. Grace is said, Madame Reylé and the eldest son Pierre cut the monumental cheese in half. (In the cantons, half of a large cheese is used, a squared-off end placed toward the embers to soften.) Madame placed the cheese on the hob close to the embers to simmer in the heat. The cheese, I found, becomes soft as butter but will not melt. One of the boys now fetched a huge earthenware tureen of baked potatoes. With a long-handled fork we each speared a potato. I scraped the soft hot cheese from the wedge, spread it thickly on my potato, sprinkled it with coarsely ground pepper and settled back to enjoy this heroic dish. While the youngest son, Jean Baptiste, poured a white wine from the Reylé vineyards I listened to tales of great vintages of other years, always celebrated fittingly with festivals by the hard-working and equally hard-pleasuring Vaudois.

Geneva, or Genève as one hears it called hereabouts, is the third largest city in Switzerland. Completely French in thought, it is a beautifully laid-out city on the southwest extremity of Lac Léman. Promenades and gardens abound. No matter where one turns, the view of Jura Range is on one side, the Alps on the other. The Rhone, one of the most rampageous and exciting rivers in Christendom, tumults through Geneva on its course to the Mediterranean, dividing the city in two parts. La Cité standing on the left bank embraces the Old Town. St. Gervais on the right rises in garden terraces wherein villas and fashionable clubs and schools are situated.

Julius Caesar thought highly of his villa on the Rhone, mentioning it with unaccustomed enthusiasm in his *Commentaries*. Geneva was already a town of considerable importance before the Romans built markets, as well as mills for grinding grain from the fertile Rhone valley farms.

The Musée d'Art et d'Histoire is repository for a remarkable collection of antiquities ranging from Etruscan to Renaissance, Baroque and Louis XVI periods. The swannery is a great attraction. Every morning at eleven o'clock over three hundred swans are fed at the Pavillon des Cygnes. This is a signal for everyone to repair to the pavilion to take coffee or apéritif.

Auberge l'Or du Rhone faces the rapids of the river. The cuisine here is in the great French tradition of Brillat-Savarin and must be enjoyed leisurely. Three hours for lunch; for dinner, an entire evening. This distinguished restaurant specializes in soups. *Petite marmite* and oxtail soup are well worth a visit here as well as *potage à l'oignon*. Renowned to gourmets the world over, La Perle du Lac displays a visitor's book resplendent with signatures that read like pages of an International Who's Who. I was served *tournedos* with flaming brandy sauce. Asparagus jellied in port wine served with turkey cutlets stuffed with truffles is indeed another epic dish. The smaller *"habitant"* restaurants in La Cité are extremely good; nearly all have terraces with a view of the river or Mont Blanc. Hotel Beau Rivage holds to an ancient lineage—a reputation for comfort and good food and besides, the old hotel has atmosphere. Hotels de la Paix and des Bergues are in the best class of Swiss hotel catering, which cannot be topped anywhere. Little Hotel Sergy has the air of a French *"petite auberge"* in Brittany.

I suggest an excursion on Lac Léman. A sail to Ferney-Voltaire on the French frontier. Voltaire all but founded the village. He lived here the last twenty years of his life. His house is a rewarding museum full of memorabilia, letters affording surprises. At Territet, on a vine-hung rock, rests a seated statue of Empress Elizabeth of Austria. A gracious, utterly lovely image of the Empress in the heyday of her exquisite beauty, before she became the disturbed woman who was assassinated by the stiletto-thrust of a nihilist on the quay in front of Hotel Beau Rivage in Geneva.

Montreux has for decades enjoyed great popularity as a year-round resort with French, British and American visitors. Its chief attractions are shops of first-class order, immense luxury hotels (such as the Montreux-Palace, Belmont and Continental), water activities, and a magnificent view of Dents du Midi. Close by and easily reached by boat, the Castle of Chillon of horrendous memory molds and growls away the years, haunted by conflicting ghosts to the last gargoyle waterspouts. The neighboring villages of Vevey, Les Planches, Châtelard, Clarens and Veytaux-Chillon claim the finest gardens and villas in French Switzerland.

Lausanne is said to "wear her tiara constantly." Old Bourg and Cité sprawl across the hills of La Côte and Lavaux—the two quarters which Lausannois call "Les Oiseaux," for singing birds hang in cages from every house, be it of high or low degree. In rue du Bourg stands the house once occupied by Madame de Staël—her *château* at Coppet on the lake is now a museum of her "personalities and summer vagaries" as the catalogue reads. In her town house she held a brilliant court during winter months. Her wigs were a weather barometer. On days promising fair she was crowned in brassy yellow coronal braids. If dull and rainy weather, she strode forth in curls black as thunder clouds. If a tempest of destructive order threatened, de Staël appeared in a fiery red contraption in disarray aburst with multicolored plumes.

Ouchy lies in the circle of the Bay of Sulpice near the mouth of the Flon, an aerial village on stilts, on the site of one built by the prehistoric lake dwellers. Handsome villas line the *plage*, famous for excellent bathing.

Vevey is a tree-shaded "seclusion of hotels, villas, and ennui gossip," remarked Suzanne Curchod, later Madame Necker, the mother of Madame de Staël, when she refused point-blank to purchase a villa offered her in Vevey at the time when she became engaged to Edward Gibbon, author of the classic *Decline and Fall of the Roman Empire*.

Yet for anyone wishing a quiet week end to rest up from a strenuous bout of travel or to plan the next leg of the journey, I recommend one of the little resort towns that line Lake Léman—Ouchy, Vevey or Clarens.

L'Envoi

And so in the autumn it seemed eminently fitting that the night before I left Austria, where I had been ranging the farthest reaches of every province for five months, I should hear music, lovely in itself and supremely well played. A concert of chamber music was held by candlelight in the great mirrored ballroom at the Esterházy Palace in Eisenstadt. The program included music for the harp and viols composed by immortal Haydn. Somehow, as I listened, the shimmering notes of the harp seemed to crystallize into all the beauty of the architecture I had seen in my travels, ranging from small orchard-hidden frescoed farmhouses in Carinthia to the great Baroque monasteries built after the Reformation when the Prince Bishops reigned over the countryside of Austria, as powerful as any emperor. I listened to a minuet composed by Haydn and intended to be played at a ball in the Vienna Hofburg. For the last encore the orchestra played a Reed Song of the Neusiedlersee. In a way it is a lover's lament, and yet a song of hope. More than this, it tells a typically Austrian story. A young herdsman will ride his horse at night into the grassy courtyard before the house of his beloved. Sitting still in his saddle, a small zither upon his knee, he will strum it, and he will sing to the night, the stars, and to the ear of his lady:

> "To the pond where it reposes
> Drop the moonbeams softly down,
> Twining their ethereal roses
> In the reeds' encircling crown."

Index